The Political Economy of Border Drawing

Arranging Legality in European Labor Migration Policies

Regine Paul

Published by
Berghahn Books
www.berghahnbooks.com

© 2015 Regine Paul

All rights reserved. Except for the quotation of short passages
for the purposes of criticism and review, no part of this book
may be reproduced in any form or by any means, electronic or
mechanical, including photocopying, recording, or any information
storage and retrieval system now known or to be invented,
without written permission of the publisher.

Library of Congress Cataloging-in-Publication Data

Paul, Regine.
 The political economy of border drawing : arranging legality in European labor migration policies / Regine Paul.
    pages cm
 Includes bibliographical references and index.
 ISBN 978-1-78238-541-7 (hardback : alk. paper) — ISBN 978-1-78238-542-4 (ebook)
 1. Foreign workers—Government policy—Europe. 2. Labor policy—Europe.
3. Europe—Emigration and immigration—Government policy. 4. Europe—Emigration and immigration—Economic aspects. I. Title.
 HD8378.5.A2P38 2015
 331.5'44094—dc23

2014029064

British Library Cataloguing in Publication Data

A catalogue record for this book is available from the British Library

Printed on acid-free paper

ISBN: 978-1-78238-541-7 hardback
ISBN: 978-1-78238-542-4 ebook

Contents

List of Illustrations — vii

Acknowledgments — ix

Abbreviations — xi

Introduction. Labor Migration Management: An Interdisciplinary Interpretive Policy Analysis — 1

Part I. Border Drawing as a Framework for Migration Policy Analysis

Chapter 1. Labor Migration Management as Meaningful Border Drawing — 19

Chapter 2. Border Drawing across Capitalist Economies, Welfare States, and Citizenship Regimes — 43

Chapter 3. Border Drawing in Context: Profiling Migration Histories and Policy Legacies for Comparative Analysis — 73

Part II. Border Drawing in German, French, and British Labor Migration Policies

Chapter 4. What Makes Migrant Workers "Legal"? Mapping Entry Regulation — 105

Chapter 5. A "Tool for Growth"? The Shared Cultural Political Economy of Labor Migration Policies — 139

Chapter 6. "Poles Don't Even Play Cricket!" Embedding Labor Migration Policies in National Socio-Cultural Norms — 164

Conclusion. Border Drawing, Policy Analysis, and the Governance of Mobility in Europe ... 192

Documents and Interviews ... 207

References ... 211

Index ... 228

Illustrations

Figures

Figure 2.1.	Ideal-Typical Norms of Classification in Labor Migration Management	70
Figure 3.1.	Inflows of Foreign Nationals to Germany (1950–2012)	77
Figure 3.2.	Origin of Foreign Residents in France (percentage by year of census)	84
Figure 3.3.	Work Permit Entries to France (1946–2010)	85
Figure 3.4.	Migration to the United Kingdom by Region of Origin (1975–2010, in thousands)	92
Figure 3.5.	Work Permits Issued in the United Kingdom (1995–2008)	96
Figure 4.1.	Classifications of Labor Migrants in German Legislation	108
Figure 4.2.	Classifications of Labor Migrants in French Legislation	115
Figure 4.3.	Classifications of Labor Migrants in British Legislation	123

Tables

Table 2.1.	Capitalist Coordination Regimes in the EU-15	50
Table 2.2.	Welfare State Regimes in the EU-15	57
Table 2.3.	Historical Citizenship Regimes and Recent Changes in EU-15	64
Table 3.1.	Origin of Newcomers and Foreign Residents in Germany (2010, in percent)	76

Table 4.1.	TCN Worker Inflows per Type of Permit and Entry Route in Germany	110
Table 4.2.	TCN Worker Inflows per Type of Permit in France	117
Table 4.3.	TCN Worker Inflows per Type of Permit and Entry Route in the U.K.	124
Table 4.4.	Comparison of Selectivity in Labor Migration Policies	134
Table 5.1.	Three Shared Economic Imaginaries of Labor Migration Policies	162
Table 6.1.	The Embedding of Labor Migration Policies in National Societal Contexts	190

Acknowledgments

The protocol of many policy analyses demands that scholars leave their judgments at the door. As this book challenges this protocol conceptually and methodologically, it comes with an early acknowledgement that the author herself is embedded in a specific social context and cannot fully escape judgment. In consequence, for the sake of credibility of research, positivist or interpretivist, readers ought to be told just why authors choose—yes, choose—to engage in specific research. No worries there, my story is brief.

When I was seven years old, the world around me was dramatically altered. Where my parents and grandparents were severely limited in their job and consumption choices, opinions, and travels, my brother and I grew up largely without these limitations. For all the unfulfilled promises that German reunification has certainly entailed for many in terms of socio-economic developments, I remain grateful that by sheer fate of being born in the 1980s in Eastern Germany rather than the 1960s—or rather than elsewhere on the globe today, for that matter—I have been able to work and study wherever and whatever I wanted in various inspiring places throughout Europe. The infamous lottery of birth is largely determined by borders: of nations, of religion, of class, of race, of gender, of time. It is my continuing emotional struggle to justify my entitlement to the mobile European life that my mom and grandma were denied at my age, and that many of my friends and colleagues are still excluded from today, that informs my perspective on migration policy through the lens of border drawing.

Hidden behind the many words on borders and migration in this book is a truly joyful research journey that would not have been thinkable without the support and friendship of several people. Foremost, I am deeply grateful for Emma Carmel's support. An exemplary mentor and a lovely friend, Emma continuously infects me with her enthusiasm for research and thoughtful passion for policy analysis. Sue Milner generously shared her expertise in detailed feedback, especially on the French case. Hedley Bashforth, Peo Hansen, Theo Papadopoulos, and Graham Room provided thorough and utterly constructive readings of draft manuscripts, and it was for Peo's encouragement that I contacted Berghahn Books. I am profoundly indebted to Emma Carmel, Hannah Durrant, Jenny Harlock, Sarah Morgan-Trimmer, Hester Kan, Michelle

Farr, and Fiona Morgan who have shaped a uniquely collegial and intellectually stimulating environment in the Governance Research Group at Bath University. They will hear the lasting echoes of our years of discussion and friendship from these pages. With a smile on my face, I often anticipated their crisp commentary while writing. I am grateful to Tina Haux who, in addition to being a lovely friend, has provided vital feedback on how to simplify dense analytical frameworks.

The time and effort that interviewees dedicated to this study is much appreciated: their generously shared accounts of what labor migration management might be all about form the heart of this research. Kind institutional and personal support by Antje Blöcker and Uli Jürgens at the Social Science Research Centre in Berlin and Alain Morice at the Unité de Recherches "Migrations et Societé" at Paris VII eased fieldwork and triggered intellectual exchange. For the memorable fieldwork, an experience I would not have traded for anything, I received generous funding from the University of Bath and the Office Franco-Allemand pour la Jeunesse. Charlotte Branchu, Luke Martinelli, and Karin Paul offered their help in the tiresome business of transcribing hours of multilingual audio files. My thanks also to my lovely housemates and regular visitors at 9B Wellsway, Odd Down, and Kelston View, who, through many divine cooking sessions, period drama screenings, cycle and walking tours, set the right context for letting research be research just often enough. On his frequent visits to Bath, Bastian Loges in particular became a much-valued companion in dialogue about research life. In the unsettling times of revising this manuscript I could rely on the financial support of the German Academic Exchange Service, and was further lucky to encounter the hospitality of Steffen Mau and his research team at Bremen University and of Helen Schwenken at Kassel University. The families Mangels-Voegt and Laudenbach-Oyen generously hosted, fed, and entertained me during my commutes between Bonn, Bremen, and Kassel and kept my spirits up during revisions.

Special thanks are due to Elizabeth Berg, Adam Capitanio, and Mike Dempsey at Berghahn Books in New York, who navigated me through the production of this book with precious advice, admirable clarity, and patience. The sharp and genuinely constructive comments of three anonymous reviewers helped make several parts of the argument clearer. I want to thank them especially and hope that they find their feedback well reflected in the final work.

Last and not least, my family and friends on both sides of the Harz Mountains have endured my absences with unwavering support and love. Above all, to my husband, Mathi: words cannot capture my joyful gratitude for your patient endurance of painful geographical separation for the sake of my research contemplations. Without ever doubting my narrative of indispensable research mobility, as you could have, you bigheartedly redrew the borders of your own dreams to include my extravagancies.

Abbreviations

BA	Bundesagentur für Arbeit (German Federal Employment Agency)
BAMF	Bundesamt für Migration und Flüchtlinge (German Bureau for Migrants and Refugees)
BIS	Department for Business, Innovation and Skills (UK)
BMAS	Bundesministerium für Arbeit und Soziales (German Ministry for Employment and Social Affairs)
BMI	Bundesministerium des Innern (German Home Office)
BMWA	Bundesministerium für Wirtschaft und Arbeit (German Ministry for the Economy and Employment)
CEC	Commission of the European Communities (EU Commission)
Ceseda	Code de l'Entrée et du Séjour des Étrangers et du Droit d'Asile (French Migration, Residence and Asylum Law)
CEU	Council of the European Union (EU Council)
CME	Coordinated market economy
CPE	Cultural political economy (shorthand for Bob Jessop and Ngai-Ling Sum's approach as delineated in chapter 1)
DDETFP	Directions Départementales de l'Emploi, du Travail et de la Formation Professionnelle (French Departmental Employment Agencies)
EC	European Communities
EU	European Union
EU-15	EU member states before accession round in 2004
EU-2	Bulgaria and Romania, accession countries to the EU in 2007
EU-8	Eastern and Central European accession countries to the EU in 2004 (without Malta and Cyprus)

GISTI	Groupe d'information et de soutien des immigrés (French migrant advocacy group)
ICT	Intracorporate transfer (of employees)
INSEE	L'Institut National de la Statistique et des Etudes Economiques (French National Institute of Statistics and Economic Studies)
IPA	Interpretive policy analysis
IT	Information technology
LME	Liberal market economy
LTR	Long-term resident / long-term residence
MAC	Migration Advisory Committee (UK institution)
MIIIDS	Ministère de l'Immigration, de l'Intégration, d'Identité Nationale et du Dévelopement Solidaire (French Migration Ministry, abolished in December 2010)
NAO	National Audit Office (UK)
OECD	Organisation for Economic Co-operation and Development
OFII	Office Française d'Immigration et de l'Intégration (French Bureau for Migration and Integration)
ONS	Office for National Statistics (UK)
PBS	Points-based (immigration) system
PSZ	Priority solidarity zones (*zones de solidarité prioritaires*, French term to define developing countries from which to avoid migrant brain drain)
RLMT	Resident labor market test
TCN	Third-country national (EU jargon for someone without EU citizenship)
UKBA	UK Border Agency
VET	Vocational education and training
VoC	Varieties of capitalism

INTRODUCTION

Labor Migration Management
An Interdisciplinary Interpretive Policy Analysis

"The good into the pot, the bad into the crop"[1]

Foreign workers are known to assuage structural bottlenecks in specific economic sectors or regions. Be it food processing, agriculture, hospitality and catering, social care work, medical professions, financial services, engineering, or information technology, migrant workers seem to play an important role in keeping entire economic sectors productive and competitive in European national economies (for the British example, see Ruhs and Anderson 2010b). In 2009, workers from abroad made up more than 13 percent of the Austrian labor force, 10 percent of the Belgian and Spanish, 9 percent of the German, and roughly 8 percent of the Italian and British (OECD 2011). Given foreign workers' central role in remedying not only short-term but also structural labor shortages, labor migration is prone to continue resiliently through economic crises (Castles 2011; Koser 2010; OECD 2013).

Yet we know full well from news stories that the economy drive of labor migration is contested in policy making. "Not always does the interest of the economy reflect that of the entire country," states Wolfgang Bosbach in the newspaper *Frankfurter Allgemeine Zeitung* in 2002. Then spokesman of the Conservative parties in the German Bundestag, Bosbach rejects economic arguments with a view to justifying the CDU/CSU boycott of the more liberal admissions regime for migrant workers proposed by the Social Democrats and Green Party. More labor migration, Bosbach explains, would mean to overburden society with social and cultural integration costs.

A decade later, Bosbach's fellow party member and Labor Minister Ursula von der Leyen welcomes liberalizations to German labor migration policies—they go way beyond what was intended in 2002—and promotes skilled labor migration as "a huge gain for all sides" in the same newspaper in May 2013. Suddenly, the economy's interest in labor migration, so fiercely contested by her colleague eleven years earlier, implies not so much burden but chief advantages for German society and sending countries.

In 2006, President Nicolas Sarkozy mentions the need to adapt French migration policies to economic needs. However, as with the German Labor Minister, labor migration means more than just economic gains to Sarkozy, albeit from a quite different angle: *"immigration choisie"* explicitly seeks to lower the share of groups who are economically less useful—i.e., family members—from the total of incoming foreigners. Labor migration means reducing family migration. In this, Sarkozy tells *Le Monde,* labor migration is a "fortress against racism." The sudden discursive link between unwanted family migration, wanted labor migration, and racism nourishes our imagination further: Does labor migration mean less post-colonial migration mean less racism?

When in spring 2012 the company running London's famous red buses recruited fifty new drivers directly from a small Polish town, the domestic yellow press was infuriated: "There are currently 2.64 million unemployed people in Britain. Critics would suggest that any number of these would have been suitable candidates to drive the iconic buses. The revelation comes as it was revealed that 160,000 Britons have missed out on employment because work was taken by foreigners" (*Daily Mail* 2012). To parts of the British population, it seems, labor migration—even when promoting the mobility of fellow EU citizens—means unwanted job competition. In this, the Brits are not alone, of course. When asked about the most important issues facing their country in spring 2011, 12 percent of Europeans mentioned concern about immigration (*Eurobarometer* 2011). While inflation, the general economic situation, unemployment, healthcare, and pensions worried even more people, the concern over immigration is likely linked to some of these chief causes for concern, especially rising unemployment. The 2009 meltdown of global financial markets, it seems, has brought national labor market protectionism back to the center stage of public debates about migration.

But then another turn in the tale: in October 2013, the British Prime Minister David Cameron tells *The Guardian* that "Eastern European immigrants should not be blamed for seeking jobs in U.K. factories when not enough young people in Britain are fully capable of doing the same jobs." Beyond the immediate economic-need argument, labor migration thus signifies the failure of the British education system to produce the skills that the economy needs.

President of the European Parliament Martin Schulz inflicts quite a different meaning of *need* in his reaction to a repeated deadly shipwreck of a boat packed with mostly African migrants offshore the Mediterranean island of Lampedusa in autumn 2013. A more liberal system of legal immigration—including the permission to earn a living—Schulz claims in *Der Spiegel,* would mean to alleviate need among poor and persecuted people elsewhere and thus "combat the sources of inhumane practices of human trafficking."

An economic necessity, a burden for societal integration, a welcome diversification of society, a due relief from unemployment for sending countries, a means to curb family reunion, a tool to overcome unwanted bonds to former colonies, a weapon against racism, unwanted competition for domestic[2] employees, a marker of educational failure in the host country, a due end to deadly attempts in unauthorized migration—which one is it? I've limited my storytelling here to only a few key tales and already the array of different meanings and objectives that policy makers (and the public) attach to labor migration policies is impressive, to say the least, maybe confusing, and probably contradictory. "Be reasonable!", Business Department officials might want to tell their Home Office colleagues, "evidence shows that the economic gains of labor migration outweigh your concerns." Every tale claims its own reason. Alas, to establish "reason" through policy analysis might be missing the point, as Deborah Stone (2012: 380) well notes: "Reason doesn't start with a clean slate on which our brains record their pure observations. Reason proceeds from choices to notice some things but not others, to include some things and exclude others, and to view the world in a particular way when other visions are possible."

This book is an invitation to take the choices laid out in labor migration management—blurry, unreasonable, and paradoxical as they might seem—seriously without taking any of them for granted. In an interpretive and interdisciplinary cross-country comparison of labor migration policies in Britain, France, and Germany, I seek to offer several contributions to the analysis of a still-emergent policy field, as I will detail now.

A Novel Policy Approach and its Analytical Implications

Faced with the different tales alluded to above, policy makers in Europe have taken pains to design more selective labor admission regimes that could somehow achieve multiple, if not all, aims at once. This concurs with Steffen Mau and colleagues (2012: 51), who claim that "liberal states have an interest in selective and controlled forms of openness." Martin Ruhs (2013) demonstrates that trade-offs between openness and rights restrictions are indeed typical of high-income economies' policies toward migrant workers. It is through selectivity then, policy makers argue, that economic gains of labor migration can be harvested while keeping an eye on socio-cultural integration, national labor market protection and development aid, too. Labor migration management seems to offer a welcome remedy for policy complexity precisely as a strategy to put "the good into the pot—the bad into the crop."

The EU world is a prime example here. "Labor migration management" was born as a designated policy approach in the EU and OECD world in the early 2000s. The image of the EU as "fortress"—which ferociously keeps non-EU nationals outside its gates and controls the borders of *Schengenland* with ever-more sophisticated means—has increasingly crumbled in this period (e.g., Carmel and Paul 2010; Favell and R. Hansen 2002; P. Hansen 2010; Roos 2013). In a tight embrace of the Lisbon Agenda's growth, competitiveness, and employment targets, the EU Commission has keenly promoted the reconciliation of foreign labor recruitment with security and protectionist concerns under the umbrella of "managed economic migration" since 2001. In a Green Paper on this issue, the Commission calls for more harmonization across the European Union: "Recognizing the impact of demographic decline and ageing on the economy, the Commission highlighted the need to review immigration policies for the longer term particularly in the light of the implications which an economic migration strategy would have on competitiveness and, therefore, on the fulfillment of the Lisbon objectives" (CEC 2004: 3). Some years later we are told that "immigration is a reality which needs to be managed effectively" (CEC 2008: 2). Similar arguments surface within the OECD with the pursuit of "a road-map for managing labor migration." In a recent policy plan, the organization argues that "labor migration management has become an imperative" for policy makers in rich economies and should be treated as a policy priority (OECD 2009: 78).

Labor migration management comes with a set of distinct presumptions with analytical implications for research. It entails three crucial policy shifts that distinguish it from previous approaches and contribute to the ways in which labor migration tales are now told: (1) liberalization of admissions as part of a competitiveness strategy, (2) a qualitative shift in recruitment approaches toward highly fine-tuned selectivity, and (3) a deepened embedding of national admission regulation in the European common market.

Firstly, the recent liberalizations of labor admissions represent a discontinuity to the official suspension of migration since the early 1970s and make it a promising and still underexplored field for comparative research. Certainly, migration continued during the "recruitment stop": "guest workers" settled against policy makers' expectations; family members followed their working spouses and entered labor markets; so did asylum seekers whose migration to Europe increased during the 1980s and 1990s; pockets for cheap foreign labor remained open, albeit informally in many cases (Castles 1986; Castles and Miller 2009). What changes with the policy reforms of the early 2000s then is not so much the empirical reality of labor migration itself but the welcoming and proactive tone of regulation (Boswell and Geddes 2011; Menz 2009; Menz and Caviedes 2010b). Britain lifted entry conditions for high-skilled and skilled workers in 2002, Germany created a new permit for high-skilled professionals in 2005, France followed suit with similar measures in 2006, Ireland established a Green Card for high-skilled migrants in 2006, and Denmark operates a "positive list" with qualified shortage professions since 2008. The return to active recruitment policies in contemporary Europe mirrors a more general tendency across the OECD world (Dumont and Doudeijns 2003).

Secondly, the recent return to facilitating labor migration entails substantive changes of directions compared to admission schemes that deserve analytical scrutiny. The list of specific policy tools that operate in twenty-first-century labor migration management is long and can certainly not be exhaustive here (see OECD 2008a). Canada, the United States, and the United Kingdom, for instance, use points-based migration systems to select workers on the basis of their qualifications, earning potential, or language proficiency. Many countries operate resident labor market tests and detailed shortage lists (e.g., France, Germany, Denmark, Spain, the United Kingdom) to recruit migrant workers into specific shortage positions on the domestic labor market. Special permits have been created to recruit workers of particular skill sets (such as the German Green Card for IT workers, or the Irish high-skilled permit). Most European countries further entertain bilateral agreements with individual sending countries that specify professions and occupations for admissions, and frequently link those to overall quotas for nationals of these countries. Regularizations are sometimes used to legalize informal workers who work in shortage professions. While amnesties are often castigated as an unsustainable Mediterranean policy tool, northern European governments have frequently resorted to regularizations as well, both in work-related and other contexts (Maas 2010; Sunderhaus 2007). To complicate things even further, we find that a vast array of different permits, each often coming with quite distinct sets of rights, is operated across the European Union.

Without yet embarking on a detailed analysis of these policy tools, their mere listing exposes a pattern of highly fine-tuned and sophisticated selectivity in labor migration and suggests a lot of scope for national variation. Georg Menz (2009: 31) suggests that managed migration entails very "carefully delineated (labor) migration channels" as well as a much "more restrictive stance towards other venues" compared to past recruitment schemes. Scholars commonly acknowledge that this selective and fine-tuned labor migration approach starkly departs from the practice of recruiting unskilled labor and sheer "manpower" in the guest worker period (Caviedes 2010; Menz 2010a; Menz and Caviedes 2010a; Ruhs and Anderson 2010b). This shift is usually ascribed to the rise of Post-Fordism in Western economies, which is mainly associated with the end of mass production, the simultaneous rise of highly specialized and flexibilized production, and the increasing relevance of the service sector. In order to account for the distinct quality of foreign labor management approaches today, policy analysis eventually "should thus be embedded within the larger discourse on the changing political economy of Europe and in the world" (Menz and Caviedes 2010a: 4). Indeed, the introduction of comprehensive labor migration policies, often including notionally quite similar policy tools, across the EU-15 at roughly the same time seems to reflect a shared economic governance agenda in post-Fordist capitalist economies.

This is where, thirdly, the European Union kicks in. Certainly, member states remain the most relevant actors in labor migration management (Boswell and Geddes 2011). National governments have so far largely resisted harmonization attempts for legal labor migration from third countries. Even when the 2010 Lisbon Treaty subsumed labor migration under the community method of decision making and thereby coerced member states into closer interaction with the Commission and Parliament, national governments have retained key authorities over specifying volumes, bilateral recruitment agreements, or further entry conditions (Carrera et al. 2011). Moreover, some member states, frequently including the United Kingdom, Ireland, and Denmark, tend to opt out of migration-related EU regulation altogether. The introductory reflections have further pointed out that when the yellow press mobilizes against foreign workers and concern about migration surfaces among part of the electorate, the option of appearing to act "tough" on foreigners is certainly not readily surrendered by national policy makers (Boswell and Geddes 2011; Cento Bull 2009; Marthaler 2008; Schain 2008).

These caveats aside, however, national regulation is deeply embedded in EU market making and its underpinning norms and values, irrespective of the lack of formalistic integration (P. Hansen and Hager 2010). The most obvious instance of common market making with regard to foreign labor movements surfaces in the area of EU free movement. Member states cannot—or only in very limited ways—control labor mobility of fellow EU nationals (note that the British tales described earlier seem to "confuse" mobility and migration in that respect). EU nationals can work, study, live, and settle in any other member state without applying for visa or work permits and they have to be treated equally to nationals of their host country. Indeed, "any invocation of national boundary to restrict these opportunities for European foreigners is considered discrimination" (Favell 2008a: 3).

The diffusion of the norms and institutions of the common market through EU mobility reach far beyond the governance of EU workers. Policy tools such as the resident labor market test—according to which domestic *and* EU workers' availability on the national labor market must be checked before any non-EU newcomer can be admitted—evidence the way in which free movement can constrain labor migration. Free movement creates a shared legal reference to a common EU labor market and workforce that cannot be ignored in labor migration management (Paul 2013). This might be especially true when disparities in member states' economic situation in times of crisis is sought to be cured—or at least partly absorbed—with internal labor mobility. The "co-production" of migration policies by the EU and member states (Carmel 2013) requires a Janus-faced policy analysis approach that can capture both shared features of labor migration management and their embedding in common market making and cross-national variation of policy tools, logics, and the norms that guide foreign labor recruitment in EU member states.

Placing the Book in a Nascent Research Field: An Interdisciplinary Commitment

This book seeks to build its strength on an interdisciplinary approach to analyzing labor migration management. I believe that this can offer substantive conceptual and empirical contributions to a nascent field of scientific inquiry that so far suffers from disciplinary eclectics. To avoid misunderstanding from the outset, I do not seek to criticize specific disciplines or scholars writing from these perspectives as such. I rather promote the epistemological argument that in policy studies—i.e., research that is guided by the desire to understand and account for policies rather than being predetermined by the concepts and methods of a specific discipline—narrow disciplinary boundaries and paradigm battles hinder rather than serve the aim of developing encompassing and critical accounts of policies and their effects on those governed through them.

Legal scholars have taken the shifting normative foundations of labor migration policies most seriously in their analysis of developments in the EU's legal framework (Baldaccini et al. 2007; Crowley 2001; Guild 2005a, 2005b; Peers 2001; Ryan 2007). The disciplinary interest in the legal principles of admission and residence allows legal scholars to identify and specify the normative underpinnings of labor migration management. They show, for instance, that admission rights for migrants frequently depend on their potential success in formal labor market participation. Legal analysts have further contributed substantially to the notion of the European Union as a source of differential rights and inequalities for migrant workers. They devote their research to assessing policy implications for migrant rights much more thoroughly than many economic and political sciences approaches can and do.

Besides this valuable commitment to scrutinizing the normative foundations of policies, however, legal scholarship tends to disregard the structural context in which the selection, design, and codification of legal principles for labor admissions operates. As they are less interested in the specific economic and public policy conditions under which legal norms emerge, they often overlook sources of variation, too. By contrast, economists and political sociologists have started analyzing precisely how the macro-economic and political conditions co-shape the need for foreign workforce in various sectors of capitalist economies and how they determine migrant workers' rights in host countries. Martin Ruhs and Bridget Anderson's (2010b) impressive volume on Britain highlights, for instance, how public funding shortages for social care reinforce the need for cheap migrant labor in this sector. Unlike in legal research, there is little consideration, however, for the entrenched logics and norms of labor migration management, as public policy is treated as a relatively stable context for foreign labor demand. Policies are not adequately disentangled as attempts to govern and structure labor inflows according to specific normative ideals. Ironically then, even though taking flanking public policies serious as structuring factors for foreign worker recruitment in different sectors, the volume downplays labor migration policies' power to reshape the very structural conditions for migrant worker recruitment.

This is more convincingly achieved in critical sociological research that examines precisely how migration policies structure relations between migrants, citizens, and employers and thereby impose consequential judgments about how the social world ought to be ordered. Illustrative are Bridget Anderson's (2013) account of British immigration control, which imposes the normative vision of "community of value" on aliens and citizens with far-reaching implications for the rights of both; or Peo Hansen and Sandy Brian Hager's (2010) analysis of EU citizenship policies as a deliberate attempt to create an increasingly utilitarian and ethnocized model of belonging in Europe. With the historical empirical depth required for these embedded studies, they can be excused for not providing comparative insights.

Comparative policy insights are offered by scholars of a political science and institutionalist political economy tradition (Berg and Spehar 2013; Cerna 2009, 2013; Devitt 2011; Menz 2009, 2010a). With a focus on the role of political parties, trade unions, employers, and non-state actors, these studies illuminate decision-making processes and actors' power struggles in labor migration management and explain cross-national commonalities and differences with regard to variable political economies and institutional environments. Especially Menz's (2009) comparative study highlights the close interaction of labor migration management with the post-Fordist political economy and its promotion by the European Union. His evidence from six countries indicates some Europeanization of policies, but also highlights that "different models of political economy shape distinct strategies for labor recruitment from abroad" (2009: 261; also 2010a).

Yet these accounts tend to underestimate variations in the normative judgments vested in seemingly "similar" post-Fordist policies, take for granted the conditions under which policy choices have emerged, and pay little attention to the structuring effects of labor migration policies for social relations in the host country and the wider world (this critique—which rests on an ontological cleavage in social science—is elaborated in the first chapter). By excluding meanings and policy effects from our studies, we miss out on the analytical harvest of legal studies and critical sociology/political economy (see discussion of interpretive approaches to follow).

Seeking to offer a more holistic account of labor migration policies—as founded on normative claims, as structurally embedded in specific socio-economic settings, and as consequential for the ordering of social relationships—this book is situated at the intersection of legal studies, political economy, and political sociology. Our comparative analysis of labor migration policies thus captures their legal principles and normative foundations (legal perspective), their emergence and governance in particular socio-economic settings (political economy perspective), comparative variations across national contexts (comparative policy perspective), and policy implications for migrants' rights (political sociology perspective).

Outlining the Comparative Policy Analysis Approach

This book maps contemporary labor migration policies in three of the largest national economies and labor-importing countries in Europe—Germany, France, and the United Kingdom. More precisely, it extracts from legislation and interviews with its makers the normative foundations of selecting "legal migrant workers" and assesses the socio-economic setting in which these norms of selection emerge in a comparative perspective.

Interpretive Policy Analysis

This book promotes an interpretive approach to policy analysis. My ontological agreement is with those who claim that "the effort to exclude meaning and values from the work of the policy analyst cuts the very heart out of political inquiry" (Fischer 2003: 216). In the first chapter, I will discuss in more detail how, by concentrating on the effectiveness of territorial border enforcement, a considerable share of migration policy studies falls short of explaining how and why specific meanings of borders between "legal" and "illegal" migrant workers emerge in the first place. Assessed from an interpretive paradigm, this misrecognizes not only the constitutive character of policies as world makers that frame, filter, and institutionalize ideas about "good," "bad," "legal," or "illegal"; it also downplays policy effects such as the unequal allocation of rights to migrant workers.

In the spirit of our labor migration tales from earlier, my analytical starting point is that (a) policies entail specific calculations of the social world and how to best organize it, and (b) these calculations depend themselves to a great deal on presupposed meanings of concepts such as "labor market," "shortage," "economic competitiveness," "citizenship," or "social justice." Policies constitute categories for thinking about—and managing!—legal workers through vesting specific meanings in admission legislation; and they thereby likewise reproduce or change the institutional anchors on which they rest. This dual perspective on meaning making through and structural embeddedness of policies follows interpretive policy analysts who claim "that meaning does not merely put a particular affective or evaluative gloss on things, but that it is somehow constitutive of political actions, governing institutions, and public policies" (Wagenaar 2011: 4). To be wholly clear: I am not in the business of judging whether the meanings vested in labor migration management are "right" or "good," achieve specific aims, or pay enough attention to alleged market needs or host society concerns. Other policy specialists perform these evaluative tasks plentifully (e.g., OECD 2009, 2011, 2012). Rather, I seek comparative comprehension of the contexts and conditions under which specific normative foundations for managing migration have emerged as policy-relevant across our three cases. In other words: who are these "good" workers who end up in the pot and why, exactly, do they or don't they? Under scrutiny then are the normative intentions and contextual reference points behind policy choices for or against specific notions of migrant worker legality.

A commitment to the historical-reconstructive paradigm in social sciences research enables this book to combine a critical analysis of the normative foundations of labor migration management with a case-oriented comparative policy analysis. We understand cases as complex configurations and follow an explanatory comparative strategy that is historically and contextually bound (Della Porta 2008). It is "by carefully attending to the empirical world," by situating each case in its political and socio-economic context, that we can seek explanation for the emergence of specific sets of norms and tools in labor migration policies (Wagenaar 2011: 10). Interpretivism then does no let functionalism in through the backdoor: context should not be mistaken for a straightforward or neutral policy informant. Rather, established institutions and consolidated sets of meanings—such as capitalist coordination regimes, welfare states, or models of national belonging—serve as sources of judgments that policy makers can *selectively* draw on in pursuit of specific policy objectives, but they might as well ignore them or even revoke them through migration policies. The first two chapters will elaborate on this conceptual point in much more depth while the analysis in the second part of the book takes pains to elucidate labor migration policies as dynamic and disturbingly incongruous examples of "meaning in action," to borrow the catchy title of Henk Wagenaar's recent textbook.

Scope of the Study

In this book I will examine and compare contemporary labor migration management across three cases. By focusing on three big European economies and labor-importing countries—Germany, France, and the United Kingdom—

the book offers more general reflections on policy trajectories in Europe. The three represent the biggest economies and populations within the European Union, irrespective of current economic and demographic troubles (OECD 2008b). Their big labor markets have attracted most migrants in absolute terms for some decades now, and they are also listed among the top ten countries receiving migrants worldwide by the International Organization of Migration (2008, 2009). Our three cases have seemingly started from similar positions—numerically at least—to develop strategies for labor migration management.

Theoretical sampling, further, starts from the premise that the British, French, and German national economies, labor markets, welfare states, citizenship, and integration regimes are varied enough to inform patterns of similarity as well as striking differences in policy making. The second chapter will outline hypothetical variation in depth. It is worth mentioning here that I aim to capture as much policy variety as possible without losing the advantages of a small-n comparison, namely to explain policy configurations across cases as multiple constituent parts in specific empirical contexts (Della Porta 2008). Regime theory suggests that France serves as a bridging case between the opposing British and German case. Aligning with the latter, France displays a capitalist economy and welfare state that diverges much from the British case (Amable 2003; Esping-Andersen 1990; Kitschelt et al. 1999b). Moreover, France and Germany usually embrace EU regulation but both have chosen a cautious approach toward free movement for new accession state members since 2004. The United Kingdom opts out of most EU directives but opened free-movement options for Eastern Europeans much more liberally. Aligning with the United Kingdom, however, France displays a similar citizenship and historical migration regime with strong post-colonial underpinnings—all while operating different integration approaches—which has traditionally been in stark contrast to the German model of ethnic belonging (Brubaker 1992; Favell 2001; Howard 2009; Joppke 2005b). This theoretical cross-pairing of cases, with France assuming a hub position in between the most different cases of Germany and the United Kingdom, promises to shed light on the relative weight of economic, social, and civic logics of organizing policies (chapter 2).

Some definitional groundwork is apt. For the purposes of this book, *migration* describes cross-national movements of people of some permanence. An individual who resides in a country of which they are not a national for at least one year is considered a migrant (Jordan and Düvell 2003). Within these limits, this research specifically covers the regulation of formal labor migration from so-called third countries; that is countries that are neither part of the European Union nor of the European Free Trade Association (EFTA, covering Switzerland, Norway, Iceland, and Liechtenstein) and are thus not covered by

EU internal market regulation.[3] The concentration on legal movements—as in legal labor migration—does not downplay the role of unauthorized migrants in the European Union.[4] I rather comprehend them as a direct effect of policies that exclude some migrant workers from legal entry to the labor market; indeed, the concept of border drawing emphasizes the chief role of legislation in legalizing some flows while illegalizing others (chapter 1). Illegality is an inherent effect of border drawing and is co-observed in our critical analysis of labor migration management.

The analysis further excludes non-work movements such as those of students, family members, or asylum seekers. While these categories of migrants dominate distinctions in official statistics and have informed clear-cut policy analyses by type of migrant (Boswell and Geddes 2011), they remain legal ideal types that are usually intertwined in practice. Our contextualized policy analysis acknowledges these empirical complications and understands labor market conditions, including informal residence and employment and the role of other migrant groups, as indispensable analytical backdrop for the interpretation of policy data. The third chapter throws robust anchors by profiling in depth the empirical contexts in which labor migration policies operate in the three countries.

Our border-drawing concept (chapter 1) seeks to examine the distinction of legal and illegal migrant workers and problematizes the neat categorization of migrant types in legislation. The same line of argument applies to my analytical focus on labor migration of third country nationals (TCN),[5] of course. This follows the regulatory distinction of labor mobility of so-called second country nationals within the European Union and national policies for the admission of workers from outside the European Union (and EFTA). When I speak of labor migration, I thus refer to the latter type. In fact, national labor migration management targets TCN workers precisely because it lacks the capacity to limit the mobility of fellow EU and EFTA Europeans. However, empirical interactions between EU labor mobility and non-EU labor migration both on actual labor markets and in legislation (remember the example of the resident labor market test) mean that policy analysis cannot ignore the EU mobility context in which TCN labor migration management operates (Paul 2011, 2013). The detailed portrayal of policy legacies and migration experiences addresses this need (chapter 3).

Overall, the contextualized comparative analysis in this book seeks to minimize the danger of reifying legal categories. Even if TCN labor migration is the analytical focus, the presence of other legal concepts such as EU mobility and their resonance in labor migration management has to be an integral part of any interpretive and critical analysis of border drawing and its effects for foreign workers.

Organization of the Book and Argument

The book contains two main parts: (I) a theoretical-analytical framework, and (II) the comparative policy analysis and discussion. The first part, titled "Border Drawing as Framework for Migration Policy Analysis," engages with the question of how to best analyze labor migration policy in comparative perspective. It introduces border drawing as an alternative framework for policy analysis (chapter 1), highlights the need to capture and compare multiple dimensions of border drawing (chapter 2), and throws contextual anchors for an ideographic comparative analysis by detailing the distinct migration experiences and policy legacies of each case (chapter 3). The first chapter introduces the border-drawing concept and its intellectual heritage. Rather than being doomed to witness the ineffectiveness of their territorial borders, states engage in "legitimate classification" as they draw borders between several legal and illegal positions for migrant workers. But how do migrants end up in the good pot, in the ideal case? Wedding the border-drawing concept to interpretive and critical policy studies in the marriage of theory and methodology, the chapter stresses the inherently normative and selective nature of border drawing and brings it to the forefront of our analytical attention. The second chapter elaborates the border-drawing framework further by investigating in potential structural sources of classification norms. Regime theories suggest that labor migration policies draw borders across an economic, social, and civic dimension, and in distinct interactions of those. This view integrates perspectives that have compared migration policies with a more singular focus on the diversity of capitalist economies, different welfare states in Europe, and citizenship regimes, respectively, and enables us to capture labor migration management—often analyzed predominantly as a matter of economic "demand and supply" or "push and pull"—in its complex multidimensionality without compromising analytical parsimony.

The third chapter carves out the context of our case-oriented comparative policy analysis. I establish a Weberian approach to comparative social sciences inquiry in which policy context itself "serves as an important explanatory variable and an enabling tool, rather than constituting a barrier to effective cross-national research" (Hantrais 1999: 94; also see Wagenaar 2011). An in-depth case profiling—with specific focus on each country's institutional setting according to regime theories, distinct policy legacies, and key features of the foreign and migrant resident population—serves the purpose of forming robust analytical anchors for the ideographic comparison of labor migration management in Germany, France, and the United Kingdom.

The second part, "Border Drawing in German, French, and British Labor Migration Policies," presents empirical findings from policy document analysis and interviews with leading policy makers in our three cases. Based on the overarching conceptualization of labor migration policy as norm loaded, multidimensional, and contextualized border drawing, three related questions for empirical analysis emerge:

- How are "legal" migrant workers selected in legislation and which policy meanings are vested in classification mechanisms? Which variations can be observed?
- Which role do economic, social, and civic classification norms play and how do these interact empirically within and across cases? How can variation be explained?
- Which sorting effects do overall border-drawing regimes entail for migrant workers?

The fourth chapter maps policies, selection tools, and legal principles by which migrant workers are chosen as legal entrants in each country. Data stem from a document analysis of thirty-three pieces of legislation (see appendices) and consultation reports up to autumn 2011, with comments on more recent developments up to November 2013 discussed in the book's concluding section. A key finding is the overwhelming comparative similarity in selecting migrant workers by skill level and by the scarcity of the skills profile they offer. Selection by skill level and labor scarcity, however, coexists with policy tools that classify legal migrant workers by their origin, by social cohesion concerns, or with annual numerical limits in highly diverse ways across our three cases. As it cannot establish any straightforward selection of migrant workers by their economic utility alone in either case, the chapter starts throwing light on so far rather overlooked norms of labor migration management as key sources of policy variation.

The fifth and sixth chapters examine the roots of at the same time similar and diverse labor migration management regimes by considering the meanings policy makers vest in migrant classifications. This is based on semi-structured expert interviews with leading decision makers (see appendices) in Berlin, Paris, and London carried out until May 2011. The fifth chapter identifies three shared economic imaginaries that operate in labor migration policies in all three cases. Shared economic judgments on the usefulness of *certain kinds* of migrant workers constitute overwhelming commonalities in border drawing by skill level and labor scarcity. While high-skilled recruitment is considered to be part of a supply-led "global" knowledge-based economy that needs facilitation, skilled recruitment counts as legitimate strategy only if a concrete domestic shortage exists. Lower skilled migration is almost entirely crowded out by the assumption of vast EU-internal labor supply. The sixth chapter demonstrates that the variable policy contexts depicted in chapter 3 inform highly diverse migration control agendas across our three cases and eventually inform nationally distinct uses of bilateral agreements, regularization practices for informal workers, or annual caps. Data show, for example, that post-colonial legacies are mapped onto economic admission strategies in the French and British case, highlight Germany's geopolitical concern with European workforce management, or point to the relevance of heightened levels of EU mobility as distinct driver of recent restrictions to labor migration in Britain.

Overall, findings portray labor migration management as much more than "a tool for growth"[6] in response to economic needs. The multidimensional policy analysis reappraises scholarly work that predominantly emphasizes the economic drivers of labor migration management. While confirming that economic utility matters, this book evidences that labor migration policies also operates as devices for the management of post-colonial relations, the control of distinctive resident populations, the activation of the resident workforce, or the strengthening of a country's geopolitical role in Europe. My discussion of more recent policy reforms (from the end of this book's data-gathering cutoff point in late 2011 up to November 2013) in the conclusion depicts a deepening of these dynamics.

We leave off where we began then: with coexisting tales of labor migration policy. To be sure, labor migration management is a reflection of policy complexity and tensions between economic openness and societal closure reactions. Yet both the conceptual and ontological engagement in part I and the comparative empirical analysis in part II of this book showcase high degrees of systematicity and orderliness behind policies as the tales are arranged in specific ways and for specific selection purposes. Far from being completely contingent, policies are structurally embedded in dominant economic production models. Yet far from being functionally determined by competitiveness and labor market conditions, labor migration management always co-governs specific populations and nationally distinct notions of work, welfare, and cultural belonging.

The precise combination of economic and socio-civic norms of border drawing bears considerable implications for migrant workers. Our discussion in the conclusion considers unequal and multi-conditional allocation patterns of labor mobility rights as powerful border-drawing effects. To pay tribute to developments after the core research span of this book, the conclusion appraises briefly any policy reform which the British, French and German governments may have initiated in the context of "crisis" since autumn 2011[7].

Our findings inform reflections on the usefulness of the border-drawing concept in migration studies and policy analysis more generally. The conclusion hence dares to promote border drawing as a holistic—that is, theory-driven and ontologically underpinned—analytical concept that is fit to capture landscapes of classification in interpretive policy studies also beyond the realm of migration. The book will hopefully convince the reader that the border-drawing lens enables us to recognize, understand, and explain in a systematic and adequately nuanced manner the emergence, reproduction, and contestation of specific normative configurations that lay at the heart of policy distinctions of legal from illegal, lawful from criminal, entitled from not entitled, deserving from undeserving objects of governance.

Notes

1. In the fairy tale "Aschenputtel," as recorded by the Brothers Grimm in German, Cinderella relies on the help of some friendly pigeons to sort lentils, asking them to put "the good into the pot, the bad into the crop."
2. Unless otherwise noted, *domestic* signifies "national" in this book. Scholars of migrants in "domestic work" as service providers in private households will excuse this flawed shorthand.
3. When I refer to third country nationals (TCN) in the remainder of the book, this excludes EU nationals plus Swiss, Norwegian, Icelandic, and Liechtenstein workers. For simplicity, I omit the additional mentioning of EFTA nationals when referring to EU workers and EU mobility rights.
4. A comparative study reports high shares of irregular migrants throughout the European Union (10 percent of total foreign population on average), reaching up to 14 percent in the Netherlands, 17.5 percent in the United Kingdom, 21.5 percent in Greece, 25 percent in Lithuania, or 34.5 percent in Romania in 2010 (Papadopoulos 2011).
5. Typical EU jargon, the term *third country national* (TCN) is used in legislation to define all nationals of non-EU countries and distinguish them from mobile EU nationals.
6. Statement of a French Migration Ministry official in an interview; see chapter 5.
7. I offer a more detailed analysis of policy change in Germany and the United Kingdom in relation to notions of "crisis" and capitalist varieties elsewhere (Paul 2014).

PART I

Border Drawing as a Framework for Migration Policy Analysis

CHAPTER 1

Labor Migration Management as Meaningful Border Drawing

> "It is in the realm of symbolic production that the grip of the state is felt most powerfully."[1]

This book sets out to understand how, exactly, states manage labor migration and how to explain variable policy approaches across Europe. How can we best conceptualize statutory migration management for this purpose? It is received wisdom that states manage migratory movements into (and sometimes out of) their territory by means of erecting and controlling borders. In an "age of migration" (Castles and Miller 2009), however, territorial borders seem increasingly permeable and unmanageable for nation-states. In consequence, many existing migration policy accounts tend to conceptualize borders as territorial demarcation lines that lose their effectiveness when migrants cross them or stay within them without permission. From this perspective, migration management fails where borders are disrespected.

Narrow border concepts such as this one underpin a lot of the discussion on managed migration in research and policy. They are problematic because they entail a bias toward physical border controls, a dichotomous notion of inside/outside, and a relative blindness toward the various stratification mechanisms applied to migrant workers *within* a state territory. Further, when measured against this book's aim of interdisciplinary comprehension and interpretive policy analysis, many accounts of migration policy—especially those written from a positivist political sciences tradition—seem to lack engagement with the normative foundations of specific border arrangements, the socioeconomic formations in which particular sets of norms emerge and gain influence in labor migration management, and the ways in which entry conditions and statuses derived from these normative decisions allocate differential sets of rights to different types of migrant worker.

The present chapter introduces the concept of border drawing as my humble attempt to overcome these conceptual shortcomings and disciplinary boundaries. I propose a Bourdieusian reading of migration management that, even though stemming from political sociology thinking, gradually enters into a fruitful discussion with legal studies and political economy as the chapter unfolds. From a border-drawing perspective, states make use of their symbolic power over "legitimate classification" to draw borders between several "legal" and "illegal" positions for migrant workers. They then allocate highly differential statuses and sets of rights to the thus sorted individuals. In proximity to authors who emphasize the relevance of policy framing for migrants' access to rights and statuses, I highlight that the legal distinction of "desired" migrant workers from those who are "unwanted" is not neutral. Rather, borders are politically inaugurated institutions that embody and institutionalize policy makers' judgments of exactly which migratory movements should count as desired or not and who can thus be labeled as a legal migrant worker. Just because these judgments are so deeply embedded in the wider socio-economic formation of European capitalism (as is well shown in a critical history of European citizenship politics by Peo Hansen and Sandy Brian Hager 2010), they cannot be assumed as a given in migration policy research.

The reader will have noticed the proximity of the border-drawing perspective to an interpretive-constructivist methodology. Indeed, my discontent with parts of the migration policy literature stems to a great deal from a wider philosophical cleavage between positivist and interpretive policy studies. From the latter angle, who counts as a legal migrant worker in labor migration management and on what basis is only fully comprehensible if we examine the multiple admission criteria and selection procedures, investigate their underpinning policy rationalities, and explain their emergence as part of the wider socio-economic formation.

This chapter should be read as an invitation to converse about contemporary migration policy studies both conceptually and methodologically speaking. It nails our colors to the mast by challenging the relative dominance of positivist accounts of labor migration management—and showing their conceptual limitations—and discusses the offerings of constitutive explanation strategies[2] and interpretive policy analysis. I seek, in best intention to comply with the quality criteria of nuanced and critical policy research, to forge an "approach to interpretive analysis [which] forms a theoretical and methodological whole" (Wagenaar 2011: 8).

Beyond Border Control: Critiquing Dominant Migration Policy Accounts

Entry and residence control count as pivotal state activities in migration studies. Indeed, we can assume that governments "want to be able to choose which people to admit, how many, for what purpose, and for how long. They do not want these decisions to be made by employers, other governments, or would-be migrants." (Weiner 1995: 12) Control claims reflect a deeper philosophical dilemma entailed in the interaction of "states" and "migration." This dilemma—and conceptual answers as to how we can best capture it—informs migration policy analysis at large, and deserves a brief résumé here. Let us commence with concepts of the state. The intrinsic link between sovereignty and territoriality in the Weberian definition of *state* emphasizes the physical borders of the terrain in which any state legitimately rules: "within a given territory" (Weber 1994). The close intersection of territory principle and nation principle in the nation-state[3] means that any physical demarcation of state equally implies—and requires—a demarcation of the population over which and for which a state can legitimately rule. Passports have been crucial in the distinction of citizens and non-citizens and represent the state's attempt to "monopolize the capacity to authorise the movement of persons" (Torpey 2000: 6). Recent comparative work expands this argument to include visa policies and showcases sovereign states' capacity to control and channel global mobility while promoting the liberal treatment of their own nationals abroad (Mau et al. 2012).

The monopoly over the "legitimate means of movement" (Torpey 2000: 7) does not just serve demarcation ends in itself; public policy largely depends on it. When we look for it, the all-embracing power of demarcation beyond migration issues becomes obvious: who has to obey traffic rules or pay taxes, who can vote, who has to serve in the armed forces, who is entitled to public schooling, healthcare or housing, whose security is protected on the state's territory and beyond it? Demarcation is essential to answering any of these questions. Without some sense of territoriality and/or population, the concept of state dissolves to a meaningless term without any reference point for its very purpose. States rely on the notion of *border* to delimit the territory on which their rule and policies apply and the number and kind of individuals that acquire rights and duties with regard to their public policy. This makes borders core ingredients of statehood; demarcation is both a key state activity of itself *and* an indispensable prerequisite for other state activities. State theorists since Weber have thus embraced the idea of a "given population" on which state apparatuses "define and enforce collectively-binding decisions" even where they depart from the territoriality principle and acknowledge multilevel forms of spatial organization, most prominently the European Union (Jessop 2008: 9).

Human migration challenges the very principle of demarcated territory and population. Fueled by globalization, "movement of all kinds across organizational borders" has become a defining feature of global economic integration (Jordan and Düvell 2003: 3). If states rely on a definition and enactment of borders to territory and population, migratory movements cannot help but trigger tensions for concepts of statehood as well as for statutory policy making. As Myron Weiner (1995) has argued, the organizing principles and functions of modern states are in constant and dire conflict with the phenomenon of human migration, informing a notion of "migration crisis."

The state-migration dilemma has important implications for policy analysis. The concern for migration in much of the present day academic and policy debate hinges on the concept of the nation-state and its ability to control its borders,[4] and thus people and their rights, on a designated territory (it is impossible to list all accounts, but a selection of relevant work might include Brochmann 1999; Castles 1995; Freeman 1998; Guild and Mantu 2011; Hammar 1990; Joppke 1998b; Mau et al. 2012; Ruhs 2013; Schierup et al. 2006). We simply cannot—or rarely—think of human migration outside the category of the state in policy sciences as long as states, or state-like entities such as the European Union, remain key providers of public policy, welfare, and security. Most research in the field thus rightly starts from the assumption that states can and shall somehow "control" their own borders. This brief overture has shown that this focus is not accidental: it embodies the deep philosophical dilemma between states—one of the most essential organizing principles of humanity—and the eternal human practice of moving across the very organizational boundaries that humanity constructs and has constructed.

Borders: A Matter of Effective State Control?

Starting from the notion of inherent conceptual tension between nation-states and migration, many scholars have scrutinized the extent to which states *can* actually control migratory movements and sought reasons for control failures. Academic debates about the "unintended consequences" of guest worker programs in the twentieth century—with workers settling rather than going back to their countries of origin—highlight that control targets have not, or at least not entirely, been met in the past (Castles 1986; Cornelius and Tsuda 2004). Frequent mass regularizations of irregular migrants (either in terms of work or residence, often both) in countries such as Italy, Spain, or Greece, but not exclusively, have time and again demonstrated the limits of regulated entry mechanisms (Peixoto 2002; Reyneri 1998; Sunderhaus 2007). Against this empirical setting, the tale of states' limited ability to effectively control their borders—and thus migration into their territory—has become commonplace in migration policy research. This is certainly most obvious in the wide reach of the so-called gap hypothesis (Cornelius et al. 2004), which claims a considerable detachment and often contradictory relationship between policy goals of restriction, regulation, and control and the rather liberal implementation practices and "unintended" or unwanted policy outcomes. It is by reviewing the main strands of migration policy literature that we can thus gain first insights in existing conceptualizations of borders and state policies' use of borders vis-à-vis migratory movements. Most influential in that respect have been neo-classic economic theory, including internationalization and globalization perspectives, rational choice as well as post-Marxist political economy accounts, multilevel governance scholarship in political sciences, but also neo-institutionalist explanations. How do these accounts treat borders and the role for state policy vis-à-vis migration?

Economic labor mobility theory, firstly, treats labor migration as a function of international trade (Ghosh 2000). Neo-classic economic theory perceives global labor markets as markets determined by demand and supply. Labor migration is believed to correspond to macroeconomic push-and-pull factors without much of a role for the state or border control: strong labor demand and high wages in industrialized countries pull migrants toward those countries, whereas bad life and work conditions, low pay, or unemployment push them away from their countries of origin (Castles and Miller 2009). Rational-choice political economy accounts of migration policy rely on this conceptualization of labor migration as a matter of global economic allocation. They presume that migration policy in liberal democracies will always be slightly expansive—irrespective of tight control targets—due to the concrete benefits employers,[5] most importantly, can expect from labor migration (Freeman 1995; Freeman and Kessler 2008). Control "gaps" and highly permeable borders emerge from the economic benefits of these very gaps for specific economic agents on the state territory. As Christina Boswell and Andrew Geddes argue (2011), the "malintegration" of tough policy rhetoric on irregular migration and more lenient implementation practices of tolerating unauthorized migrant workers is no paradox from a rational-choice perspective. Rather than representing policy failure, the control gap might entail a deliberate strategy of serving both the interests of a hostile electorate and employers' demand for cheap labor.

Some have further claimed that globalization and internationalization processes have led to the end of state control and increasing meaninglessness of nation-state borders in migration policy. With globalization's free-trade regime contributing to "a new geography of power" (Sassen 1996: 5)—predominantly visible in the establishment of transnational and international economic and trade institutions, regulatory regimes, and governance systems—we have arguably witnessed a rescaling of migration policy making to the global level. Post-Marxists have criticized that this rescaling and de-bordering process has so far not gone hand in hand with the advancement of a global regime of citizenship and migrant rights that could cushion global social inequalities caused by economic globalization (Cohen 1987, 2006; Jordan and Düvell 2003). While arguing over the guiding ideologies and directions of labor migration regimes in the twenty-first century, liberal and post-Marxist economists agree on the fundamental diagnosis of an ever-fading role for states and nation-state borders in migration control.

Neo-institutionalist strands of migration policy literature, by contrast, locate the source of limited control in liberal states themselves. The "liberal constraint" thesis identifies vital institutional constraints to effective border control and considers their source in liberal democratic constitutions themselves (Hollifield 2004a; Joppke 1998c, 2005a; Joppke and Morawska 2003). States risk losing their democratic legitimacy when excluding migrants from the liberal human rights regime that otherwise applies on their territory. Rather than reflecting an economic superimposition, states' limited ability to effectively ensure territorial borders originates from the imperatives of their very own democratic constitution principles and values. Deportation and the long-term denial of rights to residents contradict the guiding principles of democratic societies. Indeed, research has shown that the "moral political economy" of including "good" residents can even justify regularizations of otherwise "illegal" migrants in liberal states (Chauvin and Garcés-Mascareñas 2012). Courts can play an important role as enforcers of rights in that respect, as Christian Joppke (1998a, 1998c) has shown with regard to liberalizations of long-term resident rights, rights to asylum, family reunion, and access to citizenship in the European Union.

Irrespective of the probable causes of limited border-control abilities, governments, some argue, have not been inert toward potential control losses. Rather, they have engaged in strategic "externalization" of control (Boswell 2003, 2008; Lavenex 2005; Lavenex and Uçarer 2002; Mau et al. 2012), especially so in a context of economic integration in the European Union. The Schengen border co-operation framework serves as a prime example of supranational "pooling" of sovereignty with the aim of retaining control over migratory movements in an economically integrating Europe. This entails a delocalization of border control rather than a loss: rule making and implementation in migration policy are being dispersed to levels and agencies that are believed to be more capable of achieving control targets. Delocalization can also take the form of outsourcing: private actors such as air carrier companies are, for instance, increasingly involved in the detention and expulsion of irregular residents (Menz 2010b). For many, these dispersal strategies do not imply control losses over borders but enable more sophisticated control by other means, which even allows bypassing some of the domestic and economic constraints mentioned earlier (Brochmann 1999; Freeman 1998; Mau et al. 2012; Neal 2009).

In the setting of European labor migration policy, delocalization strategies mainly resonate on the EU level. Indeed, issues such as integration, rights of foreign residents, or asylum have been a matter of shared competency between the Commission and the Council since the Amsterdam Treaty came into force in 1999 (Boswell and Geddes 2011; Roos 2013). With the Lisbon Treaty, signed in 2010, guidelines for legal admissions and labor migration have also become subject to the community method of EU decision making, with qualified majority voting reigning in the Council and the European Parliament acting as co-legislator (Carrera et al. 2011). A number of scholars diagnosed a gradual Europeanization of policy making and increasing shifts to multilevel governance in that respect (Boswell and Geddes 2011; Faist and Ette 2007; Menz 2009; Roos 2013; Zincone and Caponio 2006). Certainly, member states have so far resisted a full-blown European harmonization of migrant admissions and integration, with countries such as the United Kingdom or Denmark opting out of most directives and EU decision making explicitly excluding the definition of volumes and specific criteria for admitting migrants so far. At the same time, however, some aspects of migration and integration policy, such as the rights of long-term residents or family members of migrants, are now subject to the Commission's input and have come to determine national policies (CEU 2003a, 2003b). To be sure, the EU governance of migrant rights and statuses is of itself a growing and ever more specialized industry and has direct implications for member states as well as regional migration and integration approaches (Berg and Spehar 2013; Boswell and Geddes 2011; Campomori and Caponio 2013; Carmel and Paul 2013a, 2013b). Christof Roos' (2013) analysis of the negotiation processes around several key directives demonstrates well how European Union immigration policies have even produced considerable "cracks in the walls of fortress Europe".

It would be short sighted, however, to label these dynamics as a loss of border control for nation-states. Member states are known to use the EU level—and other supranational or international arenas—as a strategic venue to bypass domestic constraints and achieve restrictive policy targets (e.g., Guiraudon 2000). Asylum restrictions throughout the European Union, for example, have been actively shaped and used by individual member states to toughen more liberal and constitutionally anchored domestic approaches. Scholars highlight the benefits of border delocalization strategies for host countries—be it within the European Union, in so-called partnerships targeting emigration control in sending states, or with private security agencies (e.g., Kunz 2013; Mau et al. 2012; Menz 2010b). While delocalization perspectives highlight states' ability to develop response strategies to weakening border-control capacities, they usually do not dispute the basic assumptions of the gap hypothesis: seldom do border-control aims and outcomes link up in national migration management. Delocalization scholarship fruitfully challenges the traditional nation-state-centric concept of borders that is echoed in most of the approaches we discussed earlier. Yet accounts often stop just short of questioning the very usefulness of geographical conceptualizations of borders in migration policy analysis[6].

Simply In or Out? Migrants, Borders, and the Definition of Legality

Have states reached the point where attempts to manage migration and control physical borders have become untenable? There are several grounds for conceptual discontent with the "control lost" / "control shifted" scenario. This book questions the analytical value of understanding borders predominantly as territorial demarcation lines, which lose their effectiveness and meaning when crossed by a migrant without authorization. There is, in large sections of the migration policy literature, a concern with effective physical border control, a rather dichotomous view on insiders and outsiders, and a relative disregard for the societal effects of defining legal/illegal migration *within* a given territory. While helping to explain how borders work or don't work once they have been set up, these accounts, I argue, tend to obstruct our view on the very process of setting up borders as one of the most powerful state activities in labor migration.

To be sure, many migration policy accounts pay surprisingly little attention to the realms where state authority is extremely visible. In an analysis of deportation policies in Germany and the United States, Antje Ellermann (2009: 6) rightly finds it "surprising … that the vast literature on state capacity has virtually ignored the study of coercive social regulation." Deportations happen irrespective of the alleged liberal constraints operating in democratic states, as we are regularly reminded by media coverage. It is not merely in the realm of deportation and removal that states attempt to channel flows into paths congruent with their policy objectives. Even where they cannot control, keep out, or deport migrants physically, states define and apply differential regimes of rights and duties to everyone living on their territory. State policies can define who is entitled to what rights, affected by which duties, benefit from what kind of public service provision, and under which conditions.[7]

States' activity of defining rights and duties and conditions for access to public goods seems somewhat underestimated in the migration-control debate. This role is most evident in their capacity to distinguish between legal and illegal migratory movements in state legislation and to attach differential rights regimes to this very distinction. Statutory laws largely—though not entirely—monopolize control over access to the provision of public goods such as welfare entitlements, housing, health care, schooling, and employment for migrants. Borders to these realms might not always coincide; being "legal" in one realm does not necessarily imply "legality" in all the others. If anything, the wide range of different permits, entry criteria, and associated residence and work rights in Europe indicates that public policy paints many different shades of legality and thus allocates rights in highly selective ways. There is a multiplicity of statuses on the legal-illegal continuum (Chauvin and Garcés-Mascareñas 2012; Ruhs and Anderson 2010a), statuses that are in themselves highly volatile and are not usually organized in straightforward hierarchies of "more-or-less" included migrants (Carmel and Paul 2013b).

Rather than limiting migration control to the enforcement of territorial borders, states construct various borders to migration through a wider set of policies that determine labor market access, welfare entitlements, and other sets of rights *within* the territory of the state.

A whole range of authors have been preoccupied with the multiplicity and distributional consequences of *internal* borders as means of ordering migration phenomena—even where they occur without authorization. Representative of a wider debate could be the following: Thomas Hammar's (1990) portrayal of subsequent "entry gates" for migrants from initial immigration to naturalization; Lydia Morris's (2002) finding of "civic stratification" of rights for different types of migrant residents, Steve Peer's (2001) notion of a "sliding scale" of rights by which migrants are gradually included in a host country; John Crowley's (2001) work on differential "internal" borders for EU free movers; but also our own reflections on the "complex stratification" of migrant statuses and rights in EU regulation (Carmel and Paul 2013b). Empirical research has shown that migration policies fuel far-reaching internal inclusion and exclusion mechanisms in that respect, with rights distributions going way beyond any binary notion of physical "in" or "out" (Banting 2000; Bommes and Geddes 2000b; Carmel et al. 2011; Koopmans 2010; Ruhs 2013; Ryner 2000; Sainsbury 2006; Schierup et al. 2006).

What unites these various scholarly perspectives is the insight that states erect various borders to labor markets, welfare states, and political communities *within* their bordered territory and thereby govern migrant populations even where they cannot control their entry or departure. From this view, borders to migration cannot be conceived of as mere territorial demarcation lines. Borders operate to distinguish people, their rights, and statuses within a given territory. Borders are not solely (and maybe not even predominantly) concerned with granting or denying access to a territory, but with regulating access to specific statuses—such as "legal" worker, family member, student or refugee—and defining the distinctive sets of economic, social, and political rights that come with this status.

Migration Policy as Border Drawing: A Bourdieusian Classification Approach

While the conceptual tension between nation-states and migration will not vanish, states can and do shape migration according to the objectives vested in policies within their territories. Instead of perceiving territorial integrity as an indicator of effective border control, this book proposes an alternative reading of migration management. It thereby adds to a growing body of work that unpacks migration policies as a means of *constructing* (rather than just reflecting) statuses of legality and illegality according to very specific normative agendas. Drawing largely on Pierre Bourdieu's work on "symbolic power" and "classification," I develop the concept of border drawing. *Border drawing* is defined as the classificatory process by which policies categorize migrants into various positions of legality and illegality according to specific predefined sets of norms. This reconceptualization of migration policy informs the later empirical analysis of labor migration management, with a particular focus on the ways in which laws demarcate and differentiate statuses, select legitimate entrants, and stratify migrant workers' access to various rights, and the justifications of all these normative decisions by policy makers themselves.

Symbolic Power and Classificatory Struggles

Outside positivist political science and rational-choice economic analyses of labor migration policies, anthropologists and political sociologists especially have problematized the notion of borders and boundaries as territorial reflection of inside and outside statuses. Bridget Anderson's sharp analysis of Britain's historical and contemporary constructions of "Us and Them" highlights the status-producing function of borders in migration policies: "International borders are commonly presented as filters, sorting out the desirable from the undesirable, the genuine from the bogus, the legal from the illegal.... However, ... borders are not simply territorial, but they reach into the heart of political space.... Laws and practices of citizenship ... may be more usefully analysed as *producing* rather than reflecting status, as creating specific types of social, political and economic relations" (2013: 2, emphasis in the original).

An understanding of borders not as neutral demarcation lines that reflect a given status of inclusion and exclusion, but as loaded classificatory systems that are being continuously produced through state policies and social practices also features heavily in race and ethnicity studies. Andreas Wimmer's work (e.g., 2008) on "ethnic boundary making" in particular showcases how ethnic markers of division are construed, filled with meaning through policy and practice, but also challenged and remade across modern societies. Like Bridget Anderson, Wimmer identifies powerful state work behind the scenes of boundary making, arguing that the organization of the modern nation-state has relied on ethnic definitions of *us* and *them* and continues to inflict those in many of its policies and thus social relations on its territory. These observations concur with Zygmut Bauman's (2004: 33) view that "the nation-state has claimed the right to preside over the distinction between order and chaos, law and lawlessness, citizens and homo sacer, belonging and exclusions, useful product and waste." By defining borders to labor markets, welfare, public services, security, or franchise in policies, states powerfully shape (though never fully determine) principles of belonging across a variety of social spheres.

But *how* exactly are borders drawn and how can we analyze border drawing empirically? Pierre Bourdieu's reflections on classification (1989, 1991, 1998) and symbolic power are highly valuable for carving out the border-drawing concept further. Bourdieu sees classifications as key mechanisms by which social positions and relations between individuals and groups are constructed and reproduced in the social world. He considers classifications as products of "symbolic struggles" over the legitimate vision and division of the social world. This means that the "space of relations," later called "social space," is not completely structurally determined but is constructed and constantly reconstructed in powerful "symbolic" struggles over classification.

While some properties of individuals—such as age, gender, race, educational attainment—are perceived as ontologically real in Bourdieu and have structuring effects as to agents' position in the social space, the way in which they structure these positions is not predetermined. Rather, a person's status and position in the social space depends to a great deal on the ascription of meaning to their individual properties in classificatory struggles and the recognition of these meanings as valid visions of difference (see also Wimmer 2008). Policies, in this reading, are preliminary codifications of meaning, temporary winner stories in the struggle over legitimate classification. Whether my language skills, my age, my biological gender, or my nationality are advantageous for (or indeed detrimental to) my entry and residence to country X is a matter of the value ascribed to these credentials in the countries' labor admission policies.

The Bourdieusian reading is akin to scholars who have examined the discursive framing of migration policies. For example, Peo Hansen and Sandy Brian Hager (2010) have traced the historical emergence of EU citizenship in respective regulation and analyzed its effects with regard to inclusion and exclusion of different groups of migrants. Their documentary research spans the whole history of the Union and demonstrates an increasing entanglement of a rights dimension (emphasizing economic belonging) and an identity dimension (highlighting a shared Judeo-Christian heritage) of EU citizenship. This, they argue, explains the notionally contradictory coexistence of a high demand for unauthorized and/or informal migrant workers from outside the European Union as cheap labor and their staging as potential security threats—especially when of Muslim faith—in need of tough assimilation measures. Steve Peers (2001) identifies four different models of "migrant" in European Community Law—workers, aliens, citizens and humans—and relates diverse policy orientations and migrant rights regimes to these. We are thus left with a four-fold classification regime that governs the produced groups according to different norms. In a similar vein, Sébastien Chauvin and Blanca

Garcés-Mascareñas (2012) show how civic or economic deservingness frames in different legislations can—within limits—inform access to more substantial rights for law-abiding and economically successful unauthorized migrants.

Other studies could be mentioned (e.g., Carmel 2011; Kofman 2002; Sales 2002), but I limit myself here to some for illustration of the analytical value that these scholars attribute to conceptualizing migration policy making as an activity of "labeling" and sorting out migrants according to specific normative visions about *good* and *bad*, *deserving* and *undeserving*. It is in this spirit that this book seeks to put Bourdieusian classification processes on center stage in migration policy analysis.

Border Drawing in Public Law

Labeling is a tricky business when it is done by states. The reader will have noted that states assume a great deal of power in classificatory struggles. This is, of course, no coincidence and is closely related to the condition of recognition that Bourdieu associates with the success of classificatory struggles. His concept of symbolic power acknowledges that not just anything goes in the shaping of social relations, and that the state enjoys a privileged role in classificatory struggles. While anyone can say and mean anything linguistically, not anyone can impose any vision of the world sociologically (Bourdieu 1991: 74). Asymmetric power relations in the social space and unequal access to "symbolic capital"—in addition to the well-known notions of economic, social, and cultural capital—found a particularly powerful role for the state in classificatory processes: "In the symbolic struggle for the production of common sense or, more precisely, for the monopoly over legitimate naming, agents put into action the symbolic capital that they have acquired in previous struggles and which may be juridically guaranteed" (Bourdieu 1989: 21).

As states enjoy a "monopoly over legitimate symbolic violence"[8] and collectively binding legislation, activities of "naming" and "labeling" are much more consequential if they are done by the state rather than by individual agents (Bourdieu 1989, 1991, 1998). If symbolic divisions, say into good and bad migrant workers, can only become influential when "recognized, that is misrecognized as arbitrary" (Bourdieu 1991: 170),[9] then certainly the state's monopoly over symbolic violence offers a powerful source for such recognition. Unlike other agents in classification processes, the state can legitimately enforce classifications drawn in public law: it is "a necessary aspect of state-law that it is coercively enforced through the use, when necessary, of physical means to compel compliance. State law is coercive as well as an institutional form of normative order" (MacCormick 2007: 54).

Eventually then, the ability to classify and define in official legislation legitimate voters, unemployment beneficiaries, pensioners, criminals, pupils in compulsory schooling, soldiers for mandatory service, civil servants, refugees, official dignitaries, or, to the point, legal migrant workers—and to equally exclude all others from the scope of these definitions and the rights or duties attached to them—must be conceived as one of the most triumphant instances of the state's symbolic power in action.[10] Speaking of Bourdieu again: "One of the major powers of the state is to produce and impose categories of thought that we spontaneously apply to all things of the social world—including the state itself." And further: "It is in the realm of symbolic production that the grip of the state is felt most powerfully" (1998: 35, 38).

Such "categories of thought"—borders between legal and illegal migrant workers in our case—are laid out deep within the realm of public law. Law can be understood as an "institutional normative order" with an "aspiration to order in the sense of orderliness" (MacCormick 2007: 11). A lot of the above-discussed migration policy literature takes the "aspiration to order" in public law for granted: while analyzing the effectiveness of admission regimes at face value, they tend to, all too hastily, discount the normative orders entailed in admission policies and misrecognize their function of sorting individuals into *legal* and *illegal* categories in the social space.

To overcome such orthodoxies, border drawing in migration policy can best be understood as the codification of a specific classificatory regime for migrant workers in public law—a regime whose very existence and emergence deserves analytical attention. When examining border drawing, we thus need to start with identifying and describing legal classifications and the principles of sorting labor migrants instigated in public law. In this book, a careful reconstruction of the key markers of division between different legal migrant worker statuses and illegal positions informs the latter analysis of the normative compass that enabled the emergence of specific border-drawing regimes. This two-fold analytical strategy is important, as it seeks to avoid collapsing legal classifications (see chapter 4) and policy makers' visions of them (see chapters 5 and 6) into one set of data. Such a strategy would hastily dismiss the possibility of similar legal classifications—say of migrant workers by skill level—but variable justifications (and thus normative drivers) for them in British, French, and German policies. Equally, similar visions of the world might not always lead to the same policy tools. In order to avoid reifications of orthodox narratives of why *legal* is legal and *illegal* is illegal, therefore, laws and justifications ought to be treated separately in analysis.

How exactly can we trace instances of legal classification? Public law is probably a grateful object of analysis for—unlike less formalistic policy documents or manifestos—its business is precisely the creation of straightforward and clear provisions for inclusion and exclusion, legality and illegality, lawfulness and punishment. Legal classifications rely on specific principles to distinguish between the very categories they seek to create. No classification works without a criterion for distinction, so it is classification criteria that we are after in analysis (see chapter 4) first. If public legislation establishes a minimum age, say of eighteen years, as a criterion for classifying those allowed to buy alcoholic drinks and those who are not, then the border to legal drinking will be manifested through age. It could just as well be gender or religion, or a combination of these. The decision of policy makers could, of course, also be an outright prohibition of any drinks for anyone—in which case we would not need to categorize people in order to regulate their alcohol-intake rights. Usually, however, public policies operate with much less universal and more fine-grained classifications—certainly so in the migration case.

As with legitimate drinkers, legal migrant workers are selected and classified according to certain principles. Anyone not matching these is deemed to either remain outside the country or occupy a notionally "illegal" position. It is by studying and analyzing classification principles and criteria, then, that we can trace the precise location of borders in labor migration. The comparative exploration of labor migration management in Britain, France, and Germany (chapters 4, 5, and 6) will substantiate this perspective empirically and offer a basis for critically discussing implications of border-drawing processes in Europe.

It goes without saying that the empirical examination of classificatory regimes needs to pay attention to their dynamic and multidimensional character. As they depend on sustained recognition, classificatory struggles are never "won" once and for all. Andreas Wimmer's (2008) work on ethnic boundaries indicates how their realm can be expanded, reduced, reinterpreted, and overcome by policies and the social practices of people affected by them. Practices aside, with each amendment of legislation or implementation practice, public law has to either confirm or redefine classification principles as well as the respective insider and outsider positions. The introduction highlighted, for instance, that the principles that guided bilateral recruitment of lower-skilled guest workers in the immediate postwar period since the 1950s is no longer applicable in twenty-first-century labor migration management. This reflects no less than a massive shift in the underlying classification principles and admission criteria that single out a "desired" migrant worker from those unwanted in admission policies.

In addition, cross-sectional policy complexity makes border drawing a rather murky business. Across the variety of policy domains—schools, pensions, health care, military, tax system, civil service, employment, and so on—individuals can be labeled as insiders and outsiders at the same time. Indeed, this recognition served as one of my key criticisms of dichotomous territorial border concepts above. Migrants can, for example, be formally entitled to enter or reside, but still be excluded from the labor market. This is the case of workers in some older member states from the recent EU accession countries, but also applies to asylum seekers who might have temporary leave to remain and access to basic health care, but are often not allowed to work or have a family life in the host country (Bloch 2008; Carmel and Paul 2013b). While this monograph is not able to trace shifts in border-drawing processes over time (some initial reflections on policy shifts in the conclusion aside; see Paul 2014 for an analysis of change in two cases), the multidimensional policy analysis established in chapter 2 seeks to do justice to the complexity of border-drawing regimes by analyzing the very interaction of multiple principles of classifying legal and illegal migrant workers.

Border Drawing as Ontology: Meaning Making and Selectivity in Migration Governance

Equipped with the concept of border drawing, the contours of our analytical framework for comparing labor migration management across different European countries become clearer. Missing is a specification of the book's ontological and epistemological position toward key paradigmatic cleavages in social sciences. I allude to the fairy tale of Cinderella to introduce this reflection. The border-drawing perspective, thus forth, enables us to identify patterns of sorting "good" migrants into the pot (i.e., granting them a legal status) and "bad" ones into the crop (i.e., condemning them to an illegal status). By comparing admission laws, we can observe, for instance, that the British points-based system differentiates between three different professional skill levels and defines three work-related tiers for work visas. In a simple analysis, this could lead to the conclusion that "good" and "bad" are distinguished according to a migrant workers' skills profile. So what? In the social world the sorting of migrants is not determined by natural laws. Borders entail a whole set of politically inaugurated principles that define the grounds on which a migrant should be classified as legal or illegal: these could include their skills profile, age, nationality, language proficiency, or their previous links to the country of destination, or they could not. The specific combination of classification principles in admission policies involve a highly selective normative vision and division of the world that should not—but often is—be taken for granted in policy analysis. As Leo R. Chavez (2007: 192) suitably points out, "illegality" is "a status resulting from political decisions made by governmental representatives, who could just as well have decided to allow migrants to enter." Seeking to understand just why a decision has been made one way and no other, this book looks behind the surface of seemingly evident classifications of legal migrant workers by their skill levels, earning potentials, cultural and geographical backgrounds, and so on. Our aim is to unpack, compare and explain the emergence of such norm-ridden classifications in their specific empirical contexts.

Accounting for Meaning Making: Semiosis in Policy Studies

The focus on *semiosis*—or meaning making—in policy analysis is by now well established.[11] Interpretive policy analysis (IPA) has become an academic trademark within social science research, including a specific research network and its own international conference with annually growing attendance. Irrespective of the range of different empirical interests, concepts, and methods surfacing in research, it seems fair to argue that IPA scholars share an understanding of policy not as something that follows general laws, rational thinking, objective reason, or surrounding structural impetuses. Instead, IPA understands policies as meaningful social artifacts that entail normative judgments about the world, seek to order it in a specific way, and are created and recreated through the formulation and communication of political arguments by miscellaneously powerful actors. In an early and influential text on the subject, Deborah Stone (1988: 306) tells us that "the categories of thought behind reasoned analysis are themselves constructed in political struggle … [as it] always involves choices to include some things and exclude others and to view the world in a particular way when other visions are possible." Whether we consider the "construction of facticity" in policy discourse (Fischer 2007), the role of "interpretive communities" in "sense-making" of the social world (Yanow 2000, 2007), the heavy reliance on "presuppositional concepts" (Wagenaar 2011), or the discursive establishment of the "parameters of the context" in policy making (van Dijk 1997); IPA accounts share a focus on the meanings policies, policy makers, and those governed by policies attach to the social world and the consequences of powerful meaning ascriptions.

IPA scholarship posits that policies such as labor migration management do not have "natural" meanings nor do they derive their meanings from social conditions in any deterministic way. Policies *mean* because they have been designed to mean a particular (and no other) thing, have been populated with specific (and no other) normative assumptions, draw on specific (and no other) existing symbolic orders, and do so in a particular (and no other) way. I have previously criticized part of the migration policy literature for downplaying the effect of labeling a migrant as "illegal" in policies. This criticism reflects a wider epistemological division in policy research into critical interpretivist accounts and positivist-empiricist policy analysis (for a good overview of the debate, see Stone 2012; Wagenaar 2011).

Indeed, governance studies—emergent in the late 1980s in an Anglo-American context—were mostly concerned with the changing nature of state policy and modes of coordination beyond markets and hierarchies. Studies captured changes in public-service design and delivery in terms of a "hollowing-out of the state" (Bevir and Rhodes 2003; Peters and Pierre 1998; Rhodes, 1996). Governance signified a change in the meaning of government and referred to "the new method by which society is governed," especially the inclusion of non-state actors in public coordination (Rhodes 1996: 46). The subsequent focus on modes on the efficiency and effectiveness of certain types of policy coordination—be they markets, hierarchies, networks, or multilevel arrangements—in large chunks of policy and governance research often implied analytical neglect of the objectives and underpinning normative assumptions instated through specific policy-making arrangements.

This lead interpretive policy analysts and critical governance scholars to criticize "the effort to exclude meaning and values from the work of the policy analyst [as this] cuts the very heart out of political inquiry"[12] (Fischer 2003: 216). Instead, they propose interpretive-constructivist methodologies to overcome positivist empiricism (see, among others, Fischer 2003, 2007; Gottweis 2003; Hajer and Wagenaar 2003a; Stone 2012; Wagenaar 2011; Yanow 2000). For example, Emma Carmel and Theo Papadopoulos (2003) usefully distinguish between modes and methods of governance (operational dimension) and the substance of what it is that is to be governed, how it is constituted through operational governance arrangements, and with what aims and effects (formal dimension). Empirical analyses of economic governance have showcased, for example, how the norms of *capitalist* socio-economic formations have become inscribed into (and are thus reproduced through) the very modes of coordination (Jessop 1997; Jessop and Sum 2006; Sum 2009). The conceptual discussions of the earlier sections of this chapter are thus of methodological character, though they are regrettably not usually explicated in this clarity. By concentrating on the effectiveness and strategies of territorial border enforcement, orthodox migration-control studies tend to fall short of explaining the emergence of the very border arrangements. Yet, taking borders for granted means underestimating their power as norm-driven constructions of legality and illegality that come to be accepted as "normal" and can thus unfold their far-reaching consequences for migrant workers' rights and perception as "good" or "bad" in a host country.

Accounting for Selectivity: A Cultural Political Economy Lens

The state's attempt to classify migrant workers into categories based on specific ideas about the meaning of legal labor migration is of course much more complex than Cinderella's lentil-sorting job. There are various types of good and bad, many in-between categories, many more statuses than just pot or crop, and there is certainly a vast choice of normative references to inform the sorting exercise. Meaning making is a complex governance process. Policy frames—say the desirability of high-skilled workers—are by no means given, even though a lot of the debate on this issue seems to take this positive policy framing for granted (e.g., Cerna 2013; Devitt 2012; Laubenthal 2012; OECD 2009; Ruhs 2013; Zaletel 2006; Zimmermann 2005). Rather, meanings are selected and vested in policies with the intention of structuring the social world according to specific norms.[13] For example, even though it is widely acknowledged in economics that lower-skilled workers can equally fill important shortages in host labor markets, it is usually only high-skilled migrants who are framed as "desired" in policy discourse (Anderson 2010a, 2013; Boswell and Geddes 2011; Ruhs and Anderson 2010b). Competing concerns such as domestic unemployment in lower-skilled job markets are believed to mitigate the economic labor demand argument. This simple example—which will be substantiated in the empirical analysis later—shows that policy rationales are not functionally determined by economic demand, for instance, but are carefully *selected,* combined, and fine-tuned in policy making.

Our analytical framework must pay tribute to the fact that classifications entail constant choices about the norms that should guide divisions. From an array of potential normative principles for classification, legislators select some and disregard others. In the case of migration policy this governance process concerns the selection of certain classification principles for legal labor admissions (skill level, for example) over others and the creation of certain rights regimes for migrant workers rather than alternative regimes. Faced with the variety of thinkable interpretations of the social world and potential tensions between symbolic orders, policy making emphasizes some aspects of the social world and ignores others. In meaning-making processes, power[14] and politics are played out through selection.

To capture this selective momentum of migrant worker classification in border drawing analytically, I frame this study with a cultural political economy lens—inspired mainly by Bob Jessop and Ngai-Ling Sum's works (Jessop 2009; Jessop and Sum 2006, 2010; Sum, 2009; Sum and Jessop 2013). This serves a dual aim: firstly, it integrates the legal analysis with the political economy perspective that I promised would illuminate the socio-economic conditions under which specific norms for sorting migrant workers can emerge and become dominant. Secondly, it creates a systematic interpretivist framework for migration policy analysis more generally, as cultural political economy (CPE) lets us examine labor migration management as *a selective meaning-making process*. More precisely, CPE serves three purposes in our study: (1) it offers a useful understanding of classification principles in border drawing as selectively framed and constructed according to specific normative presumptions; (2) it helps exposing the strategic momentum of meaning making in policy; and (3) it is particularly interested in economic formations and governance processes and hence offers a useful analytical toolbox and vocabulary for a study of labor migration as embedded in specific political economies.

CPE explains the emergence of directions and modes of economic coordination in terms of the strategic variation, selection, and retention of policy meanings and policy tools over time (Jessop 2009; Sum and Jessop 2013). Governance is hence understood as an attempt of political ordering that engages with competing interpretations and structural sedimentations in a given policy field, labor migration in our case; selects and imposes specific semiotic orders; and ultimately structures the rights and statuses of those governed through the policy according to these normative foundations. Jessop and Sum propose to study why exactly certain economic formations, policy mechanisms, and interpretations of the social world get selected, become powerful, and are retained and reproduced in collective meaning-making processes. With a view on empirical analyses, Jessop (2009: 344) introduces the analytical category of economic imaginaries, arguing that the CPE approach: "highlights the role of discursively-selective institutions in the making of economic [and social] practices and, a fortiori, economic [and social] policies. *Imaginaries* are semiotic systems that frame individual subjects' lived experiences of an inordinately complex world and/or inform collective calculation about that world. … They identify, privilege, and seek to stabilize some economic [and social] activities from the totality of economic [and social] relations and transform them into objects of … governance" (emphasis mine).

It is the analytical device of economic imaginaries that enables this book to compare exactly which aspects of the socio-economic world Britain, France, and Germany accentuate in their respective labor migration policies, which ones they choose to neglect and why. By identifying the dominant economic imaginaries of labor migration, I scrutinize the meanings and roles policy ascribes to labor migration and migrant workers, the selective character of these normative prescriptions, and the strategic and selective contextualization of labor migration management in multiple and sometimes competing normative frameworks within the wider socio-economic formation (this last point will be specified in the next chapter). The CPE analysis in chapters 4–6 thus also adds to the current elaboration and analytical specification of CPE as an emerging framework for critical policy studies (see Paul 2012a).

It is important to recollect Bourdieu's notion of symbolic power at this point: the initial (and seemingly arbitrary) selection momentum highlighted by CPE is preliminarily neutralized with the recognition and solidification of the proposed symbolic order as a shared imaginary[15]—and especially so when its normative principles have been codified in law. Policy analysis is all too easily seduced to buy into these imaginaries as given structures: the examination of policy effectiveness, or the modes, mechanisms, and levels of public policy governance is frequently decoupled from an investigation of the underpinning normative choices, their deliberation, and their constitutive causes (this criticism is stated, for instance, by Carmel and Papadopoulos 2003; Fischer 2007; Gottweis 2003; Hajer and Wagenaar 2003b; Stone 2012). The political momentum of *choosing* particular sets of meanings and vesting them in a policy continuously operates alongside that very policy and the institutions created for its effective operation; an interrelated dynamic that requires analytical unpacking.[16]

Governance processes are, at the same time, structurally embedded and constitutive of new meaning. This book takes on board this insight as one of the crucial contributions of the CPE agenda for the analysis of economic coordination processes—foreign labor recruitment in our case. The CPE authors suggest navigating between "the structuralist Scylla and the constructivist Charybdis" (Sum and Jessop 2013, chapter 4 heading). At one extreme end, orthodox economic thinking "fetishizes economic categories, naturalizes economic actions, institutions and 'laws', and neglects their ties to the wider social formation" (203). At the other extreme, radical constructivist analyses are castigated for falling into the opposite trap of misrecognizing the impact of structural preconditions of policy making. This, however, obscures the view on the power of already institutionalized social relations to delimit—though never fully predetermine and certainly not unwavering—the range of *actualizable* social formations and to thus structure the 'compossibility' of specific discourses at specific times and places.

CPE duly stresses the dynamics between construal and construction of the social world, and thus echoes Bourdieu's dialectics of vision and division, description and inscription. Classifications are seldom path-breaking but draw on some already established classification systems: cross-references to existing laws, references to the country's constitution or international human rights charters, EU Directives, specific decrees in a policy field, and so on. Bourdieu (1991) has highlighted that linguistic categorizations and new symbolic orders *have to* relate to already existing institutional structures—conceptualized as products of previous struggles over classification but precisely *not* perceived as such in the social world[17]—to derive credibility and legitimacy. Indeed, structural cross-references make meaning making possible in the first place: any semiotic system needs an already established and recognizable semiotic reference point—albeit as a point of departure for contestation—to "make sense."

This means that border drawing—as any policy making—cannot act in a vacuum or on a tabula rasa to create just any meaning. Rather, it is historically and socially embedded, and interacts with aspects of previous migrant classifications and their normative foundations. Henk Wagenaar (2011: 18) usefully discusses the power of the mostly implicit "presuppositional concepts" that offer patterns of meaning in distinct social or cultural contexts and thus silently shape our (and policy makers') understanding of what a particular policy is about. In our case, the notion that labor migration has something to do with "economic productivity" or "welfare" is a prime example of presupposition and thus needs to become part of the analysis. Jessop and Sum's empirical work, but also that of others, exposes precisely how the normative foundations of post-Fordist capitalism shape and impose organization principles such as deregulation, privatization, decentralization, competition, individualization, and so on onto societies and states and thereby reproduce themselves as ultimately neutralized categories of thought (Blaney and Inayatullah 2010; Cerny 1997, 2010).

The view on structural embeddedness, however—and this is a departure from assumed institutionalist determination of the "path dependency" kind—should not lead to an underestimation of the powerful construction of "facticity" through policy making (Fischer 2003). Statutory classifications of migrant workers might create new statuses, amend or change previous structures. Policy makers constantly "engage in shaping and reshaping the law as part of their regulatory activity" (Morgan and Quack 2010: 299–300). CPE employs the term *sedimentation* to capture the naturalization dynamics that lift the interpretations of the social world that have been chosen to matter in policy up into the higher realm of "facticity," and thus "gives them the form of objective fact of life" (Jessop 2009: 340).

Once created, classifications such as borders tend to "become hard realities, facts that constrain us, not merely norms that guide our autonomous judgment" (MacCormick 2007: 33). It is precisely this construction mechanisms by which actually quite arbitrary symbolic claims such as "we do not need lower-skilled workers" or "high-skilled workers boost economic growth" can acquire the status of tacit knowledge that is beyond contestation and serves as "fact" in future classification struggles. More than that: any classification of migrant workers in legislation, say by their skill level or by their origin, not only informs future understandings of legitimate distinctions of migrant workers in labor migration management, but it simultaneously shapes notions of legitimacy and belonging in other realms of the social world. As Anderson's recent study on British migration control evidences, the definition of "aliens" as deserving of admission where they are law abiding, contribute to economic growth, and share the values of the British nation has direct implications for citizens where they are seen not to share these values, are guilty of "welfare scrounging," or commit crimes: "There is conflict, exclusion, and failure inside as well as outside the kingdom.... The borders of the nation can also be called upon to exclude the Failed Citizen" (2013: 177f; see also Bommes and Geddes 2000a; Schierup et al. 2006).

Border drawing is not just shaped by the socio-economic formation in which it takes place, but also reconstitutes this setting through the very process of producing new or at least partially rearranging policy meanings. We turn to a specification of policy contexts and institutional settings in detail in chapter 3 to enable an anchored and case-sensitive policy analysis that pays tribute to the constitutive and structurally embedded character of border drawing in Britain, France, and Germany.

Conclusion: Border Drawing and Migration Policy Analysis

This chapter establishes the book's conceptual and methodological framework for analyzing migration policies. Departing from the migration-control literature, it problematizes orthodox views on the state's role in labor migration policy. Migration policy, I argue, is not just a matter of effective territorial border control, with states failing to close "gaps" in physical borders as part of the literature suggests. To overcome conceptual shortcomings such as the bias to territorial and dichotomous notions of borders, I have proposed a Bourdieusian reading of migration policy. This refocuses our analytical efforts to the question how states, irrespective of control gaps, sort out migratory flows in line with their normative visions. Relying on their immense (though not infinite or unchallenged) symbolic power and law making, states draw borders between "legality" and "illegality" for migrant workers and attach highly differential sets of rights to them. Eventually, migration policies can be best captured as acts of statutory border drawing that codify classifications of legal migrant workers in public law.

We have gone on to highlight the inherently normative character of all classifications that are entailed in border drawing. The reflection on interpretive policy analysis and critical governance studies has brought selective meaning making to the center of our analytical attention. As an instance of classification of legal and illegal migrant workers, labor migration management entails and imposes specific meanings of legality and illegality. This ontological position dictates a strong methodical commitment: if policies embody policy makers' attempt to construct and impose specific meanings of the social world and thereby govern it, we chiefly rely on interpretive methods (such as document and interviews analysis) to reconstruct these very policy meanings and explain their emergence in the wider socio-economic context.

Overall, border drawing forges an interdisciplinary analytical perspective fit to: identify the normative foundations of labor migration policies by exposing how admission laws classify migrant workers and analyzing the justifications for these classifications (critical legal studies), explain the emergence of specific classificatory regimes in the context of state-economy interaction patterns (political economy), and assess political ordering effects of policies on social relations, with particular regard to the distribution of rights to different kinds of migrant workers (political sociology).

Notes

1. Pierre Bourdieu, *Practical Reason* (1998).
2. In opposition to positivist causality claims, constructivist research focuses on explaining the emergence of configurations (Héritier 2008; Wendt 1998; Yanow 2006). Interpretivists seek what Héritier (2008) calls "constitutive explanations" by reconstructing what has happened, what has been said and written, and in which context specific structures and meanings have emerged. The analytical emphasis is on understanding relationships as constitutive of a social formation in its context, rather than on inferring ahistorical causes. This pursues a Weberian or ideographic comparative approach, which sees cases as distinct complex configurations that are comprehensible only in their specific context.
3. *Staatsgebiet* and *Staatsvolk* in Weber's terms.
4. This is even true for studies of supra-national organizations such as the European Union, which are viewed simply as larger entities demarcated by borders (as for the Schengen area).
5. The authors note that human rights groups share employers' and business lobbies' interest in and concrete benefit from liberal migration policies.
6. I owe this clarification on border delocalization research to an anonymous referee.
7. A good overview of the "idea of public law" in modern states is offered in Loughlin 2003.
8. The term *violence* (*Gewalt*) stems from Weber and alludes to the state's authority to use force—such as police or military enforcement—as ultimo ratio when implementing its policies and legalization.
9. Interestingly, despite not being a post-structuralist, Bourdieu defines discourse here in not so very dissimilar terms from Michel Foucault when emphasizing the power of classifications. This reminds us of internalization of discourse and technologies of the self in Foucauldian terms.
10. It is important to note that while classifications can be contested in practice, as the migration-control literature quite rightly indicates, their far-reaching implications should not be written off: classifications delimit borders of "legality" and therefore determine what exactly is to be contested.
11. Two encompassing and vivid overviews are offered by Wagenaar (2011) and Yanow (2006).
12. A similar position is promoted by discursive institutionalists who have forcefully highlighted the power of ideas in policy making and have analyzed their strength to shape institutions, actors' opportunity and constraint structures, and discourses (Schmidt 2002a, 2002b, 2008), but also the ability of ideas to adapt and survive in times of crisis, contestation or even failure (as in the case of "resilient liberalism" in Europe after the recent economic crisis) (Schmidt and Thatcher 2013). As these scholars do not group themselves to the IPA community, I use their insightful reflections on European capitalisms empirically, rather than analytically, in chapter 2.
13. Meaning making refers to intended policy effects: the attempt to impose a specific vision of the social world through legal classification of migrants finds its practical limits when policies are contested or not fully implemented. The struggle over symbolic power is relentless.
14. Jessop and Sum found CPE on a neo-Gramscian hegemony concept and a post-structuralist analysis of technologies to account for power in governance processes.
15. For example, Sum's (2009) work on competitiveness as a "knowledge brand" has indicated how the combination of certain techniques, practices, structural reference points, and meanings can become hegemonic in form of a widely uncontested imaginary.

16. A current book project of the Governance Research Group at the University of Bath (of which the author is a member), edited by Emma Carmel (also see: Carmel 2014), conceptualizes "governance as an analytical approach" in which the political ordering of social relations is analytically exposed through specific empirical interactions of policies, complex policy environments, and actors' struggles over the exact arrangement of policies.
17. I owe this clarification to one of the anonymous reviewers.

CHAPTER 2

Border Drawing across Capitalist Economies, Welfare States, and Citizenship Regimes

> "Capitalism knows only one color: that color is green; all else is necessarily subservient to it, hence, race, gender and ethnicity cannot be considered within it."[1]

> "Since the time of Homer every European ... was a racist, an imperialist, and almost totally ethnocentric."[2]

This book is an invitation to envisage labor migration management as meaningful and selective border drawing, as a normatively underpinned classification of migrant workers into "the pot" or "the crop." But what principles, exactly, guide border drawing and why are certain principles chosen to determine "legality"? This present chapter populates our border-drawing concept with empirical life: I engage with various regime literatures to develop a thorough set of assumptions about the comparative dynamics and rationalities of border drawing in German, French, and UK labor migration management.

Beyond Economic Rationalities: Toward a Multidimensional Analysis

At the heart of this chapter lies the recognition that border drawing is a multidimensional process that does not follow a set of singular norms but often combines multiple and not infrequently contradictory logics. The epigraphs borrowed from a liberal economist on the one hand and a critic of postcolonial Europe on the other mark the extreme poles within the debate. Migration scholars of course widely acknowledge the existence of multiple agendas in any one policy (e.g., Anderson 2013; Boswell and Geddes 2011; Carmel 2011; Guild and Mantu 2011), and some scrutinize the role of selective border control as a means of achieving various goals simultaneously (e.g., Mau et al. 2012). However, comparative accounts of labor migration management so far tend to focus predominantly on the economic dimension of border drawing where, following Thomas Sowell, the color of the currency should rule. Scholars highlight related economic agendas across capitalist varieties and their key role in shaping policies (Devitt 2012; Laubenthal 2012; Menz 2010a; Menz and Caviedes 2010b).

Yet a glance at policy tools such as the bilateral recruitment agreements that France entertains with its former colonies raises doubts as to whether, really, governments select migrant workers solely on the grounds of assumed economic utility. French (but not only French, as we will well see) selection by origin brings us closer to Saïd again and seems to indicate that ethno-cultural selection processes are ongoing in migration management. Andreas Wimmer (2008: 990f.) suggests that "the change from empire to nation-state provided new incentives for state elites to pursue strategies of ethnic—as opposed to other types of—boundary making" (say based on social or economic division lines). His work offers extensive evidence to propose that the ethno-cultural foundations of the nation-state are still with us in contemporary "classificatory struggles." I suggest—in this chapter and throughout this book—that Wimmer's argument needs to be extended to the case of labor migration management where analyses so far tend to overlook non-economic policy rationalities and fail to hear the socio-political and ethno-cultural undertones that resonate even *within* the common discourse of selecting "the best and the brightest" for "the demands of the national economy." The evidence from this book's policy analysis indicates that this multidimensionality is not always a matter of policy "malintegration" where the tough talk control in the socio-political realm of welfare protectionism coincides with lenient admission practices to appease both a wary electorate as well as business interests (Boswell and Geddes 2011). Rather, contradictions between economic, social, and ethno-cultural rationalities are assembled *within* legislation itself and are often indicative of an attempt to create some kind of balance in a set of often irresolvable policy tensions.

To fully grasp what labor migration management *means* and how it orders sets of rights and privileges for specific groups of foreign workers in different countries, we should neither too hastily write off migrant classifications that are not, or only remotely, related to economic rationalities, nor should we take all contradictions as malintegration of talk and practice. It would be equally short sighted—and maybe naïve—to underestimate the relevance of absences: policies' lack of linking regulation to an aspect that seems pertinent in the wider-case context entails specific normative choices and structuration effects that add to comprehension just as well. This relates to Bourdieu's claim that the entire social world is present and being restructured in classificatory processes, meaning that relations that are not touched upon in this process do not disappear but might actually be rather muted or subordinated to a novel logic of relations or principle of hierarchy.

In order to offer an adequately nuanced account of what states do (and don't do) when they "manage" labor migration, I seek to expose the very interplay of available sets of norms, their amplification or silencing in regulation. When do economic justifications dominate and silence conflicting social norms in labor migration management? How is this justified by legislators? Can normative references to social or civic models of belonging even trump economic selection rationales? For which groups of migrants is this the case? These questions matter for migrants themselves as they uncover the roots of the sets of criteria an applicant needs to fulfill to enter a given country as a "legal" worker. They equally matter for policy analysis as they get to the heart of understanding states' complex and highly selective arrangement of norms in labor migration management.

Based on a review of existing comparative migration policy studies, I identify in this chapter three dimensions of border drawing—economic, social, and civic. This follows not only T. H. Marshall's famous dimensions of citizenship, but also addresses empirical insights from joint work that examined the sets of rights granted to different migrant statuses in the European Union (Carmel and Paul 2013b). I develop ideal-typical assumptions about the role of the economic, social, and civic dimension of border drawing in labor migration management, drawing on insights from regime literatures[3] on capitalist coordination, welfare states, and citizenship models, respectively. Where possible, I include all EU-15 countries in tables and the discussion of regime literatures in order to provide a wider literature review for the interested reader, even if the rest of the book concentrates on Germany, France, and the United Kingdom. The former two share features of their capitalist coordination and welfare state approaches but have come from completely opposite sides of citizenship and migrant integration philosophies. The latter two look more similar in their liberal civic citizenship approach—with some qualifications about the exact mechanisms of integration—but could not diverge more in their socio-economic governance approaches. As explained in the introduction, this cross-pairing of cases promises to illuminate the relative weight of economic, social, and civic border-drawing norms and mechanisms (the introduction has also outlined empirical rationales of case selection). In this, France assumes a Janus-faced position connecting to both of the two most different cases—Germany and the United Kingdom.

Some methodological notes are due on my analytical usage of regime literatures: typologies such as the well-known varieties of capitalism or welfare state regimes are understood here as ideal-typical benchmarks[4] (on ideal-typical reasoning, see Hekman 1983; Weber 1994 [1919]). They provide valuable theoretical insight about the available normative frameworks in specific institutional settings, and help in generating assumptions about how these norms tend to shape border drawing in different countries. What would ideal-typical border drawing in a liberal market economy look like, or what kind of agenda would be pursued if policies were fully guided by the principles of a Bismarckian welfare state regime or an ethnic citizenship approach? The development of clear ideal-typical assumptions about expectable border-drawing dynamics (see figure 2.1) enables a later empirical benchmarking and cross-national comparison in chapters 5 and 6.

Comparing Economic Border Drawing: The Logics of Capitalist Coordination

The return to active foreign labor recruitment since the late 1990s has triggered increasing academic attention, mainly from political economy scholars. Manifold are the accounts of the economic and demographic "pressures" that lead governments across Europe to facilitate—once again—labor recruitment, and the attempts to compare the respective economic coordination responses across countries (e.g., Castles 2006; Cerna 2009; Devitt 2011; Menz 2009; Menz and Caviedes 2010b; Ruhs and Anderson 2010b). Scholarship widely agrees that the rediscovery of migrant workers as "potentially useful human resources" informs highly selective and utilitarian admission regimes: "Migrants are welcome as long as they promise to contribute to the prerogatives of a business-friendly national economic growth strategy" (Menz 2009: 31).

The comparative political economy branch of the labor migration literature predominantly highlights the economic dimension of border drawing and scrutinizes the site of capitalist coordination to explain policies. To develop assumptions about how economic border drawing tends to play out across our three cases, this section engages with scholarly work that has examined the organizing principles of capitalist coordination in post-Fordism, and the variable organization of capitalism in Europe (varieties of capitalism).

Capitalist Coordination Hegemony?
Labor Migration in the "Competition State"

For political economists the division between "legal" and "illegal" workers in labor migration management relies on the normative foundations of capitalist coordination approaches. As Georg Menz and Alex Caviedes (2010a: 2) highlight, the "structural transformation of the European political economy" creates a shared setting in Europe for "new strategies and designs of labor migration policy." To be sure, the logics of capitalist coordination constitute a chief analytical backdrop for labor migration researchers. This particularly concerns the post-Fordist character of the foreign labor recruitment policies emerging since the 1990s, especially in terms of their selective approach to recruiting "high-quality" skills (e.g., Cerna 2009; Devitt 2012; Laubenthal 2012; Menz and Caviedes 2010a; OECD 2009). From this perspective, labor migration is "another tool for growth"[5] in a post-Fordist capitalist environment. The idea is that national economies require selective labor migration to compete successfully in a globalizing economy, and that state policies facilitate economic competitiveness and growth strategies. Labor migration management becomes an adjacent of capitalist value accumulation, embodying the norms and logics of the very economic arrangement that it is designed to promote.

It is not accidentally then that Menz (2009) draws on Phil Cerny's (1997) famous "competition state" concept in his pioneering analysis of revitalized labor migration policies in Europe. Capitalist state theory goes some way in predicting economic border-drawing dynamics. With his "competition state" concept, Cerny (1997: 272) has described globalization-induced shifts from welfare state to competition state, with a changing role for state policy toward "the promotion of economic activities, whether at home or abroad, which will make firms and sectors located within the territory of the state competitive in international markets." A domestic "raison d'état" as entailed in the production of national welfare, full national employment, social solidarity, and justice has given way to a "raison du Monde" that embraces the logics of economic association and international capitalist competition (Cerny 2010). Cerny sees a strong role for the state in this context: rather than making state regulation redundant, economic globalization "necessitate[s] the actual expansion of *de facto* state intervention and regulation in the name of competitiveness and marketization" (1997: 251). In a more recent analysis of the role of states in responding to the 2008/2009 economic crisis in Europe, Vivien Schmidt and Cornelia Woll coin the term *liberal neo-statism*: "If anything, the state has become more active in managing the market.... but the state has also become more liberal in its approach" (2013: 135). Their empirical analysis demonstrates how crucial coercion and state intervention have been in the (successful) attempt to retain core ideas of neo-liberalism, such as the primacy of market competition, during crisis. This view does not only support the argument of persistent state power in open economies; it equally informs an understanding of the potential directions of economic border drawing as facilitator of competitiveness and growth in the migration domain.

Bob Jessop's famous portrayal of the "Schumpeterian workfare postnational regime" (SWPR) has diagnosed a similar tendency in contemporary state-economy relations (1999, 2002). He depicts the role of the "capitalist state" as one of securing the key conditions under which valorization of capital and the reproduction of labor are possible (2002). States, according to Jessop and Cerny, do not lose power vis-à-vis the market per se; they powerfully internalize the logics and the dynamics of the economic system. Since the 1970s and 1980s, statutory economic coordination processes have embraced Schumpeterian innovation as crucial means of wealth production and have promoted the creation of a "knowledge-based economy" that can generate, or so the belief suggests, innovation-induced growth.

This claim is evidenced further by Ngai-Ling Sum (2009), who demonstrates how competitiveness has been installed as a dominant organizing principle in economic and political governance by means of benchmarking reports and indexes. Others highlight the role of "immaginnovation" and virtuous "talents" in the Schumpeterian economy: Nigel Thrift (2010) shows that the surfacing of an affectionate discourse about talents' miraculous potential to spark of innovation and growth is frequently far removed from empirical facts as to their "real" economic value. I could name more, but these two recent studies suffice to indicate that normative assumptions vested in competitiveness and innovation agendas tend to frame and direct contemporary economic coordination. The semiotic claims entailed in "competitiveness" and "innovation" agendas can be partially neutralized in policy making, even in absence of "hard evidence" about, for example, the huge economic value of high-skilled "talents" as opposed to lower-skilled workers.

Competitiveness and innovation logics are highly likely to inform migrant classifications and admission regimes in labor migration management. Menz in particular has started to enlighten the tight link between competitiveness and migration. In order to retain attractiveness "in the eyes of long-term foreign investment" (Menz 2009: 31) and to meet national productivity and growth objectives, labor recruitment policies are designed to attract "mobile international human capital."[6] Who counts as desired "human capital"—and thus potentially as "legal"—will depend on the degree to which a migrant worker promises to contribute to competitiveness and innovation goals. This link is exceptionally apparent in the European Union's legal migration scheme (CEC 2000, 2004, 2005), which draws heavily on the Union's regulatory model of economic markets, including the key ideas of "extension and promotion of competition in the name of creating a single market" (Thatcher 2013: 194). In particular, the close links of European level migration approaches to the Lisbon Agenda's growth objectives[7] strongly reflect these market-making rationales (Carmel and Paul 2010). The Commission (2004: 3) frames this as follows: "the need to review immigration policies for the longer term particularly in the light of the implications which an economic migration strategy would have on competitiveness and, therefore, on the fulfillment of the Lisbon objectives." Some take such statements as evidence that "market-driven migrant selectivity is irrevocably becoming a major determinant of migration flows in the EU" (van Houtum and Pijpers 2007: 301); and, further, that EU citizenship itself hinges on ideals of neo-liberal labor mobility (P. Hansen and Hager 2010). Yet competitiveness rationales do not solely matter with regard to the positioning of the EU economy in competition with the US or East Asian economies; they have equally intensified competition for labor force within the European Union (Verwiebe 2004; Zaletel 2006).

Yet any empirical association of the normative foundations of post-Fordist capitalism and labor migration management cannot automatically be taken as functionally determined. Alongside critical political economists such as Bob Jessop, Ngai-Ling Sum, Phil Cerny, Vivien A. Schmidt, Colin Hay, or Daniel Wincott—to name but a few—I understand these links as political choices of policymakers who *select to* embrace specific norms at specific times while silencing or ignoring others (see chapter 1). Once made, these choices do not remain on the rhetorical level but bear material consequences for migrants in host countries by determining their status far beyond initial utilitarian admission. As Ulrik Schierup and colleagues (2006) demonstrate, migrants' social inclusion in Germany, Sweden, Italy, and Britain has increasingly depended on their economic contribution in a dominant, though slightly variable, model of "economic citizenship." More recent comparative work has confirmed that for them to gain access to social protection migrants need to prove their economic utility first (Carmel 2011; Carmel et al. 2011; Kaiser and Paul 2011). Overall, we can expect migrant workers' anticipated or actual economic contribution—expressed in terms of innovation, competitiveness, and growth norms—to shape their classification as legal or illegal in admissions and to affect the rights that come with different legal statuses.

Varieties of Capitalist Coordination

While no political economist seriously challenges the notion that some basic common organizing principles unite European capitalist economies, it is equally acknowledged that meanings of competitiveness and innovation and associated growth strategies vary considerably across countries. Menz (2010a: 45) argues that the rediscovered "appetite for labor migrants" among European employers and governments differs according to the skill levels and type of skills required in different national economies. Rather than operating one-size-fits-all admission systems, governments have developed fine-tuned responses to sectoral shortages and "only opened to workers in particular occupations, such as engineering, care-giving, or food processing" (Caviedes 2010: 70). The sectors in need of extra workers might not be the same across countries and cause highly variable classifications of migrant workers as "competition-supporting" and hence "legal." Such empirical observations draw foremost on the varieties of capitalism (VoC) literature in their comparative claims.

The VoC literature (Hall and Soskice 2001b) distinguishes two basic modes of capitalist coordination (table 2.1). The idea of institutional coherence and complementarity in economic governance serves as an analytical starting point in Peter Hall and David Soskice's (2001a) famous account of capitalist variation.[8] In order to be productive and competitive, the well-rehearsed argument goes, companies have to coordinate their activities across different institutional spheres, and they are inclined do so in a mutually reinforcing way. Different product market strategies lead to different institutional setups in support of competitiveness. The institutional spheres include industrial relations, vocational education and training (VET) systems, corporate governance, inter-firm relations and relations with the firm's own employees. VoC's crucial comparative claim is that the functionalistic interdependence of coordination mechanisms across spheres can take different, equally successful, directions: "Broadly speaking, liberal market economies are distinguishable from coordinated market economies by the extent to which firms rely on market mechanisms to coordinate their endeavors as opposed to forms of strategic interaction supported by non-market institutions" (Hall and Soskice 2001a: 33).

Both coordinated and liberal market economies feature specific "comparative advantages" as to their competitiveness. Liberal market economy (LME) firms tend to rely on radical innovation and shorter-term profitability. Current earnings and tributes to shareholder value matter most in financial corporate governance, and firms' ability to raise capital on financial markets depends on their short-term profitability. Flexibility in staff turnover is essential to adapt to changing profitability patterns, and a focus on general skills in the VET system caters for highly volatile skill needs. Competition characterizes intercompany relations (Hall and Soskice 2001a: 27–31).

Firms in coordinated market economies (CME), by contrast, tend to follow incremental innovation strategies. This is supported by trust-based relations to the financial system that guarantees capital flows regardless of profitability fluctuations in the shorter term. Companies mostly draw on a highly skilled and specialized workforce, and firm-specific skills are provided through a

Table 2.1. Capitalist Coordination Regimes in the EU-15

Variety of Capitalism	Subtypes	Country (Case)
Liberal market economies (LMEs)	Market-led capitalism (state as liberal arbiter)	U.K., Ireland
Coordinated market economies (CMEs)	State-led capitalism (state as interventionist leader)	France, Italy, Sweden
	Managed or negotiated capitalism (state as enabling facilitator)	Germany, Austria (Netherlands)

Sources: Hall and Soskice 2001a; Coates 2000; Schmidt 2002b

highly diversified VET system. Skilled workforce is retained during minor recessions and industrial relations secure corporate commitment to high-skilled jobs through wage-bargaining, long-term employment tenures, protective work councils, and so on. Firm-internal structures and trust-based corporate governance reinforce network monitoring systems that envisage long-term productivity and reputation; market shares and intra-company relations rely on longer-term trust as well (Hall and Soskice 2001a: 22–27).

VoC accounts have been criticized mainly for a dichotomous vision of capitalist coordination, institutionalist determinism, static conceptions of economic coordination, disregard of the state's role as regulator, and underestimation of economic segmentation within countries (Amable 2003; Blyth 2003; Coates 2000; Crouch 2005; Hancké et al. 2007; Hay and Wincott 2012; Kitschelt et al. 1999a; Schmidt 2002b). Nonetheless, a VoC perspective has the potential to inspire the empirical analysis of economic border drawing for three main reasons. Firstly, alternative typologies and taxonomies in critical response to VoC have mostly maintained the core analytical distinction between market-led and non-market-led economic coordination processes (table 2.1). Some have refined the category of CME according to specific non-market forms of coordination.[9] Yet the crude distinction by Hall and Soskice seems to preserve its empirical-analytical importance and thus offers a suitable source of initial assumptions about economic border drawing in comparative labor migration policies.

Secondly, the role of public policy in creating and sustain VoC—potentially also through labor migration strategies—has duly gained more attention. According to Vivien Schmidt's "discursive institutionalist" (2002a, 2008) account, policy legacies and cultural frameworks in different countries work as contextual filters that produce and reproduce capitalist diversity, with a potential to change regimes over time. Schmidt—who usefully has studied the same three countries of interest here—argues (2002b: 113) that states can act as "liberal arbiters," "enabling facilitators," or "interventionist leaders" in capitalist coordination, thus identifying three types of capitalist state discourse and policy intervention in the United Kingdom, Germany, and France (table 2.1).

Thirdly, VoC's lack of addressing labor market segmentations is a matter of analysis from a border-drawing perspective. By concentrating on a prime segment of the national economy, VoC tends to ignore large parts of the economy, some of which can be especially relevant in the empirical context of labor migration. Research on migrant employment speaks of highly segmented labor markets, often with a focus on informal economies and/or unauthorized migrant employment[10] in Mediterranean countries (Ambrosini 2001; Boswell and Straubhaar 2004; King et al. 2000; Quassoli 1999; Reyneri 2004). Studies of informal migrant labor in the German care sector or British food processing clearly evidence that labor market segmentation and informalization is no southern European problem (Geddes and Scott 2010; Lutz and Palenga-Möllenbeck 2010).

When conceptualizing migration policy as border drawing and linking it to an investigation of the selective arrangement of norms in policies (see discussion of CPE in chapter 1), VoC's inherent disregard of many economic sectors and the entirety of the informal sector becomes a matter for analysis. If our empirical analysis were to confirm LME or CME patterns of selecting migrant workers, this would simultaneously imply an illegalization or at least misrecognition of labor migration outside the prime sectors of the national economy. Eventually, any VoC-confirming finding would thus not just emphasize the state's strategic role in facilitating models of competitiveness by attracting the workforce that Volkswagen in Germany or HSBC in London require. It would moreover pinpoint the structuring effects of selective economic border drawing that, by "fashioning" an irregular workforce through highly selective admissions, equally ignores and sustains informal labor market segments (Anderson 2010b; Morice 1996; Samers 2010).

For us to fully comprehend the (selective!) governance of labor migration, we thus need to build on detailed contextual knowledge about migrant workers' role in host labor markets and economies. The case profiling in chapter 3 portrays migration policy legacies and key features of the foreign resident population in Britain, France, and Germany to form a firm anchor for our comparative analysis of labor migration management in Europe.

Typological Assumptions about Economic Border Drawing

In a policy field that has been revitalized predominantly, it seems, as an economic growth strategy just slightly more than a decade ago, capitalist coordination norms are bound to matter in labor migration management. Capitalist state theory and VoC fuel far-reaching theorizations of the normative foundations of economic border drawing. Firstly, capitalist state theory would expect migrant workers' anticipated or actual economic contribution with regard to innovation, competitiveness, and growth to co-shape their legal status and rights ascribed through admission policies in the receiving country. VoC lets us expect some empirical variations across economies. Though not being part of VoC frameworks, labor migration seems to fit well into the notion of complementarities[11] in an economy. Parallel to the VET system, migrant labor admissions would be expected to be used strategically in order to provide companies in the national economy with exactly the labor they require to be innovative and competitive. Consequently, foreign labor migration policies are likely to entail the diverse logics of LMEs and CMEs.

Due to the recent reactivation of labor migration policies, the VoC's explanatory capacities with regard to national variation in labor migration management has only begun to be assessed (Cerna 2009; Devitt 2011; Menz

2005, 2009; Menz and Caviedes 2010a). Menz's (2009: 261) research evidences regime-typical divergence in policies as "different models of political economy shape distinct strategies for labor recruitment from abroad." This predominantly concerns the variable regulatory focus on admitting workers of specific skill levels and skill compositions: "CME production patterns … require mainly highly skilled well-trained labor migrants that can easily be integrated into a high value-added production pattern.… LME production patterns necessitate a steady supply of labor migration into both low-wage low-skill service sector positions where poor working conditions and wages are combined with structural flexibility requirements lead to low staff retention" (ibid.).

Further, different labor market regimes might display different patterns of allocating economic rights to migrant workers. LMEs would tend to govern labor entries less rigidly, as lower job protection allows high staff turnover and employer flexibility. The argument would be reversed for CMEs, with higher levels of job protection potentially acting as incentives for more careful and rigid admissions initially. Initial studies of foreign labor recruitment across regime types have supported these claims (Cerna 2009; Devitt 2011).

A last claim concerns expectable interactions between capitalism and welfare. VoC scholars conceive of the more generous status-maintaining benefit levels in CMEs as a company strategy to form and maintain a workforce with high industry- and firm-specific skills (Estevez-Abe et al. 2001; Iversen and Stephens 2008). Higher social protection levels in comparison to LMEs are thus interpreted as a way of incentivizing specific skilling strategies among the workforce and sustaining the competitive advantage of CMEs. By the same token, lower protection levels of employment and against unemployment in LMEs coincide with companies' predominant reliance on generic skills. These interactions imply beneficial ramifications for migrant workers: the attempt to be attractive for high- and specifically skilled migrant workers in a CME is likely to be flanked with relatively generous sets of social rights.

From our engagement with modes of capitalist coordination emerge the following principles of economic border drawing for subsequent comparative scrutiny:

- there is a shared focus on economic utility of migrant workers with regard to competitiveness, growth, and innovation aims across countries;
- we find a focus on high and specific skills, potentially also sector specific, in CME admissions;
- but a focus on more generic and also lower-skilled migrant workers in LMEs;
- CME firms rely on more generous social and civic rights as incentive for migrant workers who bring high- and specific skills profiles to the national economy;

- we expect to find more liberal admission policies in deregulated LME labor markets;
- and more selective and restrictive labor market regulation—including admissions of migrant workers—in CMEs.

Our subsequent policy analysis (chapters 4–6) illuminates the extent to which notionally shared trajectories of post-Fordist economic coordination surface in labor migration management. It equally considers institutional sources of national divergence and their links to capitalist varieties. Our main additions to existing political economy accounts of labor migration management, however, rest in the comparative examination of economic border-drawing dynamics in interaction with social and civic ordering rationalities, to which we shall now turn.

Comparing Social Border Drawing: The Logics of Welfare State Regimes

The inadequacy of predominantly *economic* accounts of labor migration has become obvious in the postwar era. So-called guest worker programs "created the illusion that immigration was really an economic matter, and that the state could easily intervene in the marketplace to close the immigration valve," mainly during the economic downturn in the 1970s (Hollifield 1992: 73). Unintended settlements, continuing family reunions, and migrant workers' acquisition of welfare entitlements after the notional recruitment stop prove the point. The misrecognition of the social, political, and cultural implications of migration is believed to have carried adverse effects for migrant integration and social cohesion in receiving countries (Bommes 2000; Castles 1986, 2006; Sainsbury 2006). This is no surprise from a Polanyian (2001 [1944]) reading: any managed migration scheme that considers solely the economic features of labor migration falls into the trap of overlooking the "fictitious" character of labor as "commodity." Polanyists highlight the necessary social regulation of markets both for the sake of their own maintenance and of socially acceptable outcomes of economic processes (Bienefeld 2007; P. Hansen 2014). While economic calculations such as the ones discussed in the previous section might be core to labor migration border drawing, one-sided economic accounts misrecognize the fact that, once migrated, foreign workers cannot simply be expelled or moved around according to market needs. Democratic and human rights commitments render the enforcement of returns or the prohibition of family reunion and settlement untenable, just as neo-institutionalist migration scholars argue. Where a "shoving about of labor" stripped from its sociocultural clothes is endeavored nonetheless, contradictions with social inclusion policies and citizenship norms deepen and become increasingly explosive (P. Hansen 2014).

Little credit has so far been given to social and civic border-drawing dynamics in labor migration policy analyses (Caviedes 2010; Cerna 2009; Devitt 2011; Geddes and Scott 2010; Menz 2009, 2010a; Menz and Caviedes 2010b; Ruhs and Anderson 2010b). A notable exception is Martin Ruhs' (2013) recent comparison of how 46 high-income countries regulate admissions and migrant workers' rights. While not offering a case-sensitive comparison of the kind intended here, Ruhs' study demonstrates forcefully that economic openness for foreign working hands tends to come at the price of restrictive social and political rights for migrants. If we acknowledge that markets are socially embedded and always regulated in a specific societal context, the interplay of economic with other impulses for regulation needs to be analyzed more carefully. In order to widen our analytical radar, this section discusses welfare states as main sites of social border drawing, while the third section considers formal citizenship models as sources of civic-cultural border-drawing norms.

Migration into Welfare States: Selecting "Legitimate" Contributors and Beneficiaries

The recent interest of migration scholars (though not labor migration analysts) in comparative welfare state research acknowledges that welfare states "constitute key arenas within which issues of inclusion and exclusion are mediated" (Geddes 2000: 152). A welfare state angle on labor migration management achieves two things: firstly, it illuminates a blind spot of political economy accounts of labor migration by shifting the analytical focus from economic utility considerations toward social border-drawing norms. Secondly, the social dimension of border drawing seems particularly important for TCN newcomers. While they are excluded from EU mobility and social rights portability and cannot yet access long-term resident rights (Geddes 2000), subsequent social inclusion dynamics are almost written on the wall for policy makers who take admission decisions. Thomas Hammar's seminal work (1990) has shown that while many foreigners lack "formal" citizenship rights in European host countries, they have often obtained "substantial" citizenship rights, especially with regard to welfare entitlements. Hammar labels this status "denizenship".[12] A welfare state perspective hence captures vital internal border-drawing mechanisms that operate below the level of formal citizenship, and sharpens our analytical lens to the potential impact of denizenship and social inclusion pathways on border arrangements.

For more than a decade (and now revived during the economic crisis), the erosion and retrenchment of mature European welfare states in times of "austerity" (Pierson 1998, 2001; more recently Hay and Wincott 2012) have been discussed as triggers for redefining the "community of legitimate welfare receivers" with restrictive effects for migrants (Bommes and Geddes 2000a). Associated with increasingly multicultural societies seems to be an erosion of welfare state support (Kymlicka and Banting 2006), as welfare solidarity and generosity are believed to be weaker in contexts of increased ethnic heterogeneity and large-scale migration (Alesina and Glaeser 2004; Nannestad 2007). Policy responses to the notably contentious relationship between welfare and migration include further exclusions of non-nationals from access or a general retreat from the solidarity community. Processes of "racialized exclusion" feature prominently in welfare state retrenchment (Schierup et al. 2006); migration is "nested within more general debates about the future of welfare provision" and has thus become a major piece within the jigsaw puzzle of welfare state reforms (Geddes 2000: 153). A restrictive social inclusion stance toward migrants in general might equally trigger wider reconstitutions of welfare state models. Scandinavian countries—often heralded as the Eldorado for social rights—have started redefining their universal rights regimes in an attempt to keep "unwanted" migrants excluded from generous welfare provisions, hence forging a model of "neoliberal" belonging (Sainsbury 2006; Schierup and Ålund 2011). Bridget Anderson's work on Britain (2013) offers key lessons as to how social rights are constantly under pressure for "undeserving" migrants and "Failed Citizens" alike. These studies suggest that mature Western European welfare states, in times of retrenchment and eroding welfare support, have also renegotiated social inclusion for migrants. Welfare chauvinism is most noticeably directed toward asylum seekers and family members (Bloch and Schuster 2002; Peers 2001); yet, migrant workers, too, are likely to be affected by the shifting normative foundations for social inclusion.

While most studies focus on the comparative social stratification effects of welfare systems on migrants *after* they have entered the host country (Carmel et al. 2011; Schierup et al. 2006), there seems to be less interest in welfare states' role in shaping ideas about inclusion and exclusion at the point of admissions themselves. An exception is certainly Andrew Geddes' claim that "by providing access to, or exclusion from, welfare support, European states have sought to welcome some forms of migration while deterring others." This goes beyond general signaling effects: if the welfare state really is "an 'internal' method for the regulation of migration" (Geddes 2003a: 153), labor migration management is likely to engage with the specific social inclusion pathways of the welfare state ex-ante when picking norms for admission.

It is time then to consider the comparative relationship between welfare state norms and labor migration management as key driver of social border-drawing dynamics. From a cultural political economy perspective, welfare states provide certain policy logics that can be employed selectively in admission policies to serve specific selectivity goals regarding labor migration. Ideas about welfare provision, contributions, and entitlements are frequently incorporated into border drawing to shape categorizations of migrants as potentially "beneficial" or "harmful" for a country's welfare system. In economic research (e.g., Borjas 1994, 1999; Dustmann et al. 2010) this has begged the question of which kind of migrants contribute to funding (welfare) states. Sociological studies have been more concerned with which groups of migrants are classified as "deserving" of welfare entitlements and provision (e.g., Anderson 2013; Carmel et al. 2011; Sales 2002; Schierup et al. 2006). In order to inspect the ways in which the variable normative frameworks implied in different "ways of doing welfare" (Sainsbury 2006) structure admission policies for foreign workers, we now turn to welfare state regime theories.

Welfare State Regimes

What can regime theory tell us about the potential dynamics of social border drawing? Gøsta Esping-Andersen's seminal work (1990) triggered now long-standing debates about the variable organization and underpinning political objectives of social policy and welfare provision. For Esping-Andersen, the welfare state is not only "a mechanism that intervenes, and possibly corrects, the structure of inequality; it is, in its own right, a system of stratification. It is an active force in the ordering of social relations" (ibid: 23) Welfare regime theory exposes how different countries organize welfare and explains the emergence of regimes in their historical and political context. More importantly from our interpretivist border-drawing perspective, this literature engages with the fundamentally different logics of stratification to be found at the heart of diverse welfare state clusters (Arts and Gelissen 2002), and highlights diverging normative foundations of social policy in different countries (van Oorschot et al. 2008). Let us thus rehearse the different welfare state logics and their likely implications for social border drawing in labor migration management.

In his distinction of worlds of welfare capitalism, Esping-Andersen traces three ideal-typical regimes, characterized by their varying levels of decommodification and mechanisms of social stratification (table 2.2). Liberal welfare states offer residual welfare provisions, modest social insurance plans, and

Table 2.2. Welfare State Regimes in the EU-15

Regime type	Country (case)
Liberal-Residual (Anglo-Saxon)	U.K., Ireland
Conservative-Corporatist (Continental)	Germany, France, Belgium, Austria, (Netherlands)
Social-Democratic (Scandinavian)	Sweden, Finland, Denmark
Mediterranean (Latin Rim)	Italy, Spain, Portugal, Greece

Sources: Esping-Andersen 1990; Leibfried 1993; and Ferrera 1996

modest means-tested benefits. Strict entitlement rules and means testing produce low decommodification levels.

Policies concentrate on the provision of a basic safety net while promoting individual responsibility and the provision of income through the labor market. The welfare state serves as a "compensator of last resort" (Leibfried 1993: 127). Some have taken issue with the resemblance of all Liberal regime countries with regard to assumed low redistribution levels. Francis G. Castles and Deborah Mitchell (1993) have argued that targeting through taxation or the transfer system in the United Kingdom and Australia, for instance, can imply lower post-transfer inequality levels than in the Netherlands (usually seen as a more egalitarian regime). Yet the fundamental reliance on market income as a means of welfare provision remains a shared feature of Liberal welfare states.

Conservative-corporatist welfare states provide social rights with reference to occupational statuses. Entitlements are usually proportional and originate from an individual's labor market participation and the associated social insurance contributions paid into the *Sozialkassen* and *Caisses Sociales*. Named after the historical inventor of the social insurance model, former German Reichskanzler Otto von Bismarck, this Bismarckian model uses wage replacement rates to achieve proportionality between contributions and welfare entitlements. The Bismarckian welfare state eventually works as "compensator of first resort" in cases when income from labor market participation fails (Leibfried 1993: 127). The relative preservation of previous income and status in case of unemployment, sickness, old age, and parental leave (etc.) by means of relatively generous replacement rates bears modest decommodification effects. However, dependence on the market is held up over the life course as benefit levels for most types of welfare provision depend almost entirely on prior employment (Palier 2010b: 42).

Social-Democratic welfare states, lastly, tend to endorse universalism of social rights and target a "maximisation of capacities for individual independence" (Arts and Gelissen 2002: 142). They promote social equality on a high provision level beyond a minimum safety net and thereby offer high levels of decommodification and redistribution. This model "crowds out the market … and constructs an essentially universal solidarity" among citizens (Esping-Andersen 1990: 28). It creates a strong role for the welfare state as public employer and promotes female labor market participation. Scholars later extended the typology to include a so-called Southern, Mediterranean, or Latin Rim model (Bonoli 1997; Ferrera 1996; Leibfried 1993), which departs from the Corporatist-Conservative model mostly by its strong emphasis on familialistic welfare provision, clientelist politics, and a large informal economy. Later typologies included the post-Communist Eastern European countries and East Asian economies as well (Arts and Gelissen 2002 offer a good overview).

As any typology, welfare state regime theory continues to trigger criticism as to the empirical validity of types (see ibid.). Hybrid models and structural changes of the types identified by Esping-Andersen more than twenty years ago have been suggested (e.g., Hinrichs 2010; Palier 2006; Weishaupt 2010). Moreover, common pressures such as demographic aging, budget constraints, competitiveness politics, or deindustrialization are believed to fuel convergence of different welfare states in practice (a good overview of the convergence debate is offered in Starke et al. 2008). However, recent studies of several indicators[13] have demonstrated that welfare states in Europe only display moderate convergence (O'Connor 2005; Scruggs and Allan 2006; Starke et al. 2008). A recent in-depth scrutiny of welfare change trajectories in Continental Europe equally indicates that irrespective of incremental reforms, there are "no instances of brutal departure from Bismarckian ways of thinking and doing" (Palier 2010b: 31). Colin Hay and Daniel Wincott's recent *Political Economy of European Welfare Capitalism* indicates that the politics of retrenchment "has, in effect, produced reversion to cluster 'type'" (2012: 193). Maurizio Ferrera confirms that, while neo-liberal ideas have launched an "aggressive attack" on European social policy norms and austerity measures have certainly constrained welfare budgets across the Continent, "social protection has been (and still is) a key pillar of Europe's 'way of life'" (2013: 106)—a pillar which retains room for national interpretations of welfare.

While this is not the place to discuss reasons for convergence and divergence of European economic and social policy regimes more generally (Colin Hay and Daniel Wincott offer a brilliant and heterodox analysis in this respect), we note that Paul Pierson's famous claim that "the core structures of most welfare states are not in jeopardy" (2001: 456) seems to remain valid even more than fifty years after their inauguration in most Western European countries. We expect the diverging logics of welfare provision, distribution, and redistribution—from means-tested assistance, to flat-rate benefits, and contributory benefits—to shape different pathways and mechanisms of inclusion for migrant workers. Welfare regime theory thus generates valuable assumptions about the normative foundations of social border drawing across different countries.

Typological Assumptions about Social Border Drawing

Depending on the normative basis of different "ways of doing welfare" (Sainsbury 2006), migrants might acquire welfare entitlements either through labor market contribution (Bismarckian welfare states), or via their status as residents and tax payers (Social-Democratic and Liberal welfare states). The level of benefits also varies alongside the generosity and redistributive structure of the welfare state. Research on migrants' social integration has confirmed the claims of welfare regime theory. There seem to be regime-typical inclusion pathways for migrants, with Scandinavian universal social rights regimes being more integrative than Liberal or Bismarckian regimes (Morissens and Sainsbury 2005; Sainsbury 2006). The contributory logic of Conservative welfare systems also seems to matter for migrants' social inclusion: while the strong work orientation of the Bismarckian insurance model "appears to dovetail nicely with labor migration, enhancing the social rights of foreign workers … employment has been a central condition for a residence permit and the right to abode" (Sainsbury 2006: 234f). As Bismarckian welfare entitlements rest on labor market participation and associated contributions to social insurance budgets, stable employment has quasi automatically generated social rights such as old-age pensions for labor migrants and their families (e.g., German guest workers; Bommes 2000). This picture differs considerably from Liberal-residual welfare states such as the United Kingdom, where "the easy access to the labor market indicated by high levels of participation in the labor force is accompanied by high exposure to old and new social risks in the flexible labor market" (Banting 2000: 41). Comparatively meager social rights and minimum flat-rate benefits, which are more often than not detached from workers' previous employment status, are meant to set an unremitting incentive for migrant residents to seek for income and welfare through paid work.

More recently, Ruud Koopmans (2010) has demonstrated that both Bismarckian and Liberal welfare regimes—for diverse reasons—bear employment-incentivizing effects for migrants: the former disciplines foreign workers to contribute economically in order to boost their own future entitlement record; the latter exposes them to rather extreme social hardship when unemployed and thus stimulates labor market activity. With their emphasis on universal social citizenship, the more generous Scandinavian welfare states have seemingly generated greater levels of social inclusion (e.g., Sainsbury 2006), but also created weak incentives for migrants to integrate into the labor market (Koopmans 2010). These reflections strengthen the assumption that different social inclusion pathways are anticipated and negotiated in labor admission policies. This book thus inquires to what extent and how admission policies in Britain, Germany, and France draw on specific normative foundations of welfare provision and what selection rationales, exactly, social border drawing fulfills in the overall classification regime. What can we expect for our comparison then?

Empirical research on migrant inclusion in Bismarckian welfare states has singled out the labor market as main gateway to moderately generous benefits that are "earned" through contributions. French and German policies are likely to link labor market access and social integration of migrant workers more closely and ex-ante. There is less reason to do so in the liberal United Kingdom, as social inclusion does not follow as directly from in-work contributions and is usually reduced to means-tested flat-rate benefits. As Bismarckian welfare states largely rely on formal employment to sustain social funds for pensions, unemployment, or health care, policies would also tend to favor skilled employment, which can be expected to contribute a stable and high level of contributions as a percentage of their wage.

As many "Bismarckian" countries also happen to fall into the CME category, associated with companies' demand for high and specific skills in the VoC literature, the focus on skilled migrant employment might even be amplified. A competitiveness regime that competes less on price but on quality of products is likely to treat investment in social and skills policies—including for migrant workers—not necessarily as "competitiveness-corrosive" but as "enhancing" and stabilizing (Hay and Wincott 2012: 129f.). However, as to work is to become socially integrated—at least in theory—in France and Germany, culturally selective tendencies in labor migration management might render exclusion from the labor market of certain groups of migrants a prime strategy for avoiding the building up of longer-term entitlements for groups deemed undesirable[14] from other perspectives (see next section).

In case of the Mediterranean and Liberal welfare regimes, the less generous welfare provision and detachment of prospective benefits from employment offers fewer grounds for tight enforcement of labor market borders or strict selectivity as to the "quality" of the migrant's job. Scandinavian countries, lastly, have lately taken issue with migration and started to redefine generous universal social rights to render access for foreign residents more conditional—a measure that has been criticized as welfare chauvinism (Schierup and Ålund 2011).

In anticipation of the social entitlements migrants obtain while residing and working in a host country, labor migration regulation can be expected to introduce additional access requirements and safeguards against "misuse" and welfare reliance, boost incentives for contribution to welfare funding, and promise generous benefits to highly sought-after migrant workers while excluding others. Reflections in this section direct our comparative analysis of labor migration management toward the following chief norms of social border drawing[15]:

- Equivalence between (anticipated) social insurance contributions and social rights in Bismarckian welfare states suggests tight regulation of labor market access.
- Anticipated labor market success is pivotal for admissions in Bismarckian welfare states as social inclusion is "earned" through successful economic contribution.
- The logics of enforced market reliance in Liberal welfare states create a weaker link between labor market success and social entitlements and, eventually, less of an incentive to regulate foreign labor admissions tightly.

- However, tax funding of many benefits in Liberal regimes might trigger welfare chauvinism and restrictive stances on labor migration when "reliance" on benefits is deemed a risk.

Again, the relation between welfare and labor migration management is not seen as functionalist here: the assumptions above serve as a benchmark to examine how and why labor migration policies selectively draw on some welfare state norms, but not others, or combine social entitlement logics with specific economic or civic normative frameworks. Chapter 6 in particular highlights the importance of social border-drawing mechanisms and shows policies that arrange them with coexisting, sometimes competing, logics of capitalist coordination or ethno-cultural belonging.

Comparing Civic Border Drawing: The Logics of Citizenship Regimes

Citizenship has long been the defining category for border construction in migration policies. The "invention of the passport" nourished ever more elaborate distinctions of citizens and aliens in Europe since the Napoleonic era (Torpey 2000). In a Weberian state-theoretical view, these legal distinctions have been essential for defining "mutually exclusive sovereign states" (Joppke 2005b). It is hence not surprising that migration scholars have taken pains to compare modes of inclusion linked to passport citizenship for migrants in different countries, and that the focus on civic inclusion is one of the most unyielding in comparative migration research (Bauböck et al. 2006; Brubaker 1989, 1992; Favell 2001; Howard 2009; Joppke 1998a, 2005b, 2010; Koopmans et al. 2005). These studies examine the conditions under which migrants can acquire permanent residence and, predominantly, formal citizenship status[16] in different countries.

Given this rich intellectual engagement in migration studies more generally, it is surprising that the impact of citizenship regimes and specifically ethnic notions of belonging has stayed largely under the radar in contemporary labor migration policy analyses. To be sure, the acquisition of citizenship is usually (but not always) a late step in migrant workers' integration process, reaching from physical entry (migration) over settlement and denizenship (integration) to naturalization (Hammar 1990). While economic and social rights might be granted immediately or at early stages after initial migration to workers, the acquisition of a host country's passport would open access to civic rights such as non-expulsion, encompassing protection by that state, and voting rights in national elections. This might make the citizenship regime literature appear like a far-fetched anchor for the analysis of labor admission policies.

There are two key issues with a too hasty neglect of citizenship norms in the labor migration policy realm. Firstly, the experiences of the guest worker era have abundantly demonstrated how initial worker recruitment can lead to large-scale settlement and eventually naturalization without policies ever intending this (Castles 1986; Rogers 1985). Experience has certainly heightened governments' awareness of the human face of "economic" migration and they took note of citizenship and integration trajectories far beyond their initial economic and social concerns. Civic integration pathways can be expected to form a normative backdrop in border-drawing processes even where initial admission of foreign workers is the key aim. Secondly, the economic utility drive of past labor admission regimes was dotted with ethnic and racial selection rationales—as chapter 3 will show in more detail for British, German, and French policy legacies—and it would be naïve to assume that ethno-cultural frames of belonging have vanished or become irrelevant as markers of good and "legal" migrant workers in the twenty-first century. Quite to the contrary, contemporary European integration studies expose plentifully the ethnic undertone of EU mobility and citizenship policies (Favell 2008b; P. Hansen and Hager 2010; P. Hansen and Jonsson 2011, 2012).

Thus a civic dimension of border drawing enters our analytical stage, with citizenship and integration regime research in particular promising to shed more light on the potential normative foundations of civic border drawing in labor migration management.

Citizenship and Civic Integration Regimes

Those who study migration through the lens of citizenship and civic integration mostly scrutinize the regulation of passport acquisition and the underpinning philosophies of *nation*, *citizenship*, and *integration*. Research in this domain features a dual focus on historically established migration policy paths stemming from specific migration experiences and historical recruitment strategies as well as more abstract "philosophies of integration" (Favell 2001) and currently adopted civic integration practices, institutions, and mechanisms, and the links of these practices to historical constellations in distinct host countries.

The main distinction of citizenship regimes has been between "civic" and "ethnic" models: in the former, classifications of citizens and aliens run alongside political belonging and are usually related to territorial birthright or "jus soli". In the latter, ethnicity or consanguinity form a descent-based division line and enforce "jus sanguinis." France, the Netherlands, and the United Kingdom in Europe, but also the settler countries in Northern America and Australia, serve as examples of civic citizenship, whereas Austria, Germany, or Italy traditionally represent the ethnic citizenship camp. Especially the contrasting cases of France and Germany as prototypes in their respective category—famously introduced in Roger Brubaker's historical account of citizenship regimes—continuously pull analytical weight, despite being castigated for overdrawing and stereotyping empirical phenomena (Brubaker 1992; Joppke 2010).

Variable citizenship models are widely understood as historically embedded configurations (table 2.3).[17] Marc Howard (2009) argues that colonial experience promoted the idea of civic inclusion as it triggered a vivid exchange of populations across territorial boundaries. Additionally though, civic inclusion relied on early democratization to establish legal principles for universal political rights. Accordingly, both France and the United Kingdom—colonial powers with an early onset of democratization in the nineteenth century—have developed a "historically liberal" approach to migrants' formal integration. In the opposite corner of the matrix we find countries that have neither been lasting or influential colonial powers nor early democracies (e.g., Germany or Austria). These are characterized by their restrictive[18] and ethnically biased citizenship policies. In the absence of strong colonial bonds, these countries neither had experienced relevant population exchanges, nor did legal principles of a liberal democracy force them to expand rights beyond ethnic bonds to their foreign residents. Another explanatory factor in the emergence of ethnic citizenship models is the historical importance of Diasporas. Christian Joppke (2005) shows how migration and citizenship policies in Germany and Israel have strived to create and maintain an imagined national community that can overcome geographical dispersal. Citizens are connected through common descent, history, language, or their religion, rather than their physical presence in a common political community.

Civic citizenship models might have emerged in a shared context of early post-colonial democracies, but they have subsequently taken rather different

Table 2.3. Historical Citizenship Regimes and Recent Changes in EU-15

Historical civic citizenship (colonial 'haves')	Historical ethnic citizenship (colonial have-beens and have-nots)	Recent regime changes
	Austria, Denmark, Greece, Italy, Spain *(pan-ethnic approach)*	*Restrictive continuity*
Netherlands *(late democratization meant more restrictive policies until 1980s)*	Finland, Germany,[a] Luxembourg, Portugal *(pan-ethnic approach)*, Sweden	*Liberalising change*
Belgium, France *(assimilation approach)*, Ireland, U.K.		*Historically liberal*

a. Howard (2009: 119ff) assumes a 'restrictive backlash' in German liberalizing tendencies due to the mitigation of a much more liberal citizenship package proposed by the Social-Democrat/Green government in 2001 in negotiations with the Conservative opposition in the upper chamber of parliament (also see: Green 2007).

Sources: Howard 2009; also Brubaker 1992 and Joppke 2005b

pathways. Scholars divide post-colonial regimes further into multicultural citizenship models (the United Kingdom and the Netherlands) and assimilation regimes (mainly France; see also Bonifazi 2000; Brubaker 1989, 1992; Castles 1995; Freeman 1995). Adrian Favell (2001) argues that despite their similar colonial past, demographic situation, and economic development in the postwar era, Britain and France developed quite different public "philosophies of integration." French policy makers have embraced a myth of Republican shared political identity that forged a participatory and assimilationist citizenship model. Quite contrary to this, the British approach, Favell argues, has tolerated and promoted ethno-cultural difference with the purpose of sustaining "moral public order" and social cohesion based on a consensus around "good" race relations and tolerant multiculturalism.

Despite their common tendency to enable naturalization for longer-term residents, both approaches have been associated with different sets of policies toward foreigners and ethnic minorities. In the case of French assimilation, the creation of a shared national identity is a normative and deontological goal of civic citizenship policy making. Overcoming group differences is a key target of assimilationist policies. By contrast, group identity is actively preserved and promoted in multiculturalist regimes (Favell 2001; Kymlicka and Banting 2006; Miller 2006). Both integration approaches have emerged as attempts to deal with ethnic diversity in two globally integrating colonial empires. Regardless of incremental policy changes[19] the normative foundations of *belonging* and *community*, through their codification in public law, have acquired the status of institutionalized reference points of civic belonging that are likely to inspire migration policy debates at large. As the analysis will show, France in particular struggles with its legacy of civic inclusion and inflicts in its labor migration policies a forceful and rather explicit effort to revoke a historically emerged model of belonging.

As it followed ideals of ethnic belonging and excluded migrant workers from civic integration processes, Germany has not treated the incoming "guest workers" as potential new citizens so that they often remained aliens by passport even in the second and third generation. At the same time, migrations from a Diaspora of ethnic Germans were welcomed as citizens even if they lived abroad for several generations (Green 2004). This approach of simultaneous ethnic inclusion and civic exclusion of foreigners (also associated with Austria and Italia, for instance) has been interpreted as attempt to hold together national identities of geographically dispersed ethnicities in a historical context of territorial border re-demarcations in the various wars in Europe in the nineteenth and twentieth centuries (Joppke 2005).

Mediterranean countries, by contrast, are perceived as migration "newcomers" or "emerging," and still in search of a migration regime and appear to be rather "uncontrolled" (Boswell 2007). In this, southern Europe displays a clear bifurcation into post-colonial and ethnic regimes that might impact labor migration flows and policies. Italy historically followed an ethnic inclusion pattern similar to Germany, readily granting passports to Italian descendants and their family members in Argentina for example. Spain and Portugal, by contrast, experienced early migration movements across their colonial empires and have early on developed privileged (labor) admission schemes for post-colonial migrants, mostly from Latin America. Early imperial collapses were counterbalanced with pan-ethnic citizenship models that emphasized Hispanic or Lusophone bonds across the world (Joppke 2005b). Selection by origin is likely to remain an important normative category of migration regulation in that context.

Since some decades, EU citizenship and mobility add another layer to country specific accounts in citizenship studies. Labor mobility in the whole Union is at the heart of the European common market project as "one of the most immediately visible and highly valued of the rights of persons living in the EU" (Baldaccini and Toner 2007: 6). Based on the transformation of mere free movement of workers into "EU citizenship" with the Maastricht Treaty in 1992, EU nationals count as "quasi-citizens" who are to be exempted from border controls and migration policies within the Union (Guild 2007). Certainly, there are limitations to an encompassing EU citizenship comparable to the sets of rights coming with nationality of a member state. Mobility for Eastern European workers has been restricted after the 2004 and 2007 enlargements, mobility provisions are uneven across member states and regions, and are contested during the ongoing economic crisis (Carmel and Paul 2013a; Maroukis 2013). It is further unclear under which conditions EU nationals can be expelled from another member state and whether family members automatically count as EU citizens, too (Guild 2007). Yet the point worth highlighting here is that "EU provisions on free movement exercise an important constraint on member states' national prerogatives in the area of migration policy" (Boswell and Geddes 2011: 200).

Typological Assumptions about Civic Border Drawing

To be sure, the sharp distinction between models is empirically superseded and hybrid models are observed in practice today (Joppke 2010). Yet civic integration approaches continue to vary considerably in Europe. Even if labor migration management might not be predominantly concerned with migrant workers' option of later naturalization, the long shadows of prospective civic integration are nonetheless projected onto socio-economic selection and initial admission. Indeed, the liberalness of a country's citizenship regime as a looming logic of integration and settlement might bear direct consequences for admission governance. For example, in Britain a restrictive border-control regime has come to be understood as the very precondition for "good race relations," social cohesion, and a relatively liberal citizenship regime (Favell 2001) and is thus likely to also affect policy makers' calculations about the acceptability of labor entries—especially when facing large numbers. French assimilation targets could bear similarly restrictive entry effects if economic utility concerns are mingled with ideas about "successful" assimilation.

Further, privileged labor market access offered to ethnic Germans who enter as newcomers but count as citizens might restrict or rhetorically invalidate entry routes for others. The civic principles of migrant inclusion in the United Kingdom and France might render such attempts to select workers by their origin implausible or even unlawful. At the same time, research shows that decolonization has created distinctly "post-colonial" labor geographies involving specific ethnic relations across "mother" countries and a former empire. Not surprisingly then, France has filled labor market shortages with Francophone post-colonial migrants since the 1960s (Joppke 2005b), and the United Kingdom has experienced and partly promoted work inflows from its former colonies (Schain 2008; Solano and Rafferty 2007). While these labor geographies are specified as policy contexts in chapter 3, evidence on post-colonial and ethnic admission patterns suggests that labor migration management has to engage with civic norms of belonging—be it in an affirmative of rejecting manner.

We have already discussed above that the legal obligation to grant European free movers entry to the domestic labor market on equal—or almost equal— terms is likely to further shape entry options for workers from outside the European Union. EU mobility might serve as a welcome justification for the targeted restriction of admission routes for groups of TCN workers who might seem undesirable within ethno-cultural frames of belonging (Favell 2008b; P. Hansen and Jonsson 2011; McDowell 2009; Paul 2013). Consequently, even if concentrating on labor migration policies for TCNs in general, we have to consider either privileged or deliberately restricted entry provisions for ethnic Germans, post-colonial "associate" nationals in France and the United Kingdom, and uncontrolled mobility of EU free movers as powerful classificatory systems with the potential to shape the meaning of borders to "legal" work migration more generally.

Lastly, the "unintended consequences" of the so-called guest worker period increased governments' caution in matters of labor recruitment as they are confronted with potential automatisms of settlement and family reunion (Castles 1986, 2006; Cornelius and Tsuda 2004; Rogers 1985). Several countries have introduced circular migration routes to prevent longer-term residence or settlement; a trend supported by the EU and OECD (CEC 2005; OECD 2009). These restrictive tendencies could invert even the most liberal citizenship approaches and might particularly entail attempts to loosen post-colonial ties or those associated with past admission systems in more ethnically and culturally selective labor migration policies.

Overall then, the following principles of civic border drawing emerge:

- Selection of workers by their origin works along the lines of post-colonial (in civic citizenship regimes) or ethnic belonging (in ethnic models). Depending on the stability and weight of these normative foundations, origin might surface as privilege or disadvantage in labor admission policies.
- EU citizenship and mobility might trigger restrictive tendencies for labor admission policies from third countries and, by default, add another level of selection by origin.
- Multiculturalist integration regimes anticipate social cohesion and public order effects of labor migration, while assimilationist regimes focus on the likely success of a migrant worker as a cultural and political member of the community.

The above reflections suggest that both the rather short-term rationalities of economic competitiveness and productivity in economic border drawing, and the medium-term social inclusion pathways anticipated in the social border-drawing dimension are likely to interact with civic norms of belonging. The main contention here is that distinct patterns of civic inclusion, such as EU mobility and citizenship or ethnic repatriation, form influential regulatory backdrops in the design of labor migration policies.

With our discussion of the civic dimension of border drawing, we have seemingly drifted away from an understanding of labor migration policy as economic growth strategy. To be clear, the point of this chapter is not to play down the strong economic drivers behind any attempt to govern entry and residence of foreign workers. Rather, when leaving the terrain of one-dimensional labor migration policy analyses and reappraising evidence from *across* the capitalist coordination, welfare state, and citizenship regime literatures, our examination strategy has to be geared toward interactions between the economic, social, and civic border-drawing dimensions.

It is no coincidence then that an increasing branch of comparative citizenship studies examines the reconstitution of citizenship models in the light of wider economic transformations—and precisely the ones described for economic border drawing earlier in the chapter. This seems to trigger, for instance, contractualization tendencies in integration and naturalization practices across Europe, as the need to "earn" one's citizenship or secure residence through economic performance grows. A study of the admission regime for high-skilled workers in the United Kingdom, for instance, shows that "a 'moral' conception of citizenship is invoked in the notion of a 'good' citizen predicated on primarily economic grounds." (Kiwan 2010: 334)

Trajectories like this underline the intersectionality of citizenship and integration frameworks with those of capitalist coordination. Similarly, research on the interactions between welfare retrenchment, budget constraints, and ethnicized social exclusions speaks of multidimensional migration policies from the perspective of the welfare state (Schierup et al. 2006). Ultimately, while recognizing the valuable contributions of individual regime literatures to understanding how specific dimensions of border drawing shape policies, the reflections in this chapter inform a multidimensional comparative analysis of labor migration management. This sets out to capture, compare, and explain more adequately the complex interactions of economic, social, and civic norms in British, French, and German definitions of "legal" migrant workers.

Conclusion: Toward a Multidimensional Analysis of Border Drawing

This chapter has identified an economic, social, and civic dimension of border drawing from comparative migration policy research. Capitalist coordination systems, welfare state regimes, and citizenship models, respectively, inform theoretical assumptions about the normative foundations of classifications applied to migrant workers (figure 2.1). Jointly, these assumptions form an ideal typical yardstick for our data analysis in chapters 4–6. While each border-drawing dimension provides valuable comparative assumptions of itself, the one-dimensional analytical focus in labor migration policy research, usually favoring the economic dimension, impedes our sensation for the multiple, partly contradictory, and sometimes chiefly non-economic foundations of labor migration management. Our empirical analysis makes variable labor migration policies across Europe explicable through a nuanced reconstruction of the various constituent parts of a multidimensional—and by no means straightforward—policy configuration.

In line with cultural political economy and interpretive policy analysis (chapter 1), we have further rehearsed border drawing in its normative and selective nature. Any empirically found interplay of the diverse border-drawing dimensions (economic, social, and civic) and their specific normative baggage will not occur in a self-assorting, predetermined, or accumulative manner. Rather, this interplay itself is the very object and product of governance. Depending on the ordering purposes that policy makers inscribe in the classification of "legal" and "illegal" migrant workers, they select norms and entry criteria carefully and arrange them within policies. Meanings from the economic, social, and civic realm can be chosen to matter, be emphasized, or be ignored. In this context, our analysis considers the structuring impact of each border-drawing dimension as a source of normative foundation in the classificatory process.

Yet, we are equally attentive to policies' power to set into motion (intentionally or not) far-reaching transformations of economic, social, and civic institutions themselves. Viewed through the prism of labor migration management, a relational analysis thus informs a critical engagement with wider trajectories in the governance of citizenship, welfare, and capitalism in Europe.

Border-Drawing Dimensions		
ECONOMIC	**SOCIAL**	**CIVIC**
(idealtypical assumptions for diverse...)		
Capitalist Coord. Regimes	*Welfare State Regimes*	*Citizenship Regimes*
focus on economic utility of migrant labour (competitiveness, innovation)	tight regulation of labour market access, anticipation of labour market 'success', and 'earned' integration in Bismarckian social insurance system	Selection by origin based on post-colonial (civic citizenship regimes) or ethnic belonging (ethnic models) surfaces as privilege or restrictive tool in admission policies
high/specific skills focus in CMEs versus generic skills focus in LMEs		
use of generous welfare benefits to attract high/specific skills in CMEs	enforced labour market self-sufficiency in Liberal residual regimes	EU free movement imperative implies restrictive trade-offs with TCN admissions
tighter regulation of initial labour market access in CMEs due to higher job protection	weaker and non-proportional link between work and welfare rights creates less incentive to regulate admissions tightly in Liberal regimes	Multiculturalist integration regimes require anticipation of social cohesion and public order effects of labor migration
more liberal admission regimes in deregulated LME labour markets	tax-funding of benefits (esp. in Liberal, but also in Social-Democratic regimes) might cause welfare-chauvinist backlashes	Assimilationist regimes focus on likely success of migrants as cultural and political community members
national varieties of policy discourse in market capitalism, managed capitalism and state capitalism		

Interact in selective definition of classification principles

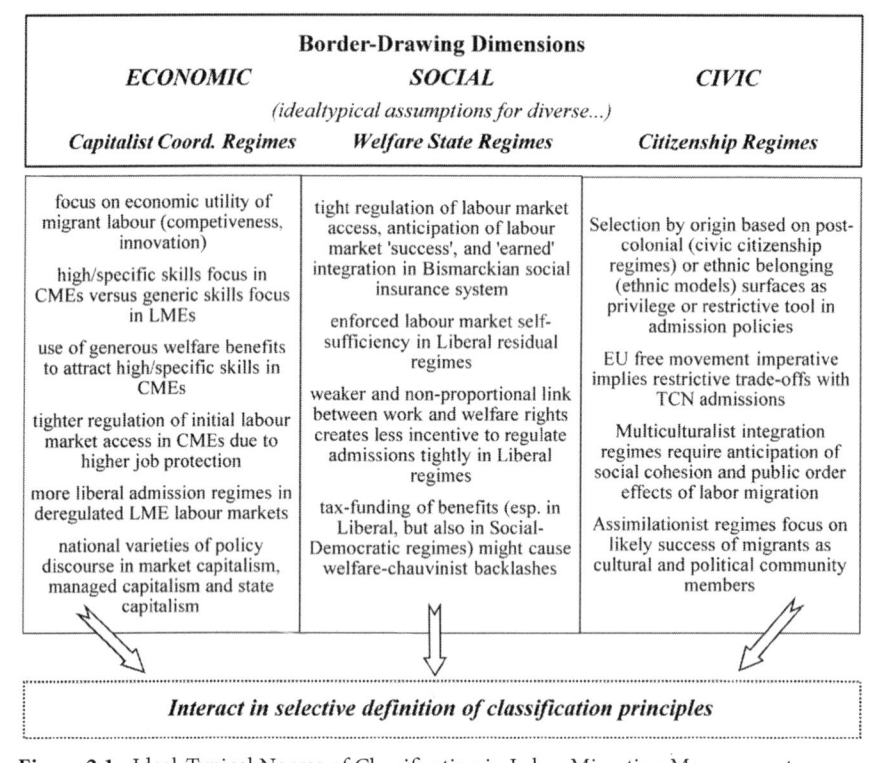

Figure 2.1. Ideal-Typical Norms of Classification in Labor Migration Management

Notes

1. Thomas Sowell, American economist at Hoover Institution, Stanford University.
2. Edward Wadie Saïd, Palestinian-American intellectual and scholar of colonial literature.
3. For brevity, typologies focus on EU-15 countries that represent the pool for case selection (see conclusion of this chapter). Equally, the aim of this chapter is not to give a detailed account of each EU-15 country's position in different typologies. The mapping of different typologies informs an initial sense of the broader empirical field of border drawing, informs case selection, and serves as a benchmark for the empirical analysis.
4. This consciously disregards the changing nature of empirical types, and potential for

convergence and divergence between them (for welfare regimes, see Arts and Gelissen 2002; for varieties of capitalism, see Blyth 2003).
5. This is a catch phrase used by a French interviewee from the Migration Ministry to summarize this growth perspective.
6. Employers have played an active part in leading governments to include competitiveness rhetoric in their migration policy making (Menz 2010a).
7. Mainly targeted at growth and competitiveness and job creation in the EU economy
8. This idea has been developed on the basis of the French regulation school tradition (Hollingsworth 1997; Hollingsworth and Boyer 1997).
9. Coates (2000) distinguishes between state regulation and trust-based coordination; Kitschelt et al. (1999) between national and sectoral coordination.
10. It is important to keep these two—informal employment in the black economy and employment of unauthorized migrant workers—apart analytically. While they often coincide, especially in the southern European debate, their confusion neglects the large shares of native workers in the informal economy (i.e., in undeclared jobs) and the share of unauthorized migrants who might work in regular jobs and pay social insurance and taxes on those.
11. This notion can be criticized as policies and sub-systems of the economy and social-market relations are more complex and contradictory in practice. Yet I argue that the state's attempt to create a coherent and complimentary economic governance strategy is visible in the realm of migration policies. Whether this attempt it is eventually successful or whether it is hampered in practice is a question beyond the realm of this thesis.
12. The EU Directive (CEU 2003a) on long-term residents is the first document to legally acknowledge and guarantee the relatively secure residence status of denizenship.
13. The studies cited use decommodification, replacement rates, social expenditure, welfare state generosity, or at-risk-of-poverty rates after social transfers.
14. I owe deeper reflections on the inherently contradictory logic of Bismarckian social inclusion via work—automatically inclusive for those who work but for the same reason also used as a justification of not granting labor market access when longer-term settlement of some groups is deemed undesirable—to the comments of an anonymous reviewer.
15. For reasons of brevity I disregard a detailed discussion of Social-Democratic and Mediterranean welfare state regimes here, as these types will not figure in the comparative analysis.
16. In this section, *citizenship* refers to formal passport citizenship that foreign workers gain by the acquisition of a nationality, not a wider definition of social citizenship, for example. Civic integration and Citizenship as aspects of "civic border drawing" relay aspects of classification related to legal residence, formal integration, and the creation of political and cultural communities, rather than to economic and social features or processes.
17. Howard (2009) also indicates recent regime changes based on liberalization tendencies (such as introduction of jus soli elements, non-ethnic naturalization practices, or dual citizenship). Simultaneously, post-colonial civic citizenship models have been increasingly restricted in the past in some countries. The case reviews in chapter 3 will take account of policy legacies and recent developments in Germany, France, and the United Kingdom in more detail.
18. For Howard, restrictiveness is characterized by tough naturalization requirements, the absence of dual citizenship options, and the equal absence of jus soli elements in the acquisition of nationality (2009: 27).

19. Recent changes have softened the sharp division between assimilation and multiculturalism. France has seen the introduction of multiculturalist policy tools to recognize group identities, while language tests requirements for naturalization or obligatory language courses introduced elements of assimilation in Britain and the Netherlands, for example (Brubaker 2001; Koopmans et al. 2005; Kymlicka and Banting 2006).

CHAPTER 3

Border Drawing in Context
Profiling Migration Histories and Policy Legacies for Comparative Analysis

> "To explain something in an interpretive manner is to situate it in its proper context. By grasping the context we make sense of whatever it is that needs to be made sense of."[1]

According to Henk Wagenaar (2011:110f.), "meanings are actualized in a specific context-in-use, depending on the particular historical circumstances and the specific intentions, challenges and possibilities that actors face." Without an elevated degree of case familiarity and in-depth acquaintance with the historical and political context of each case, comparative—and especially interpretive—policy analysis can only scratch the surface of a phenomenon under scrutiny. I thus follow those who argue that a nuanced ideographic account of cross-national similarities and differences requires in-depth comprehension of case specificities (Della Porta 2008; Hantrais 1999, 2009). If we are to understand why policies attach specific sets of meanings to the definition of migrant worker "legality", we need to be aware of the array of available normative claims in the wider policy context. What contextual features do policies incorporate, struggle with, ignore, or accentuate as meaningful? It is this chapter's task to provide the foundations for the thick contextual description required to make sense of the various constructions of "legal" migrant worker in Britain, France, and Germany and their justifications.

I carve out case contexts by locating each country in the regime literature discussed in chapter 2, then delineate key policy legacies, and specify the context in which labor migration policies have been reactivated in each case. In ideographic research designs, case profiles are more than mere descriptive portrays; they form indispensable analytical anchors for the subsequent explanation of cross-national policy variation. It is by understanding cases' relationships with specific sending countries, their legacies of regulating different types of migration, their embeddedness in the European Union, and the relevance and positions of specific migrant groups in the labor market, that an authentic appraisal of emerging policy meanings can be ensured. Mainly drawing on secondary literature on our three countries, this case profiling fulfills the important job of identifying key landmarks for the subsequent policy analysis.

Germany Between Europeanness and Demographic "Pressure"

Our case profiling starts with Germany, which the regime literatures depict as a stereotypical CME, Bismarckian welfare regime and ethnic belonging citizenship model. The case is marked by the Europeanness of its foreign workforce, aided by a simultaneous lack of significant post-colonial ties. The dominance of intra-European labor exchanges is long-standing: it has been visible in the guest worker era with preferential recruitments from Europe and its Eastern backyard (mainly Turkey and former Soviet territories) and large asylum inflows mainly from the Balkans in the 1990s. This expanded Europeanness has been forged systematically in bilateral agreements post-*Wende* and through liberal integration of ethnic Germans, while non-European recruitment has been largely suspended since the 1970s. In the midst of increasingly influential scenarios of demographic decline and severe labor shortages, German policy makers have decided to revitalize active TCN labor recruitment in the new Millennium.

Managed Capitalism, Bismarckian Welfare, and Legacies of Ethnic Belonging

Germany's economic governance regime is widely regarded as a stereotypical coordinated market economy (CME) that features all of the characteristics outlined in the original varieties of capitalism approach (Hall and Soskice 2001a). The particular categorization as "negotiated" or "managed" capitalism (Coates 2000; Schmidt 2002b) alludes to German economic coordination practices (e.g., for wage bargaining) in which social partners negotiate without much state intervention. State intervention thus plays a role of "enabling facilitator" in support or moderation of the economic self-governance of employer associations and trade unions (Schmidt 2002); and even more recent liberalizing reforms seem to have retained a strong role for the state as "re-coordinator" who can "tweak" radical market-liberal ideas to fit them into the equally desired institutions of the social market economy (Schnyder and Jackson 2013). Besides a generic focus on economic utility and competitiveness, the specific German location in capitalist regime theory lets us expect a policy focus on high and specific skills with specific incentives to attract these migrant workers through labor migration management (see also Menz 2009). Moreover, as relatively secure employment (and social) rights prevail for the sought-after skilled and high-skilled workers in CMEs, we can expect a rather tight regulation of initial labor market entries despite the job market flexibilizations (figure 2.1).

This claim is further fed by welfare state regime theory, which has us expect relatively generous social rights for those who are successful in the formal labor market and thus suggests that labor migrants' employment success is anticipated carefully at entry. According to Gøsta Esping-Andersen's (1990) famous typology, Germany serves as the paramount example of a Corporatist-Conservative regime. While some highlight the hybridization of the German model with elements of a liberal regime in employment policies and aspects of the Scandinavian activation approach (Hinrichs 2010), the organizing principles of status maintenance and rights acquisition via labor market participation have by no means lost all relevance. The close link between work and welfare can be expected to matter in labor admission policies: either as incentive to attract migrants of specific skill levels, or as a shield against migrant workers whose labor market participation does not promise to be successful, at least not in terms of social insurance contributions.

Lastly, German citizenship policy making has usually been associated with the ethnic belonging model and a specific Diaspora context (Joppke 2005b), even though a partial shift toward civic citizenship has been diagnosed more recently (Green 2001; Palmowski 2008). Guest workers and their German-born descendants have long been excluded from formal citizenship, while ethnic Germans have been "repatriated" quite smoothly. The privileged legal standing of EU nationals on (several-times-enlarged) Union territory has created an additional instance of selecting foreign workers by their origin with potentially restrictive effects for TCN workers.

Germany's European Migrants: Utility Meets Geopolitics

Almost 3.3 million individuals with a foreign passport worked in Germany in 2009 and accounted for 9.4 percent of the workforce (OECD 2011). A glance at the composition of registered foreign residents in Germany (table 3.1) reveals historical links to specific sending countries and past political recruitment decisions. The overriding Europeanness of migratory movement to and foreign residence in Germany is striking when compared to France and the United Kingdom. This is the result of several past political decisions and policy contexts: (1) the deliberate exclusion of most non-Europeans from guest worker recruitment agreements after the Second World War; (2) a simultaneous lack of relevant colonial labor exchanges with other parts of the world; (3) a strongly promoted civic integration of ethnic Germans from Russian terri-

Table 3.1. Origin of Newcomers and Foreign Residents in Germany (2010, in percent)

Origin of Newcomers (total: 798,282)		Origin of Foreign Residents (total: 6,753,621)	
Poland	14.5	Turkey	24.1
Germany (emigrant returns)	14.4	EU-14 countries	24.0
Romania	9.5	*Italy*	*7.7*
Bulgaria	5	*Greece*	*6.2*
Hungary	3.7	Former Yugoslavia (without Slovenia)	13.3
Turkey	3.5	EU-12 countries	12.1
Italy	3	*Poland*	*6.2*
United States	2.3	GUS states (without Baltic states)	6.8
Serbia	2.1	Others	19.6
China	2		
Others	40.2		

Source: BAMF 2011b

tories up to the early 1990s; (4) the principle origin of many asylum seekers from the Balkans; and (5) the specific geopolitical shifts at Germany's Eastern borders in the 1990s and 2000s. Together, these elements constitute a veritable German geopolitics of migration and labor recruitment in an expanding Europe. The historical relevance of "guest workers"[2] from the wider European continent leaves its traces in foreign residence statistics to date, with Turkish residents accounting for almost a quarter of all foreigners living in Germany in 2010, and Italians and Greeks[3] jointly making up another 14 percent. In response to severe labor shortages after the Second World War, Germany decided to recruit large numbers of predominantly unskilled male workers in the 1950s and 1960s in bilateral agreements with labor exporting countries. From the first agreement in 1955 until the suspension of recruitment in 1973, annual entries of newcomers more than quadrupled, peaking at almost one million in 1970 (figure 3.1)[4]. The foreign resident population in Germany grew accordingly, from 686,000 in 1961 to 3.9 million in 1975.

This recruitment history bears important sedimentations in contemporary German labor migration management debates. The lack or, to be more precise, early loss of colonial links goes some way in explaining the European character of migration to Germany. Some argue that unlike their homologues in post-colonial contexts—especially France and the United Kingdom—German policy makers in the 1950s and 1960s were able to shape foreign labor recruitment according to a European ideal, including Turkey at Europe's backyard, and deliberately excluded workers from other parts of the world (Schönwälder 2004).

Further, while policy makers had treated labor migration as an economic strategy without much consideration for long-term societal effects (Castles

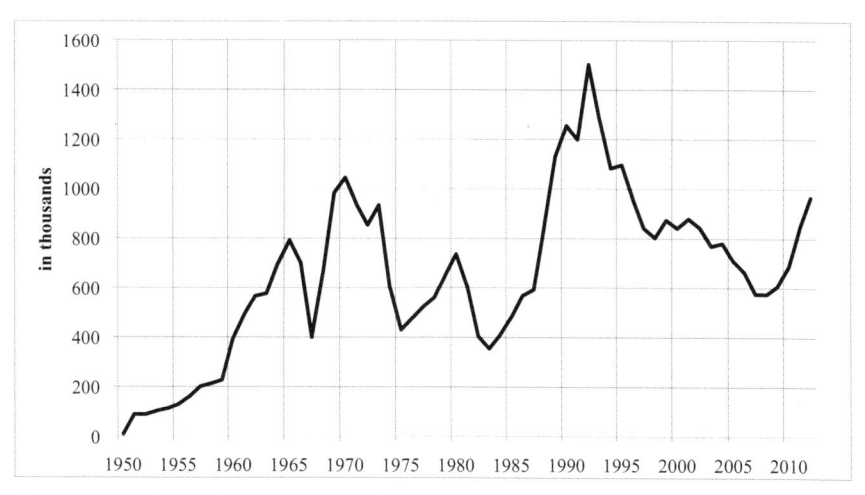

Figure 3.1. Inflows of Foreign Nationals to Germany (1950–2012)
Source: Statistisches Bundesamt 2011, 2013; until 1990 without GDR.

1985, 1986; Rogers 1985; Werner 2001), settlement of "guest" workers and their families was already mature when the government announced the recruitment stop in 1973 (Triadafilopoulos and Schönwälder 2006). With family reunion kicking in, entry numbers continued to increase substantially to an intermediate peak of 4.7 million residents in 1981, before leveling off (BAMF 2009a). Initially, policy makers did not perceive any need to establish effective integration measures or to offer viable naturalization paths to the newly entering workforce (Castles 1985; Cyrus and Vogel 2007; Green 2007; Triadafilopoulos and Schönwälder 2006). Instead, until a legal reform in 2005, Germany remained firmly attached to the ethnic belonging model of citizenship that excluded most guest workers and their German-born children from access to German nationality (e.g., Green 2004).

This treatment starkly contrasts with the welcoming attitude toward ethnic Germans who were accommodated as co-nationals during most of the second half of the twentieth century. Triggered by the territorial re-demarcation of Europe in the immediate postwar years, high numbers of ethnic Germans left the former German territories in the East. From 1950 to 1986 about 1.34 million ethnic Germans repatriated mostly from the territory of postwar Poland. Ethnic German entries increased massively after the end of the Cold War, mainly from former Soviet territories, with another 1.05 million individuals entering between 1986 and 1990 (BAMF 2011a; Hensen 2009). Some instances of public hostility apart, their integration has been straightforward in legal terms, as the German constitution automatically grants citizenship to ethnic repatriates whose German heritage has been acknowledged. Moreover, the "simulation"[5] of standard full-employment welfare biographies for ethnic German newcomers has facilitated their social integration according to the Bismarckian logics of status maintenance that we discussed in chapter 2 (Bommes 2000).

More recent developments suggest a decreasing relevance of ethnic selectivity as the preferential treatment of ethnic Germans declined throughout the 1990s. A quota for newcomers was established in 1993 and limited annual entries to approximately 200,000. Given more restrictive policies, public hostility, as well as the eventual surmounting of the post–Cold War momentum, the chapter of ethnic German repatriation appears pretty much closed in contemporary Germany (Joppke 2005b). Indeed, annual entries dropped to 35,000 in 2005 and further to less than 8,000 since 2006 (BAMF 2009b: 54).

Albeit without intent, the social inclusion logics of the Bismarckian welfare state have further worked in favor of foreign nationals who could not access civic integration paths. By contributing to the social insurance system, migrant workers have acquired welfare entitlements such as unemployment insurance or a state pension. Several observers have highlighted this mechanism of socio-economic integration, with due warning that the status maintenance logics of the Bismarckian welfare state have also cemented unequal labor market positions and exclusionary patterns for foreign workers (Bommes 2000; Kaiser and Paul 2011; Koopmans 2010; Morris 2002; Paul 2012b). A major socio-economic integration hindrance is seen in the lower educational attainment, formal skill level, and labor market participation of second and third generation "guest worker" residents (Thränhardt 2004; von Below 2007), the irony being that their parents or grandparents had once been recruited in their very capacity as cheap low-skilled laborers. Overall, decreasing relevance of the ethnic inclusion model and positive experiences with socio-economic integration of those who contribute successfully in paid employment has created a policy context in which anticipated labor market success and social insurance contributions are likely to trump other principles of selecting legal migrant workers for admission.

Asylum seekers represent the third large migrant group in Germany. Asylum seeker figures rose considerably during the late 1980s and 1990s, with a peak in 1992 (more than 440,000 newcomers). Table 3.1 indicates that these migrations originated mainly from the disintegrating Yugoslavian territories in the 1990s, and have rendered Serbs and Montenegrins the second largest non-EU population in Germany (Huddleston and Niessen 2011). Rights for asylum seekers have been curtailed in a context of increasing public hostility and welfare retrenchment in the 1990s, a debate that was recharged in autumn 2012 when large numbers of mainly Roma minorities from Serbia and Macedonia started seeking refuge in Germany (*Der Spiegel* 2012). Until and unless they are officially recognized as refugees, asylum seekers cannot work in the initial months of their stay in Germany. They are denied access to social insurance benefits and "earned" socio-economic inclusion pathways (Kaiser and Paul 2011; Sainsbury 2006). When rejected as refugees but not expellable immediately, asylum seekers usually obtain a toleration (*Duldung*). *Duldung* is no legal status but a provisional classification of a migrant until further notice that comes with highly insecure residence rights, a marginalized position in the German labor market and society. Some observers argue that despite these caveats, *Duldung* offers some recognition to otherwise fully illegalized residents (Morris 2002). Contemporary German labor migration policies address this phenomenon specifically, as I will discuss in chapter 4.

The semi-legal status of *Duldung* also explains lower levels of expected unauthorized residence in Germany. Theo Papadopoulos (2011: 33, table 2.3) estimates the share of irregular residents for the total foreign population at 4.5 percent in Germany in 2008. This figure might seem relatively low compared to France (8 percent) and the United Kingdom (17.5 percent), and lower than the EU-27 average (10 percent). However, studies of specific sectors such as domestic care highlight their structural reliance on migrant workers, often in informal employment (Lutz and Palenga-Möllenbeck 2010). Another particularity of the German case, the geographical proximity to a now-vanished outer border of the European Union, might also go some way in explaining lower current levels of unauthorized residence. Many especially lower-skilled construction and household service workers entered Germany from the East after 1989, with many supposedly lacking an official permit to do so. Even when European Union enlargement turned Eastern Europeans from TCN into fellow EU nationals, workers from Poland, Latvia, and others still experienced major restrictions to their labor mobility and some have sought semi-legal employment in the meantime. In this context, the false use of the "self-employed" or "posted worker" category as easier entry is widely cited (Cremers 2011, 2013; Dølvik and Visser 2009; Woolfson and Sommers 2006).

Yet even if they were in irregular employment, Eastern European workers did not count as unauthorized residents when enacting their right to move (though not to work) within the European Union since 2004. Their status has further been formalized with the establishment of full free movement in May 2011. Gradually formalized access to cheap labor in Eastern neighboring countries has considerably changed the geopolitical and legal context of foreign labor recruitment in Germany. Shifting weights in the foreign workforce are visible in the drop of the Turkish (down 1 percent point from 2009 to 2010 alone) and simultaneous increase of the Eastern European share (BAMF 2009b, 2011b). More than a third of all newcomers came from Eastern European member states and another 20 percent originated from other EU countries in 2010 (BAMF 2011b). Gradually expanding to include new territories in the East, Eurocentric geopolitics constitute a constant marker of German migration policy making more broadly, and the labor admission regime in particular.

Demographic Pressure? The Cautious Reform of German Labor Migration Policies

The notion of an expanded European labor pool as backdrop for recruitment surfaced soon after the German reunification in 1990. This event had created huge labor demand—especially construction workers were on demand on the then biggest construction site in Europe in Berlin. Immediately after the fall of the Berlin Wall, the German government negotiated recruitment agreements (*Anwerbeabkommen*) with Poland and other Eastern European countries[6] to channel cheaply available workers into the construction industry and other sectors experiencing severe shortages (Menz 2001). Some of these agreements remain in place to date, but most have or will become redundant with full free movement for EU accession countries after the 2004 and 2007 enlargements. This post–Cold War expansion of the intra-European labor market at Germany's Eastern porch has severely limited the scope for other TCN labor migration: as "labor markets have looked East" (Favell, 2008b: 704), border drawing alongside a prospective EU vs. non-EU divide has gained momentum in German labor migration management. Prospective EU nationals of accession and candidate countries have been treated benevolently. At the same time, the fear of losing control over Eastern European migration triggered the German decision to operate transitional limitations to free movement until May 2011 for EU-8 nationals and until 2014 for Bulgarians and Romanians. We witness an ongoing cautious but decisive embedding of German labor migration policies within the still-expanding intra-European labor market—including Croatia, Serbia, and Turkey as more or less hotly debated accession candidates.

The gradual integration of the former communist East into the European Union apart, a serious debate about the economic virtues of labor migration has gained ground since 2000, catalyzed by the planned introduction of the German "Green Card" for IT specialists. Due to massive labor shortages in the IT sector (vacancies between 75,000 and 150,000 had been reported in 2000; see Werner 2001) then Chancellor Gerhard Schröder called for the recruitment of specialists from outside Europe. Schröder's initiative decisively answered the notorious question of whether or not Germany was a country of immigration with the affirmative, and contributed to a wider belief that, after all, the national economy "had to attract highly skilled immigrants to remain economically competitive" also from outside the European Union (Green 2007: 112). Certainly also underpinned by a change of government toward a Social Democrat-Green lead after sixteen years of Conservative rule, this view significantly changed the parameters of the policy debate and contributed to a reappraisal of the German policy paradigm of non-immigration country and reluctant migrant integration (see also Menz 2009).

The demographic rationale cannot be underestimated in its chief role as a continuous driver of German policy change. Unlike France and the United

Kingdom, Germany experiences shrinking in the overall population, and low fertility rates paired with aging particularly reduce the relative share of the working age population. While population projections estimate a population growth by four million people in France and by more than three million in the United Kingdom between 2010 and 2050, the German population is expected to shrink by around eight million. The trend is not just prospective: in 2010 the proportion of the population aged sixty-five and over has been much higher in Germany (20.4 percent) than in France and the United Kingdom (16.8 and 16.6 percent, respectively; Eurostat 2008). While not precluding the potential layering of economic utility reasoning with other agendas in German labor migration policy making, or the potential misuse of the demographic argument as a fig leaf for other migration control goals, the demographic context means that a German pledge for foreign labor recruitment is likely to be—at least to some extent—genuinely linked to perceived pertinent and endemic skills shortages. This matters especially in comparison to France, as we will see, where shortage recruitment is not just an economic agenda but seems to serve the purpose of replacing the available resident workforce from former colonies with workers from Europe.

Faced with the demographic decline scenario, an Expert Commission—the so-called *Süßmuth-Kommission*[7]—was charged with proposing legal changes (Unabhängige Kommission "Zuwanderung" 2001). Besides a citizenship reform and a revisited integration approach, the Commission proposed a points-based system for labor migration. While such a stark policy shift had been compromised after strenuous political struggles in the second legislative chamber *Bundesrat* (Green 2007), the Migration Law came into force on 1 January 2005 (Bundesrepublik Deutschland 2004) and introduced cautious liberalizations of admission rules. Compared to the large-scale recruitment in the 1950s and 1960s, only around 29,000 employees came to Germany in 2007 and slightly more than 26,000 in 2009 (Parusel and Schneider 2010: 60f.),[8] confirming the highly selective character of post-Fordist labor recruitment discussed in the introduction. However, the Migration Law has certainly provided some space for skilled entries. Against the backdrop of looming demographic workforce shrinking and labor shortages, legislation has even been liberalized further since—most recently in July 2013—expanding light-touch admission procedures from high-skilled to skilled professions and, for the first time in its history, also to TCN youngsters applying for vocational training courses.

France Between Post-Colonial Belonging and "Immigration *Choisie*"

France epitomizes characteristics of state-led capitalism and Bismarckian welfare provision, sharing vital economic and social coordination features with Germany. It moreover serves as prime example of a post-colonial civic citizenship regime—just as the United Kingdom—but with a distinct focus on assimilation and political citizenship. The country has a history of utilitarian guest worker recruitment that privileged European workers, but post-colonial inflows mainly from the Maghreb and Sub-Saharan Africa have gained relevance after decolonization. Attempts to loosen these ties and restrict post-colonial migration have been highly politicized, especially given the frequent unauthorized residence and informal employment statuses of migrant workers from former colonies in France. Torn between economic utility rationales and struggles over post-colonial belonging, the recent revival of TCN labor recruitment in France operates in an especially politicized environment that sets it apart from the other two cases.

State Capitalism, Bismarckian Welfare, and Post-Colonial Republican Citizenship

According to varieties of capitalism scholars, French economic coordination shares some CME characteristics with Germany: a focus on high- and specific skill recruitment, trust relationship between firms, and sectoral coordination patterns (Amable 2003; Kitschelt et al. 1999a). However, some French particularities provoked an initial categorization as "unclassified" (Hall and Soskice 2001a). There seems to be a more important role for statutory regulation in a "state-enhanced" model of French capitalism, with the state acting as an "interventionist leader" that actively shapes conditions for firms' competitiveness (Schmidt 2002b). In a *dirigiste* tradition, France has relied on tools like direct ownership—in 1981 the French state owned thirteen of its largest twenty firms—indicative planning, and strategic research subsidies to strengthen competitive sectors. Credit allocation favored the creation of "national champion" industries and even seemingly liberal privatizations were strongly directed by state interests (Culpepper 2006; Hancké 2001; Loriaux 2003). Cutting across the realms of administrative and business elites, a discourse of national economic interest has arguably produced a sturdy social fabric for state-enhanced economic coordination in France (Loriaux 2003). Beyond the assumptions drawn from the CME type of capitalist governance (figure 2.1)—skills targeted in labor migration, sectoral organization of recruitment, and tight regulation of admissions in highly regulated labor markets—we can expect French regulation to enact a more proactive and directing role in labor recruitment than Germany. *Dirigiste* governance approaches have shown their resilience even in the face of a rhetorical turn towards more market liberalism, especially under the Presidency of Nicolas Sarkozy. As well argued in a recent study, his response to the economic crisis in 2008/2009 represents a retreat back to Keynesian stimulus policies, greater state intervention, promotion of French business, bail-outs, state-enforced mergers, and 'economic patriotism' (Gualmini and

Schmidt 2013). Labor migration policies are thus prone to entail a focus on the national economic position of France in the world, rather than being mere facilitating responses to companies' demands like in the German model.

The French welfare state has been categorized alongside the German one, with comparable presumptions for labor migration policies (chapter 2). However, recent research documented shifts away from a social insurance model toward social protection as an instrument of workfare, employability, and competitiveness, and eventually describes "dualizations" of the Bismarckian tradition of status maintenance and a more market-based liberal social-protection system (Palier 2010a). Dualization tendencies might work differentially in labor migration policies: to attract well-sought-after (and well-paid) migrant workers with the promise of status maintenance, and to exclude lower-paid and unauthorized migrant workers from access to anything more than basic entitlements.

The French citizenship and integration model traditionally hinges on notions of political community, civic belonging and jus soli, and assimilation. Chapter 2 indicated how Republicanism might disqualify any attempt to select workers by their origin or ethnicity; yet, at the same time, France's colonial legacy forges special relationships with sending countries and the special treatment of EU citizens can be expected to layer the civic citizenship model with classifications based on migrants' origin. The notion of post-colonial belonging and "Francophonie" are further likely to obstruct overly utilitarian labor recruitment approaches.

Between Europe and Francophonie:
Unresolved Questions of Post-Colonial Belonging

Around 1.5 million foreign nationals worked in France in 2009, accounting for 5.8 percent of the workforce (OECD 2011). The smaller share in comparison with Germany is certainly due to easier naturalization practices and jus soli citizenship, which turned more foreign residents and their children into French nationals, even though the 1990s and 2000s have seen restrictions to this liberal civic integration model (Hargreaves 2007). The composition of the foreign resident population (figure 3.2) in France reveals the increasing relevance of residents from former colonial territories and a simultaneous decrease of the European share among the foreign resident population. While more than 60 percent of foreigners originated from what is now the EU-27 in 1975, this share has declined to just over 30 percent in 2008. Residents of North African descent are most numerous today with Algerians and Moroccans being the most important minority groups in 2005 (Huddleston and Niessen 2011). We also observe a growth of the Southeast Asian and Sub-Saharan African resident population, especially since the 1990s. The changing composition of

84 | *The Political Economy of Border Drawing*

the French foreign resident population represents a testimony of the shifting influences on (labor) migration to France, which I will detail below.

Given male population declines in several wars and low mobility rates within France, migration had been identified as a response strategy to demographic shortages as early as in the nineteenth century (Freedman 2004; Hollifield 2004b; Weil 2005). The first guest worker contracts were signed before the First World War, and the foundation of the *Societé Générale d'Immigration* institutionalized foreign worker recruitment from 1920 onward. The French government responded to continuously high labor demand by designing specific entry routes for migrant workers with a 1945 decree (*Ordonnance*), giving the recruitment agency the monopoly of admitting foreign workers (Weil 2005). In practice, however, official recruitment procedures were undermined by employers and the agency mainly acted as a "clearing house" for the recruitment of unauthorized migrant workers (Hollifield 2004b: 189). This "laissez-faire approach" to labor migration (Hargreaves 2007) provoked large increases in annual admissions, with peaks in the mid-1950s, mid-1960s, and an all-time high in 1971 when almost 180,000 newcomers were registered (figure 3.3).

The economic utility focus was, however, always accompanied by ethnocultural selection hierarchies (Spire 2005, 2007). Before World War II, a migrant's assumed ability to assimilate easily into the French society, nation, and army benignly shaped admission decisions (*étrangers assimilable*; Weil 2005). Even though the *Ordonnance* laws did not comprise official country-reserved shares for entries, ethnic hierarchies of recruited newcomers mattered: foreigners were selected[9] "à la carte" (Spire 2005) under the discretion of prefectural decision makers in line with internal presidential orders. The assumption that foreigners of the same race and confession would integrate smoothly, informed a recruitment hierarchy in which ranged Catholics of white European

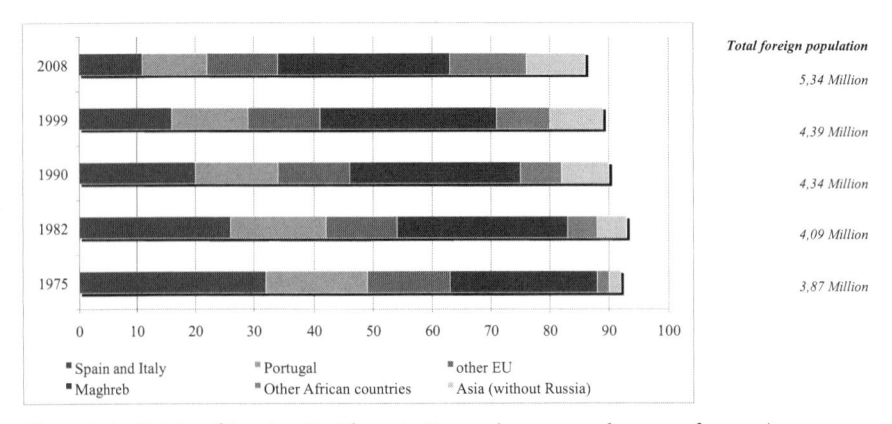

Figure 3.2. Origin of Foreign Residents in France (percentage by year of census)
Source: INSEE 2012.

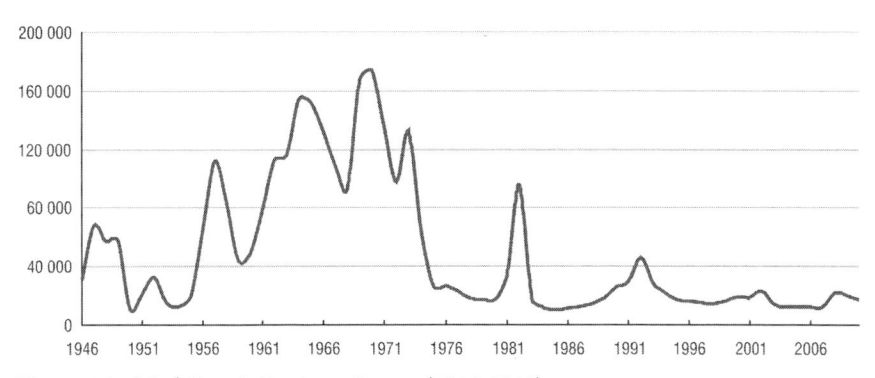

Figure 3.3. Work Permit Entries to France (1946–2010)
Source: INSEE 2012: 147, with friendly permission of reuse from http://www.insee.fr.

descent (Italians, Spaniards, Portuguese, Belgians, and Poles) before black and Muslim descendants of French colonies (Hargreaves 2007). Bilateral recruitment agreements with several European countries institutionalized this selection by origin and ethnicity. The residence patterns in the earlier twentieth century clearly mirror this ethnically biased labor recruitment policy: Spanish, Italian, and Portuguese workers accounted for almost half of all foreign residents in 1974 (figure 3.2).

This pattern of excluding non-European workers in "guest worker" recruitment applies to Europe more generally and is believed to have informed ethnically motivated labor selectivity, which has by no means lost its appeal in contemporary migration management (P. Hansen and Jonsson 2011; Schönwälder 2004). We will come back to this argument in the book's empirical chapters. Only when the European labor pool could no longer satisfy demand did the French government start recruiting Tunisians and Moroccans. The *Maghrebin* share of the foreign population grew to become the largest single category by 1982, regardless of the government's attempts to counterbalance these flows with more Italians, for instance (Joppke 2005b; Spire 2005). The simultaneity of high labor demands and decolonization in the 1960s rendered the approach to select workers by their utility and their European descent and assumed cultural proximity unworkable. Special postcolonial relationships and the former colonies' claim of linguistic and cultural proximity (*Francophonie*) to the former imperialist sovereign fueled increasing inflows from now independent territories.

Algerians, for instance, benefitted from free movement across French territories until the status of French overseas region was lost with Algerian Independence in 1962, and even preserved parts of this right up to date. With numbers as high as 180,000, Algerian workers contributed many hands to the French labor market between 1949 and 1955 (Weil 2005: 84). They have accounted for between 11.6 and 14.8 percent of all foreign residents in France since the 1960s, replacing Spaniards and Italians as biggest ethnic minority group in 1982 (INSEE 2005). Sub-Saharan migration commenced in the mid-1960s, after most French colonies (e.g., Senegal, Ivory Coast, or Cameroon) gained independence in 1960. In light of these developments, the previously promoted European dominance of migration and settlement began to cease and flows from former colonies gradually acquired vital importance as a policy context for labor migration management.

The shifting migration realities in post-colonial France triggered political tensions and far-right backlashes. Notably, the decision to suspend labor recruitment officially for economic reasons rather exploited the venue of the recession in the early 1970s to pursue a wider ideological agenda (Laurens 2009), more specifically the concern about ethnic and social cohesion under conditions of growing post-colonial migration. The recruitment stop did indeed lead to a stark drop in annual admissions in the mid-1970s, but as elsewhere, a full suspension of foreign worker recruitment was not applied, with sectoral exceptions operating in agriculture, medical professions, or for woodcutters. The principle of selective utilitarian recruitment in response to labor shortages certainly survived (GISTI 2009b). Adding to that, family reunion rights were guaranteed with a court ruling in 1975, and many family members—mostly from former colonies—joined the foreign workforce in France. By 1974 the immigrant population in France seemed well established at 7.4 percent of the total population has remained relatively stable ever since (INSEE 2005).

As political tensions and politicization of migration policy continued to grow after the recruitment stop, an "ethnicization" of migration policies unfolded and brought the previously rather hidden ethnic hierarchies of guest worker recruitment to the fore (Hargreaves 2007). The administration and part of the public opinion viewed especially North-African Muslims, even when French citizens, as an "enemy within" and ascribed to them rather grim integration outlooks (Dine 2008; Hargreaves 2007).[10] Restrictions aimed to discourage new entries and encourage exits from former colonies, and were tightened further in response to the electoral successes of the far-right Front National party in the 1980s and 1990s. Scholars evaluate the continuous political strength of Front National as most strenuous hurdle to liberalizing citizenship and migration policies in contemporary France (Howard 2009; Schain 2008).

In this rather hostile atmosphere, legislation passed in the 1980s and 1990s (with some exceptions regarding citizenship and naturalization under socialist rule) was mostly concerned with limiting eligibility for work authorization and long-term residence. Family reunion rights, access to citizenship, and the stable residence status (ten-year permit) have been curtailed and the highly restrictive Pasqua laws introduced tough policing and detention of irregular migrants (Hargreaves 2007; Menz 2009). In this context, civic Republican citizenship and assimilation, while officially based on "color blindness" and universal political rights, were increasingly filtered through an ethnicized kaleidoscope: the target of most restrictions were Muslim North-African and black Sub-Saharan migrants whose share at the irregular foreign population is known to be especially high, and whose risk of informality has been (some argue deliberately) heightened with the "zero" migration approach since 1974 (Morice 1996; Samers 2003; Samers 2010). The pragmatic handling of ex-post regularization during the postwar labor recruitment boom is certainly anachronistic: informality of employment has been increasingly criminalized and has a potential to marginalize especially migrants of post-colonial descent further.

The politicization of migration, post-colonial belonging and citizenship did not only provoke far-right backlashes and legal restrictions; it equally triggered vocal protests from migrant advocacy groups, human rights lobbyists, the political left, and intellectuals who expressed concern about departing from the Republican tradition of forging a civic political community.[11] This is particularly visible with regard to the very vocal public support for unauthorized workers, which is so far unparalleled in our other two cases. Estimates assume that between 150,000 and 800,000 *sans-papiers* were living on French territory in the 1990s and 2000s (Aubusson de Carvalay 2008). The share of undocument migrants is only slightly higher than in Germany (0.46 compared to 0.40 percent of the total population) and much lower than in Italy (0.62), the United Kingdom (1.05), or leading Greece (1.7; Papadopoulos 2011: 40, table 2.5).

The augmented politicization and open contestation of migrant "illegality," however, divides the French case from others. For example, detention and expulsion orders for unauthorized workers and residents lead to sit-ins and hunger strikes of the so-called *sans-papiers* in 1996 with large support by the civic society, especially trade unions and left parties. Similar protests reoccurred in the 2000s (Barron et al. 2011). The wide spread and vocalized solidarity with these workers in France contrasts especially the British case where a depoliticized toleration and marginalization of a larger irregular migrant working population has been observed (Wilkinson and Craig 2011). The different public perception of unauthorized workers partly explains the occurrence of amnesties[12] in France in the 1980s and 1990s as an attempt to reconcile a distinctly *political* civic citizenship model with informal and/or unauthorized employment and realities. The political struggle between defending an encompassing citizenship model that is impartial to ethnicity and economic utility on the one hand, and the attempt to restrict migrant rights, cut off post-colonial relationships, and focus on migrants' economic utility on the other is very much ongoing. This historically emerged political minefield forms a distinct policy context for labor migration management in contemporary France.

Toward "Immigration Choisie": The French Rediscovery of Labor Migration

Labor shortages in specific sectors and regions and the increase of the tertiary sector informed an "early and clear concentration on skilled migration" in France, which softened the general recruitment stop (Menz 2009: 146). Beginning with the Chèvenement Law in 1997, facilitations for high-skilled labor migration, initially of scientists, have been envisaged in a more systematic manner with the strong support of employers. In 1998 an internal administrative circular advised prefecture decision makers to fast-track applications of information technology specialists (ibid.). The most encompassing reactivation of TCN labor admissions, however, is embodied in the Sarkozy II Laws that came into force in 2006.

Labor migration has been a pet subject of Nicolas Sarkozy's presidency campaign in 2007. Still home secretary in 2006, Sarkozy wanted to "profoundly transform immigration policy in France" (Marthaler 2008: 389). The main aim was to tailor flows to the country's economic needs and to choose entries on economic grounds (*"immigration choisie"*), rather than having flows "imposed" (*"immigration subie"*) through family reunion. The *immigration choisie* agenda co-occurred with the introduction of an integration contract for newcomers, mainly targeted at family members, a further tightening of entry conditions and assimilation requirements for the non-work migration routes, a toughened fight against irregular entries and residence, and the abolishment of automatic access to permanent residence rights after ten years of (also irregular) residence. In the aftermath of the ethnic minority riots in urban Paris in 2005, assimilation and ethno-cultural belonging were back on the agenda and layered the labor migration debate.

Reactivated labor migration policy under President Sarkozy suggested that levels of professional inflows should be boosted to 50 percent of all entries by 2012. This was meant to ensue mainly from a number of new labor migration routes and permits to be discussed in the next chapter, but also from discouragement of entries via non-work routes and settlement of those not "chosen" (Le Président de la République and Le Premier Ministre 2009). A cabinet document expresses the need to fast-track visa delivery for high-skilled foreigners "who respond to the needs of our labor market" (CICI 2011: 12). *Immigration choisie* signals desirability of professional migration while at the same time transmitting a clear message of unwantedness to other resident groups. The direct link of the labor migration agenda to the aim of reducing family flows—not seen as such in the German case—indicates a strong conflation of economic recruitment rationales with the aim of restricting rights for specific resident groups in France. This suggestion is further supported by rather comfortable demographic circumstances on the French labor market where, unlike in the

German context, workforce shrinking does not seem to figure as a pertinent issue yet (Eurostat 2008). The conflation of labor recruitment with migration control has also been visible in the much-debated Hortefeux Law that, in 2007, introduced a procedure of exceptional regularization of unauthorized workers on a case to case basis and enabling them to regularize employment that has been defined as a shortage on a specific shortage list (read more on this policy tool in chapter 4). Hortefeux maps the management of migrant irregularity directly onto labor admission policies.

The *immigration choisie* agenda seems to show modest effects, with professional entries having climbed to 25,000 in 2008 compared to around 18,000 four years earlier (Sénat de la République Française 2010) and family member entries decreasing in the same period. Notwithstanding these slight changes, professional migration is still far from forming 50 percent of inflows as the Sarkozy government had suggested. The subsequent analysis in chapters 4–6 will highlight, however, that the symbolic message entailed in French labor migration policy—a warm welcome to high-skilled and skilled labor migrants and a skeptic approach toward other foreign residents, to say the least—should not be underestimated.

Adding to this, the recent concentration on Romanians and Bulgarians as recruits for unskilled and skilled labor market shortages evidences a revival of ethnic recruitment hierarchies that privilege European workers. While France, just as Germany, approached mobility of workers from new EU member states cautiously at first and applied temporary restrictions, French labor migration management has provided advantageous entry routes for new EU nationals, also including Croatian workers since summer 2013. The enlargement of the intra-EU workforce might add further to a policy of breaking with more global migration dynamics and Francophone models of belonging that have evolved in the French post-colonial setting.

Britain Between Laissez-Faire, Post-Colonial Downsizing, and Border Control

The British case is characterized by its diametrically opposite location in capitalist economy and welfare regime literatures. Categorized as liberal market economy and liberal residual welfare state, the United Kingdom should rely much more on market-based logics of border drawing than France and Germany. At the same time, it shares with France a post-colonial heritage and civic citizenship model. Yet, the United Kingdom's multiculturalist integration regime and island geography implies a comparatively strong focus on external border control. British migration policy has been oscillating between countervailing normative visions of economic openness, tough border control, and post-colonial detachment. As the liberal policy approach of New Labour in the 2000s—provoking the highest entries of foreigners to the United Kingdom in decades—and recent restrictive policy changes under a Conservative-led government in 2010 evidence, the battle over the guiding norms of labor migration management is ongoing. At the same time, one of the largest estimated population of undocumented migrant workers in the EU-15 and large inflows from EU accession countries jeopardize the tough control approach and sustain economic liberalism in practice.

Market Capitalism, Welfare "of the Last Resort," and Multiculturalist Citizenship

While the United States served as typical example of an liberal market economy in Peter Hall and David Soskice's varieties of capitalism typology, the United Kingdom has usually been associated with market-based modes of economic coordination as well, mainly under a heading of "market capitalism" (Clasen 2005; Hay and Wincott 2012; Schmidt 2002b). According to Vivien Schmidt, the British state acts as "liberal arbiter" in response to economic demand. Economic pulling horses are high-end financial and insurance services in the City of London, and sectors relying on radical innovation such as biotechnology, software development, or telecommunications. These require more generic and transferable skills that are responsive to production strategy shifts. UK companies have also competed well in sectors with low skill requirements and lower technological investment needs, such as foods or beverages (Schmidt 2002b: 132). British market capitalism is expected to imply a concentration on more generic and also lower skills in labor admission policies (Menz 2009). Moreover, the British labor market has been deregulated in the Thatcher era and bears crucial elements of the LME "hire-and-fire" philosophy (Estevez-Abe et al. 2001; Schmidt 2002b). A liberal approach toward incoming foreign workers can arguably be afforded in a deregulated labor market with few long-term commitments, high turnovers, and less far-reaching social entitlements.

Despite its Beveridgean[13] tradition, the United Kingdom has developed into one of the most liberal market-based welfare systems in the European Union under the influence of economic recessions, the Thatcher government's turn toward monetarism, and New Labour's "Third Way" (Hay and Smith 2013; Rhodes 2000; Schmidt 2002b; Taylor-Gooby et al. 2004). This tendency has further been underpinned by strong shifts toward welfare-to-work with a "competitive individualist ethos" that has surfaced much less in Continental Europe (Dean 2007: 586; Peck 2001). This individualism importantly includes elements of "privatized Keynesianism" in which state policies sustain low interest rates and highly competitive credit markets to enable people to buy property, thus increasing their assets and the ability to 'cash them in' when needed, all with a view of reducing reliance on social transfers (Hay and Smith 2013; Hay and Wincott 2012).

Liberal labor admission policies can be afforded, it seems, where foreigners' labor market participation creates no generous entitlements to welfare benefits and workfarism has even been shown to act as an incentive for foreigners' keen labor market integration in the United Kingdom (Koopmans 2010). However, the tax funding of benefits and the residual approach to social policy also tends to incite fiercer eligibility debates than in contexts where social insurance or universalism logics operate (van Oorschot et al. 2008). We might expect welfare-chauvinist responses to migrant unemployment, even though recent research does not find a significant correlation between welfare and attitudes to multiculturalism in Britain (Evans 2006).

Similarly to France, the United Kingdom has pursued a civic citizenship pathway that contradicts any ethnic bias in migrant admission and integration policies. However, special ties to former colonies might nonetheless inform positive or negative selection by origin. In sharp difference to France, lastly, the British multiculturalist integration approach has supported cultural and ethnic difference; following the aim of sustaining "moral public order" and social cohesion through managing internal race relations and group rights (Favell 2001). In this reading, tough control of the outer borders serves as key prerequisite for a liberal integration and citizenship approach inside. This tough border control focus, while seemingly ensuring the success of civic integration and social cohesion, contradicts the liberal economic policy design that VoC scholars have us expect. It is not surprising then, as the following account of migration legacies will show, that migration policies in the United Kingdom tended to oscillate between economic laissez-fairism and societal closure, with most far-reaching implications for the rights of post-colonial and unauthorized workers.

Britain's Ongoing Quest: Imperial Labor Market, Zero Migration, and Laissez-Faire

In 2009, 2.8 million foreigners formed part of the workforce in Britain, accounting for an 8 percent share (OECD 2011). According to recent Eurostat data, the largest minority groups were Indians, US Americans, and Pakistanis in 2008 (Huddleston and Niessen 2011). As in the French case, post-colonial bonds continue to shape the British migration policy context, with entries from the Old Commonwealth (Canada, Australia, New Zealand, and South Africa), New Commonwealth (mainly the Indian sub-continent and Sub-Saharan regions), and the United States being dominant throughout the past forty years (figure 3.4). Especially entries from India, Pakistan, and several African countries have increased since the mid-1990s while the relevance of Old Commonwealth entries decreased. These post-colonial migration dynamics have been

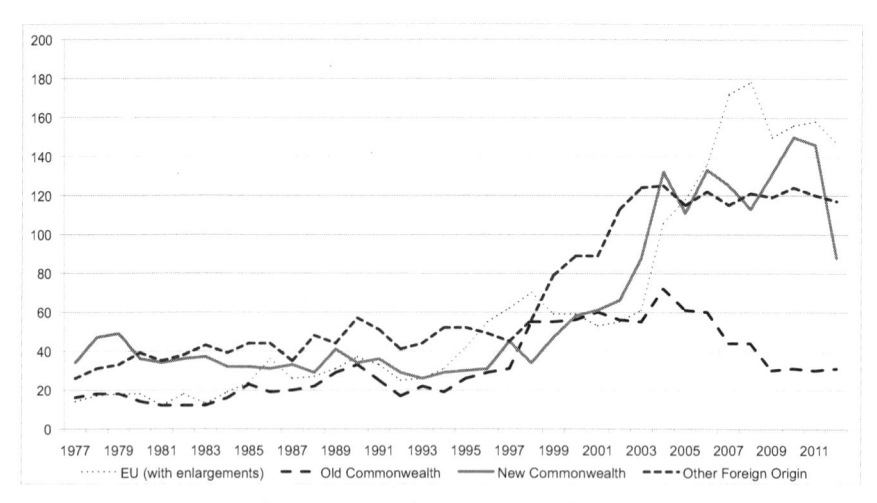

Figure 3.4. Migration to the United Kingdom by Region of Origin (1975–2010, in thousands)
Source: ONS 2008, 2011 (International Passenger Survey).

accompanied by considerably higher numbers of EU newcomers, especially in the new Millennium. The contemporary composition of the British foreign workforce is the result of the UK's changing geopolitical embeddedness in a post-colonial setting and in Europe as well as a liberal labor market, as we will see in the following.

Britain featured a different demographic and labor-market situation than France and Germany and did not need to import workers systematically (Schain 2008: 142). For most of the nineteenth and earlier twentieth century the country could rely on three sources of "internal" migration: arrivals from Ireland, returns of emigrants from the former colonies, and Commonwealth newcomers. None of these were considered "foreign" and did not need permits to enter and work. This liberal phase lasted until 1962 and allowed "almost uncontrolled" entries (Düvell 2007). Economic interests were conflated with perceived moral obligations created by imperialism so that the "drive for labor" followed imperial paths initially (Wilkinson and Craig 2011).

Commonwealth migration was characterized by mass entries mainly from the Black Caribbean since the late 1940s (peaking in the 1950s) and India and other Asian countries since the late 1950s. Between 1953 and 1962, net migration from the New Commonwealth reached around 485,000, with West Indians accounting for almost half of all entries, and Indian and Pakistanis for another 15 percent approximately (Layton-Henry 2004: 302, table 8.1). The government viewed labor entries of "British subjects" benignly and highlighted the cultural and linguistic links within the Commonwealth; indeed, policy makers at the time "imbued a profound sense of imperial obligation and noblesse oblige" (Randall Hansen 2000: 245). Simultaneously, the emerging multicultural citizenship approach emphasized newcomers' right to be different, as long as moral public order was maintained (Favell 2001).

Some sectors have deliberately seized the colonial labor pool in the postwar era: the Colonial Office imported nurses in the late 1940s to staff the newly founded National Health Service (NHS) and has thereby created "an imperial labor market for nurses" (Solano and Rafferty 2007: 1055). The utilitarian "drive for labor" exploited the imperial labor geography and left traces in the composition of the foreign workforce (Wilkinson and Craig 2011). Yet, just as in France, studies exposed unofficial ethnic recruitment hierarchies that gave preference to (white) European or Old Commonwealth workers over (black) workers from African and Asian colonies (McDowell 2003; Schain, 2008).

Ethnicized policies were endorsed more openly since the early 1960s when increasing concern about race relations[14] fueled a more restrictive and selective approach to migration and citizenship. The Commonwealth Immigration Act (1962) introduced a work entry voucher system with quotas for Commonwealth citizens born outside the United Kingdom who were not in possession of a British passport. This created an unprecedented distinction between an inner core of British citizens by birth or by passport, and a dubious category of Commonwealth citizens. While not being counted as aliens, the latter now had only limited free movement rights, which were linked to their economic utility (only those working in a shortage profession could enter). Later acts solidified the distinction between UK and Commonwealth citizens, turned the latter into aliens eventually (Immigration Act in 1971 and British Nationality Act in 1981), and restricted their access to work and residence further (see also Schain 2008).

These policy directions have been interpreted as "post-colonial downsizing" (Geddes 2003b), an attempt to cut off the moral obligations from Britain's imperial legacy and to redefine Britishness in more exclusive ways. Downsizing and tougher entry control seemed to offer a pragmatic response to growing concerns about social cohesion and public order and established "good race relations" internally and strict entry control externally as the two sides of the same multiculturalist coin (see also Favell 2001). However, this process was filtered through a racialized sieve and created differential treatment by migrant origin (Layton-Henry 2004). The introduction of the patriality principle in the 1970s, for instance, enabled family reunion of those with well-established family ties on the British Isles while excluding others from similar rights. While the policy did not restrict family reunion for nationals of certain descent per se, the socio-demographic composition of Old and New Commonwealth societies and the earlier migrations from the former to Britain implied that nationals from African and Asian territories were almost excluded by default (ibid.).

Eventually, while the United Kingdom remains among the most liberal citizenship regimes, restrictions since the 1960s indicate an increasing control bias and a downplaying of the post-colonial legacy that implied racialized classification effects (Randall Hansen 2000; Joppke 2005b; Layton-Henry 2004). The main difference to French post-colonial migration management is the earliness (1960s rather than 1980s) and relative ease of detachment from former colonies. With a view on Adrian Favell's (2001) "philosophies of integration," the pragmatic citizenship approach in the United Kingdom seemingly precluded serious politicization when restrictions were established. This of course is in sharp contrast to France where a political understanding of belonging fuels ongoing debates about the legitimacy of rights restrictions that are seen, by some, as an attack on Republican values. Moreover, the United Kingdom dealt with decolonization pragmatically and proactively, trying to avoid conflict, while France defended its empire against independence movements longer and more desperately.

The restrictive border control approach in the 1960s and onward has earned the United Kingdom the image of a "zero-immigration" country (Layton-Henry 2004). Yet, strong economic interests to fill specific labor market gaps continued to matter just as they did in France and Germany. Employment of migrant workers thus continued in the public sector (mainly NHS), but also the textile and car industries (Geddes 2003b). Consequently, the number of work permits issued continued to rise from about 60,000 in 1961 to almost 70,000 per year in 1971 (Clarke and Salt 2003). Even the recruitment ban of the early 1970s, while triggering sharp drops of annual admissions, never cut entries back to "zero" as the rhetoric of the time suggested. The ban on recruiting unskilled and low-skilled foreign workers from outside the European Economic Community (EEC) came into force in 1972. While hitting the newly defined "aliens" from the Commonwealth, high-skilled workers from anywhere and Europeans in general could still enter. Work inflows thus remained stable at a lower level (20,000 to 15,000) in the late 1970s and early 1980s (ibid.). Indeed, the scope for recruiting high-skilled and skilled hands when economically necessary remained large.

Other flows added to the labor pool after recruitment was suspended and kept overall inflow figures relatively stable after 1973 (figure 3.4). Family reunion especially from the New Commonwealth augmented after work routes were closed. Still, in 2009, 11 percent of new entries were family related and almost equaled the volume of the work routes of the points-based system (PBS; Migration Advisory Committee 2010a: 76). The biggest increase in migration over the last decade could be observed among students, with Tier 4 of the PBS contributing to two-thirds of all entries in 2009 (ibid.). The English-speaking and internationally renowned university system in Britain triggers a considerably higher student share among the foreign resident population compared to France or Germany. Especially—but not exclusively—Chinese students have come in ever-growing numbers in the new millennium, and some suggest that they not seldom add to the unauthorized migrant labor market when overstaying their student visas or working more hours than their visa would allow (Shen 2005).

Estimates single out the United Kingdom as a much bigger unauthorized migrant labor market than France, Germany, or even Italy, with 17.5 percent of all foreigners supposedly being irregular (Papadopoulos 2011). Mick Wilkinson and Gary Craig (2011: 189) claim that the deregulated labor market has fueled irregularity: though policy discourse labels those migrants as "unwanted," their economic activity is seemingly tolerated. A widely discussed example of this "willful negligence" (Wilkinson and Craig 2011) is the practice of using gang masters in agriculture or catering to squeeze low profit margins. Mostly unauthorized laborers, often from China, live and work under frequently inhumane conditions, without free-movement rights, for very low or sometimes no wages at all, and under the constant threat of being fired or reported to the police as "illegals" (Brass 2004; Geddes and Scott 2010; Pai 2008). Even though granting by far less humanitarian protection then the other two cases,[15] a deregulated and less tightly controlled labor market can also be expected to offer plenty of unauthorized employment opportunities for rejected asylum seekers.

In a residual welfare system without status maintenance logics and, the NHS apart, missing universal welfare entitlements, the economically driven toleration of migrant irregularity is likely to compound migrants' social exclusion and to fashion precariousness and exploitability more severely than elsewhere (Anderson 2010b; Sainsbury 2006; Wilkinson and Craig 2011). This seemingly confirms the assumption that Liberal welfare states control labor admissions less tightly de facto, whatever the official control rhetoric might suggest. The lack of open politicization of migrant irregularity creates less pressure for regularization compared to France. The missing link between unauthorized work and post-colonialism—in contrast to France—seems to preclude a feeling of obligation toward for instance Chinese "irregulars." More critical voices suggest that the further marginalization and criminalization of unauthorized migrant workers and residents under the tough migration control regime adds to their economic usefulness as vulnerable laborers in a LME and serves as a moral deservingness pretext for strict welfare-to-work policies toward the native resident population (Anderson 2010b, 2013). Ultimately, economic laissez-faire policies and tough border control could coincide more smoothly than expected in our discussion of regime literatures in chapter 2.

Yet Another Tale of Openness and Closure?
Labor Migration Struggles in the United Kingdom

The legal entry of foreign workers has been liberalized considerably in the United Kingdom in the new millennium, more than elsewhere in Western Europe, to support economic growth and fill labor shortages. Given the different demographic situation, with the UK working-age population growing rather than declining, the policy shift seems to rest on different rationales than in Germany. Of course, labor market mismatches can fuel shortages regardless of a large domestic labor pool, but the argument in favor of revitalized TCN worker recruitment in the United Kingdom hinged on endogenous growth assumptions and human capital theory much more than elsewhere. New Labour's open economy philosophy triggered significant shifts in labor migration policies, especially the establishment of supply (rather than demand) oriented recruitment mechanisms and the introduction of a points-based system in 2008 (Düvell 2007; Layton-Henry 2004; Menz 2009; Schain 2008; Somerville 2007).

While some facilitation for highly skilled individuals had already been introduced in the earlier 1990s under Conservative supremacy, more considerable changes to the British labor migration system started to surface in 2000. The New Labour government expanded the restrictive work permit system and initiated both a Highly Skilled Migration Programme (HSMP) and a Sectors-Based Scheme (SBS) for lower-skilled migration. The former attracted mainly finance and IT specialist, medical professionals, and business managers; the latter was targeted at substantial shortages in food processing and hospitality. The number of HSMP admissions increased rapidly from initial low levels to peak at over 28,000 in 2007; SBS approval numbers remained lower than the projected annual quota (for detailed information of work permit schemes and statistics, see Clarke and Salt 2003; Salt 2009). By far the biggest entry channel, however, was the work permits system for skilled workers in shortage professions.[16] Sectoral labor shortages and the facilitation of high-skilled entries have thus jointly fueled substantial increases in work permits issued per year (figure 3.5).

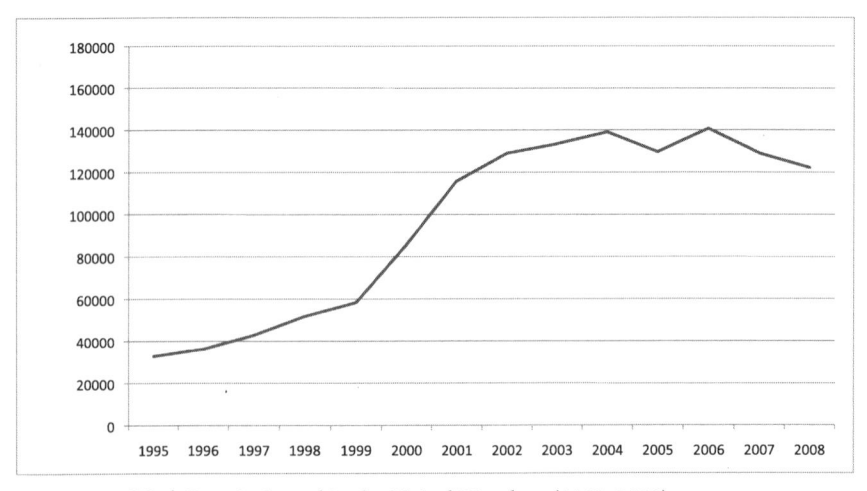

Figure 3.5. Work Permits Issued in the United Kingdom (1995–2008)
Source: Salt 2009: 92, table 5.1, with friendly permission from the author.

In 2008, the government consolidated all work routes into a points-based system (PBS). Then Home Secretary Charles Clarke (Home Office 2006: foreword) described the introduction of the PBS as "the most significant change to managed migration in the last 40 years" to set out more transparently than before who is allowed to come and work in the United Kingdom and under which conditions. Prime Minister Tony Blair viewed labor migration as "essential for our continued prosperity" (Home Office 2005: 5). In short, the spirit of the PBS was initially very welcoming toward TCN workers indeed in pursuit of an endogenous growth strategy that targets and recruits high-skilled migrants regardless of the domestic labor market situation. The subsequent chapter specifies selection mechanisms and underpinning classification principles of the PBS.

The relative openness to migration from the enlarged EU after the 2004 accession constitutes an important marker of the British labor migration management context. As one of only three EU-15 countries (with Ireland and Sweden), the United Kingdom has granted EU-8-nationals immediate full labor mobility. The Worker Registration Scheme counted almost 950,000 entries from these countries between May 2004 and March 2009, with most newcomers being Polish. While numbers of labor entries from the EU-8 initially rose sharply from May 2004 until 2006, estimates indicate drops in 2007 and 2008 (Office for National Statistics 2009). Unlike EU-8-nationals, Bulgarian and Romanians need permission to work in the United Kingdom unless they qualify as highly skilled workers. Lower-skilled jobs have eventually been withdrawn from the SBS in July 2005, with EU-8 nationals, Bulgarians, and Romanians exclusively filling respective shortages. Trade-offs between a liberal approach toward free movement and (reduced) entry options for TCN workers become evident in this respect and will be explored in more depth in the empirical analysis to follow.

Numerical policy effects are remarkable compared to Germany and France: from 1999 to 2008 almost 800,000 work permits were issued (figure 3.5), and that is in addition to the large inflows of Eastern Europeans since 2004. Very much in contrast to France, work and studies (38 and 32 percent, respectively) were the two single most important motives for migration in 2008, by far outnumbering family motives (16 percent; Office for National Statistics 2009). The comparatively higher absolute and relative numbers labor market newcomers in the 2000s seem to have been sparked off by a revived tradition of economic liberalism and utilitarianism under New Labour, very much in line with the country's categorization as LME.

Recent policy developments, however—or maybe rather eventually—counteract the liberal economic approach. Fueled by the economic downturn in 2009 and the inauguration of a Conservative-led government with a restrictive migration agenda in 2010, the pledge for "British jobs for British workers"[17] and tougher entry restrictions has leaped back onto the public agenda—and amplified its resonance ever since. The predominant gist of reforms since 2010 is one of ever increasing restrictions, tougher interpretations of skills requirements and multiplied controls of migrant residents (OECD 2012, 2013). Low-skilled migration is currently suspended and entry criteria in the PBS were tightened up initially in 2010. After Conservative Home Secretary Theresa May announced a reduction of net inflows to the "tens of thousands not hundreds of thousands" until the end of the current parliamentary term (2015) in late 2010, limitations such as an annual cap for high-skilled and skilled entries followed swiftly (UKBA 2010). 2012 saw the abolition of the post-study work route—contrary to liberalizing developments in France and Germany—the introduction of a minimum earning requirement for Tier 2 skilled workers as well as a so-called cooling-off period before a visa holder can reapply for another Tier 2 work visa after theirs has expired. In 2013, some of the restrictions were relaxed again for PhD students (who can look for work after their degree), student entrepreneurs, and intra-corporate transferees, but requirements for qualifications and conduct were further tightened for skilled workers.

These changes represent a turnaround from New Labour's economically driven laissez-faire approach to labor migration—not dissimilar to the immediate postwar period—back to a tough control mode. The oscillation between economic liberalism and tough border controls over the course of time indicates the dynamism of selective policy arrangements: the shifting weights of competing normative claims and policy meanings in labor migration management. At different points of time, policy makers in the United Kingdom seem to have picked either the economic utility side of migration by favoring liberal labor recruitment in support of the capitalist coordination model in a liberal market economy, or focused on securing public order, cohesion, and successful multiculturalism within the country by tough external control and limited entries. However, the significance of migrant employment in informal and irregular labor markets suggests that the current control backlash might have a largely symbolic function and forces continuously demanded migrant labor underground at best.

Conclusion

The case profiling has carved out the interpretive context for the subsequent comparative policy analysis in a case-oriented research design. This has exposed similarities and case-specific features that, as the remainder of the book will show, form decisive contexts for contemporary labor migration management. All three cases operated a utilitarian approach to foreign worker recruitment as a response to at times immense labor shortages after the Second World War, France even earlier than that. The utilitarian logic has survived throughout the twentieth century, continued on a smaller scale even after a common recruitment ban in the 1970s, and was revitalized widely in the late 1990s (United Kingdom) and early 2000s (Germany and France) when all three countries returned to active TCN labor recruitment policies. Further, a shared pattern of privileging migrant workers of European origin has surfaced during guest worker recruitment in France and Germany, while British migration policies introduced differential treatment between former colonies in the Western World and those in Africa and Asia. In all three cases we find that selection by origin constitutes another chief principle of migrant classification, thus confirming the claim that economic utility considerations and ethnicized definitions of belonging have been conflated in European migration governance since the early days (P. Hansen 2000; P. Hansen and Hager 2010).

The post-colonial settings in which French and British policies operate clearly distinguish these two cases from Germany. In both cases, post-colonial newcomers and residents have not only been prime targets of past migration management attempts, but the legacy of colonialism is still visible in contemporary migration and settlement patterns and thus likely to form a vital backdrop for policies. The conflation of labor migration policies and the management of post-colonial legacies seems most pronounced in France, with the *immigration choisie* agenda explicitly linking the two. At the same time, discontent with restrictions of a traditionally inclusive model of civic belonging has been vocalized loudly in public protests and manifestations in support of regularizations of unauthorized migrant workers. This is not the case in the United Kingdom where detachment from the former Empire has kicked in earlier and happened more smoothly. Rather, British migration policy has been oscillating between economic openness—most recently with New Labour's liberal approach toward EU free movement from Eastern Europe and TCN recruitment—and tough border control throughout the past decades. The contemporary rediscovery of the control mode by the Cameron government is jeopardized in practice, however, by one of the largest populations of unauthorized migrant workers in Europe whose position as exploitable laborers seems to benefit a deregulated labor market in the liberal market economy.

In lack of significant post-colonial links, German governments have co-shaped a distinctively European foreign resident and labor pool. The German geopolitics of migration and labor recruitment have sought responses to labor demands of the national economy in a gradually expanding Europe. EU enlargement also "solved" part of the migrant irregularity issue at Germany's Eastern porch, while irregular residents from elsewhere can benefit from "earned" integration when economically successful. Europeanness and

Bismarckian integration pathways apart, concern over the socio-economic integration prospects of a large Turkish minority prevails.

Notes

1. Henk Wagenaar (2011: 23)
2. This official term (*Gastarbeiter* in German), suggesting that workers can be recruited temporarily and somehow made to leave when their labor is no longer needed, was part of the policy philosophy at the time, and has seen a more recent revival (Castles 2006; OECD 2009).
3. Historical ties through bilateral agreements apart, the current economic and employment crisis in Europe and its severe effects on countries such as Greece, Spain, or Italy can be expected to feed heightened labor mobility within the European Union. Greek migration has increased by 84 percent from 2010 to 2011, for example (Süddeutsche Zeitung 2011).
4. Even though figure 3.2 displays also non-work inflows to Germany due to unavailability of disaggregated data, we can nonetheless read major tendencies for labor entries from it.
5. German pension calculations, for instance, would include working-age years not spent in Germany in order to avoid gaps in the entitlement record.
6. Treaties were moreover concluded with Hungary, Croatia, Slovenia, Bosnia, Macedonia, Romania, the Czech Republic, Slovakia, Bulgaria, Latvia, Turkey, and Serbia and Montenegro (see Menz 2001).
7. Named after Rita Süßmuth, a senior conservative member of parliament (CDU), migration expert, and former Speaker of Bundestag, who was appointed to chair the commission.
8. With inflows registered mainly from the United States, India, China, Croatia, Bosnia and Herzegovina, and the Russian Federation (jointly accounting for over 50 percent of admissions).
9. The institutionalization of this hierarchy has been quite visible with installations of ONI offices in Milan rather than Istanbul or Rabat, for instance (Weil 2005: 83).
10. Hargreaves (2007) traces stigmata of "hard-to-integrate" Muslims in public perception, with the term *immigrant* bearing strong connotations with ethno-religious features. Dine (2008) criticizes "dishonesties" in the Republican citizenship model in this context: irrespective of their French nationality individuals of Muslim belief and North African descent are often criticized for a "failure" to integrate, conflating assimilation goals with ethnic-religious hierarchies.
11. Interviewees from trade unions and migrant advisory groups insist that the political engagement with the values of the French Revolution, predominantly égalité, is much more central in French public discourse than elsewhere in Europe. Indeed, from the author's experience, a more technocratic approach surfaces in Germany and the United Kingdom.
12. Several governments tried to cease societal tensions and public protests by partially regularizing informal workers. In 1997, for instance, 170,000 migrants benefitted from an amnesty.
13. This had included a universal healthcare system and constituted a Keynesian social-liberal postwar welfare settlement based on full employment.
14. While the term "race" is publicly banned in other contexts (in Germany it implies unwelcome connotations to the Nazi regime and Holocaust), in Britain "race relations"

Migration Histories and Policy Legacies | 101

      embrace real or perceived differences between ethnic groups and aims to improve their relationship to each other, retaining political relevance to date.
15. The United Kingdom granted asylum to roughly 6,600 individuals in 2009 while Germany accepted 37,500 (2008) and France 18,100 individuals (2009; Huddleston and Niessen 2011).
16. Of an annual average of almost 125,000 newcomers between 2000 and 2008, around 84,000 per annum were skilled entries.
17. Then Prime Minister Gordon Brown's pledge of "British jobs for British workers" was used by domestic protesters at the oil refinery at Killingholme in 2009 when Total UK decided to employ Italian and Portuguese workers for maintenance work.

PART II

Border Drawing in German, French, and British Labor Migration Policies

CHAPTER 4

What Makes Migrant Workers "Legal"?
Mapping Entry Regulation

"Die Zulassung ausländischer Beschäftigter orientiert sich an den Erfordernissen des Wirtschaftsstandortes Deutschland unter Berücksichtigung der Verhältnisse auf dem Arbeitsmarkt und dem Erfordernis, die Arbeitslosigkeit wirksam zu bekämpfen."[1] (§18 German Migration Law)

"Pour répondre aux besoins de recrutement de certains secteurs économiques, la France a souhaité mieux organizer l'immigration professionnelle et faciliter l'accès de ressortissants étrangers à des métiers choisis."[2] (Ministère de l'Immigration 2010c)

"Managed migration is not just good for this country. It is essential for our continued prosperity." (Tony Blair in Home Office 2005: 5)

In the theoretical reflections preceding our case profiles much attention has been devoted to the distinction of "legal" and "illegal" migrant workers. This book is dedicated to understanding the construction of legal migrant worker categories in the process of border drawing, seeking to comprehend which norms guide the sorting of "the good into the pot" in labor migration policies, and explaining why they have been selected and arranged in a specific way. In order to grasp and compare in depth the sets of norms that guide the admission of foreign workers in Germany, France, and the United Kingdom this chapter consults operative laws. The first chapter has established a perspective that understands public law as the key governance mechanism through which normative visions—which kind of migrant worker should count as legal or illegal, under which conditions, and with what kinds of rights?—are consolidated into social structures. The first query for our interpretive policy analysis thus emerges: how does labor migration regulation select and classify migrant workers?

This present chapter maps the classification of TCN workers as legal labor migrants at the point of admission in our three countries—thereby not least offering an in-depth overview of the current state of affairs in German, French, and British labor migration management. The legal document analysis includes all relevant laws, decrees, and ministerial specifications that have been operative during the interviewing period in each case, up to autumn 2011 (appendices), but also includes reflections on more recent developments. In order to map classification regimes, the chapter asks which permits migrants can obtain in each country, under which conditions and requirements. My engagement with these inquiries has fed into classification maps, a visual representation of the ways in which policies in each country select and classify legal migrant workers[3]. These maps (figures 4.1, 4.2, and 4.3) capture the whole classification set and serve the reader as compasses to navigate a complex policy field. In the systematic fashion of tree diagrams, the document analysis has traced each possible selection step in legislation, each potential division of admission routes, multiple pathways to work permits, and criteria for admission. In this manner, I gradually reconstruct from policy documents the underpinning principles of classifying migrant workers.

This amount of analytical detail[4] is indispensable in interpretive policy analysis: only on the basis of a comprehensive and nuanced cataloguing of policy tools, mechanisms, and principles can the guiding norms of migration management credibly and plausibly be reconstructed in the next analytical steps (chapters 5–6). For easier navigation through the complex legal infrastructure for labor migration, each country section is structured according to main selection principles following classification maps and also contains basic statistical information on entry numbers for the different legal categories of migrants. The final section of the chapter summarizes similarities and differences in the legal infrastructure of labor migration in Germany, France, and the United Kingdom, and thus lays the foundations for the subsequent comparative scrutiny of the meanings and normative claims entailed in border-drawing processes.

Migrant Classification in Germany: Skills, Skills, Skills … and Origin

The German *Zuwanderungsgesetz* has been interpreted as a cautious shift toward active migrant worker recruitment, integration, and residence management (Green 2007; Triadafilopoulos and Schönwälder 2006). As evidenced in the epigraph, the law speaks to a range of different agendas, from meeting the needs of the German national economy to protecting the domestic workforce from unemployment. How does the Federal Republic select and classify incoming foreign workers on these seemingly ambivalent grounds?

Choosing Migrant Workers by Skill Level

The German legal infrastructure for TCN labor admissions implies a clear distinction between high-skilled, skilled, and unskilled entries, which informs a three-fold classification of migrant workers on the most generic level (we will see soon how these are further split up and complicated). The Migration Law defines three different skill levels[5] and associates them with different provisions and permits. Currently, legislation defines high-skilled jobs as "leading" graduate positions in academia and elsewhere, skilled jobs require an equivalent of a three-year German vocational training, while every other job is considered unskilled. Different selection criteria, residence, and labor market inclusion pathways follow from this three-fold distinction (see German classification map, figure 4.1).

Selection by skill level certainly guides admission decisions, but with an important tweak. Migrant workers need to pass a residence labor market test (RLMT) if they want to work in Germany, including also most high-skilled entry routes (this is not the case elsewhere, as we will see later). The RLMT establishes scarcity of labor as a key selection principle and permits foreign recruitment into shortages only. A valid job offer is the prerequisite of legal foreign labor recruitment in Germany; there is no supply-driven category for newcomers. In many cases, the demand-led recruitment mode is strengthened further by asking the Federal Employment Agency (*Bundesagentur für Arbeit*, or BA) to not only supervise the functioning of the RLMT but to consent to recruitment decisions before work-residence permits are issued. The BA takes the general employment situation into account and blocks admission if German unemployment is particularly high (this can also be related to a specific sector or region). Exceptions from this rule include predefined shortages, bilateral agreements with sending countries, or particular skill targets: high-skilled migrant workers, scientists, IT specialists, and domestic graduates do not need BA consent to obtain a permit. This means that the logic of classifying migrant workers by skill level cuts across the scarcity principle.

Favoring Domestic Qualifications

The 2005 Migration Act and subsequent amendments introduced significant exceptions to the principle of protecting domestic employment by means of the RLMT. This chiefly regards graduates of German universities and those who were trained in the vocational education system or acquired equivalent skilled work experience in Germany. An amendment of the Migration Law (*Arbeitsmarktsteuerungsgesetz*) abolished the RLMT for graduates of German universities in 2009 (BMAS 2008b). With a specific permit they can search for

108 | *The Political Economy of Border Drawing*

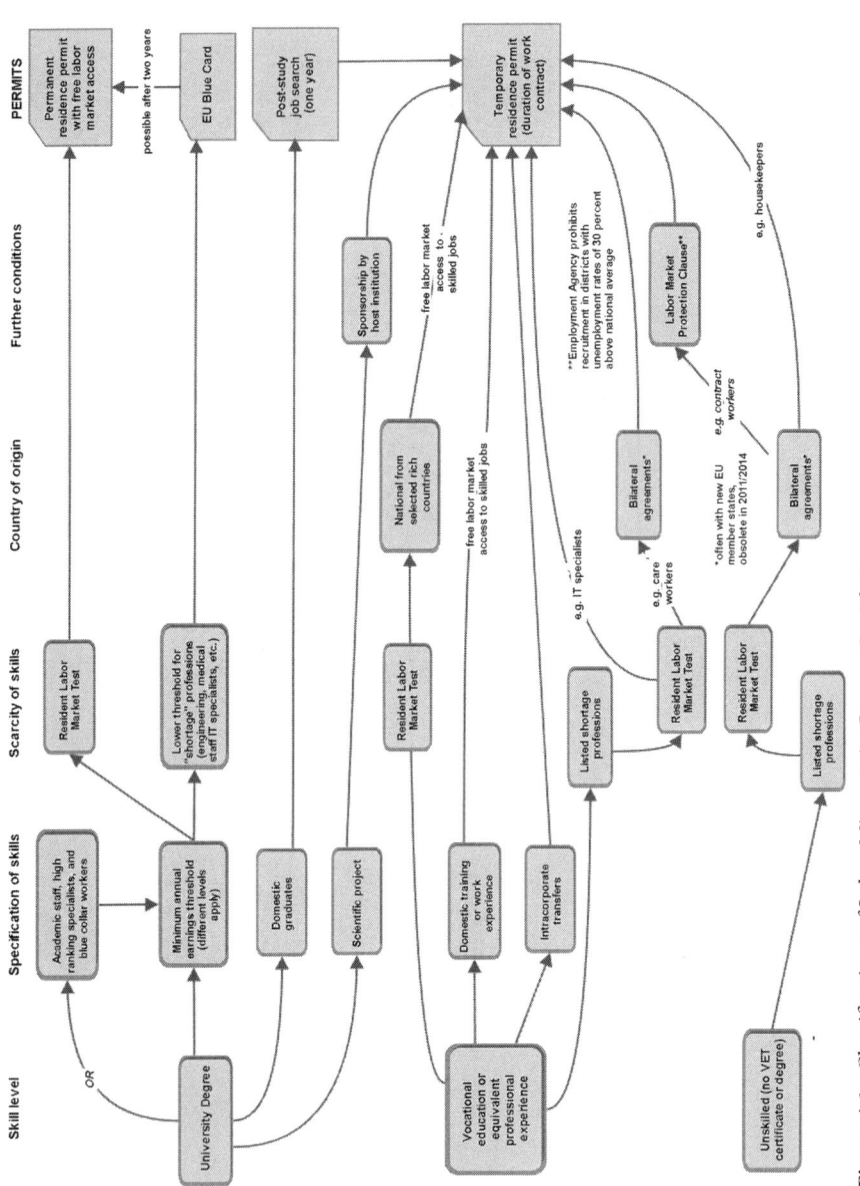

Figure 4.1. Classifications of Labor Migrants in German Legislation

jobs in their academic specialty for up to a year—a temporary exception from the job-offer requirement. If they are successful they can access a found job without subordination to domestic and EU workers and obtain a temporary residence permit. Migrants with German or equivalent vocational education and training and graduates from German schools abroad can also accept a job offer on equal footing with Germans and EU nationals. This needs to be in a VET-skilled profession, at minimum, and the Federal Employment Agency can veto their recruitment if unemployment is higher than average in the district under consideration (BMAS 2008b; Bundesrepublik Deutschland 2008).

Liberal provisions also benefit tolerated residents[6]: if they have worked in Germany for at least three years as skilled workers, without interruptions and without relying on social benefits in at least the last year of employment, they can legalize their status and switch to the temporary residence permit. Applicants also have to demonstrate sufficient German language skills, sufficient housing for themselves and their dependents, and a clean criminal record. Their professional skills, expected utility for the labor market, but also demonstrated linguistic and social integration capacity can thus aid foreign residents overcome the insecure residence situation in *"Duldung"* and advance their position in the German labor market. Provisions discussed so far speak of a beneficial treatment of TCNs with domestic qualifications and work experience. The German labor migration regime rewards successful educational and economic inclusion of foreign residents in Germany and facilitates entry of Germanophone workers from abroad. This recalls our theoretical reflections in chapter 2 on the notion of earned entitlements in the contribution-based Bismarckian welfare state. The definition of legal migrant workers and preferential selection of those who have already contributed in the German educational system or labor market seem to pivot on notions of "earned" migration with elements of culture-based models of belonging.

Facilitating Settlement and Recruitment of High-Skilled Workers

Even though most labor migrants are subordinated to German and EU workers in admission decisions, the RLMT procedure is entangled with further selection procedures that inform differential work and residence statuses for migrants. Distinction in migrant classifications is predominantly organized around different skill levels, with the high-skilled routes being the smoothest in terms of admission procedures and the most advantageous in terms of rights (see figure 4.1). One of the novelties of the Migration Act in 2005 has been the introduction of a permanent residence permit for high-skilled individuals (*Niederlassungserlaubnis*, §19 Migration Law). This allows highly qualified foreigners to settle immediately, without integration requirements (e.g., language classes) and with full access to the German labor market. By contrast, the standard temporary residence permit is for designated jobs only, fixed term, and does not offer free labor market access before a migrant worker has a record of three years of social insurance contributions in regular employment. German legislation clearly establishes a categorization of migrant worker rights by skill level. Indeed, the entitlement to immediate settlement with full labor mobility is one of the most beneficial rights regimes for high-skilled workers worldwide.[7] The comparably easy access to settlement pathways from first admission for high-skilled professionals has a potential to offset the comparatively strict German naturalization and citizenship regime. In its departure from temporary permits that enforce circularity, it also represents a paradigm shift from former guest worker approaches.

Who can obtain the beneficial permanent residence permit then? Legislation concentrates on scientists with special knowledge in their field, high-ranking academic teaching and research staff, and blue-collar specialists outside universities with earnings above a specific threshold (Bundesministerium des Innern 2004: paragraph 19/2). The earnings threshold itself has been subject to major revisions since 2005. It has been lowered from a sum of over €80,000 initially to €66,000 in 2009–2010 at the time of interviewing. Irrespective of this liberalization, the *Niederlassungserlaubnis* has so far only benefitted a tiny minority of high-skilled individuals in academia and leading specialist positions each year (see table 4.1). This might change significantly as the second Merkel government has lowered the threshold considerably again

Table 4.1. TCN Worker Inflows per Type of Permit and Entry Route in Germany

	2006	2007	2008	2009	2010
Permanent work-residence permit (§19 AufentG)	80	151	157	169	219
Temporary work-residence permit (§18 AufentG)	29466	28761	29141	25053	28289
Scientists and researchers permit (§20 AufentG)	–	–	64	140	211
Post-study work switch to employment (§27/3 BeschV)	2742	4421	5935	4820	5676
IT-specialists (§27/2 BeschV)	2845	3411	3906	2465	2347
Other specialist graduates (§27/2 BeschV)	1845	2205	2710	2418	3336
Permit for nationals of rich countries (§34 BeschV)	3757	4821	5617	4724	4999
Intra-corporate transfers (§31 BeschV)	4783	5419	5655	4429	5932
Contract workers (*Werkvertragsarbeitnehmer*)	20002	17964	16576	16209	17981

Source: BAMF 2010, 2011

in 2012, to currently €48,000. Since entry figures are not yet available for 2012, it is so far impossible to fully evaluate implications of this most recent policy liberalization here. Yet, given that the new threshold is roughly congruent with entry salaries of many academic jobs in Germany, it seems fair to suggest that a broader group of TCN workers are now able to access the high-skilled settlement permit.

Scientists and researchers including PhD students that fail to obtain a *Niederlassungserlaubnis*—for instance due to lower annual earnings—can benefit from RLMT exemption. They can work on a fixed-term project in Germany since 2007, but data in table 4.1 indicates that entries of scientists have been rather limited so far. Lastly, intra-corporate transfers (ICT) can enter a German leg of their firm without RLMT for specific purposes like installing software or machinery, or training staff to do so. Their residence is fixed for the duration of the exchange project and cannot exceed three years. The project-based nature of these entries means that they are not treated as migrants with settlement pathways, but as globally mobile project professionals. Integration measures such as language courses are also irrelevant for these newcomers.

More recently, Germany has transposed the EU Blue Card for high-skilled workers and added a new legal category to its labor migration regime. Interestingly enough, this EU-induced regulation does not replace, but complements the settlement permit in a nationally specific way (Cerna 2013). In its German incarnation the Blue Card can be issued without RLMT to foreign graduates who earn at least €44,000. Following a logic of scarcity again, the earnings threshold is lowered further to €33,000 in so-called shortage professions (*Mangelberufe*) such as engineers, IT specialists, and medical staff (BMI 2011). Blue Card holders are less privileged than settlement permit holders as they can obtain secure settlement with a two years delay.

Identifying the Scarcity of Migrants' Skills

Most widely used is the temporary residence permit (*Aufenthaltserlaubnis*), which requires a RLMT and enforces the preference of domestic and EU workers on the labor market. German legislation further distinguishes between skilled and unskilled routes toward *Aufenthaltserlaubnis* with quite different selection mechanisms. The classification map (figure 4.1) highlights very well the several paths and differential conditions that can lead to a temporary residence permit and reiterates the fact that procedures imply more conditions visually. Of the roughly 28,298 temporary resident permits issued in 2010, approximately a third were in unskilled professions while the rest entailed skilled employment (BAMF 2011b: 70). Apart from the standard RLMT operation in most cases, the key selection tool for all skilled and unskilled recruitment is a shortage list issued by the Labour Ministry (BMAS 2008b; BMWA 2004).

These lists specify sectors that are prone to experiencing labor shortages and are therefore provided with easier access to foreign workers.

In listed skilled shortage occupations[8] (*Fachkräfte*) individual TCN recruitment is possible if a migrant proves VET-equivalent qualifications that match a listed shortage. If a migrant's specific skills profile fits they can enter without further selection steps. An example of skilled shortage entry is the Green Card that became a part of the skilled entry route with the 2005 Migration Law. The Green Card targets specialists with a university degree in IT-related subjects and allows them to work in Germany once they passed the RLMT without further conditions. This provision was extended to encompass other specialist graduates such as medical doctors in 2009. The skilled specialist routes have been equally popular in the late 2000s: together with domestic graduates they account for almost 40 percent of all temporary residence permits issued in 2009 (see table 4.1). Chefs, language teachers, and blue-collar specialists can also enter once they display matching qualifications and pass the RLMT. Access to skilled jobs without RLMT is enabled for ICT and domestic graduates, as mentioned earlier. For those two categories, the selection logic of scarcity is replaced with one of global labor exchange (ICT) or favoring of domestic qualifications (as discussed above).

Considering unskilled jobs,[9] lastly, we find that additional labor market protection tools operate to ensure labor scarcity against the backdrop of potential domestic unemployment. For example, a specific clause within provisions for contract worker recruitment blocks admissions if the company wanting to recruit from outside the European Union has reduced employees' contractual working hours (*Kurzarbeit*) or is planning to lay off regular workers. The same applies if the employment district under concern suffers from unemployment 30 percent above average (BA 2009a: 14f). While the Employment Agency's role in anticipating labor market effects of foreign recruitment seems to be more of a legal formality for high-skilled and most skilled shortage workers, provisions are very detailed, specific, and protective with regard to unskilled routes. In addition to the tighter control focus of unskilled labor recruitment, a circular migration regime forces unskilled workers to leave Germany after a maximum stay of three years. Further, tight control of unskilled entries is coupled with strict selection by migrants' origin, a last classification principle we need to examine.

Selecting Newcomers by their Country of Origin

Unskilled newcomers with less than German VET-equivalent qualifications can come to work in Germany only if the unskilled shortage list,[10] a bilateral agreement with a sending country, and a successfully passed RLMT jointly admit it. In addition to scarcity, the principle of selection by origin is obligatory for unskilled workers. It is important to note that some skilled professions also rely on bilateral recruitment, for instance care workers are exclusively recruited from Croatia (BA 2009b). For these groups of workers, selection by skill level, scarcity of skills, and country of origin is highly intertwined. This exposes a conflation of different border-drawing principles whose precise meanings and rationalities will be discussed in chapters 5–6.

Most bilateral agreements regulated labor entries from new EU member states until free movement was fully established in May 2011 (e.g., housekeepers, BA 2009c). This reflects a continuation of the post–Cold War recruitment arrangements described in chapter 3. In 2012, bilateral agreements encompassed only one extra-EU sending country: seasonal workers from outside the European Union and skilled care workers can enter from Croatia exclusively (BA 2009b). The special connection to Croatia—then an accession candidate to the EU for July 2013—in the selection of labor migrants represents an interesting issue to be investigated further in interviews, even though annual recruitment is quite low with 62 entrants in 2009 and 112 in 2010 (BAMF 2011b: 85). Bilateral agreements also operate for so-called contract workers.[11] The EU-8 countries apart, nationals of Turkey, Bosnia, Croatia, Serbia, Macedonia, and Kosovo can obtain a work-residence permit for two years, with the further restriction of potential annual quotas defined by the Labour Ministry and the three years maximum stay (BA 2009b). We witness a continuation of the pronounced concentration on EU and European sending countries that chapter 3 has already indicated (see table 3.1). Bilateral agreements moreover draw on preexisting links with other former labor exporters such as Turkey, but also include the former Yugoslav countries that fueled considerable asylum flows to Germany in the 1990s.

Beyond Europeanness and historically emerged bonds in bilateral recruitment, there is evidence of a positive selection of workers from rich, industrialized, and arguably culturally similar countries. Nationals of a few handpicked countries[12] are able to work in any skilled job with a temporary permit if they pass a RLMT and thus are subject to a more liberal shortage recruitment regime than most other TCNs. This liberal provision is strictly reciprocal and it has benefitted between 3,700 and 5,600 workers annually over the last decade (see table 4.1). Chapter 6 will discern the rationales behind this liberal niche in German labor migration border drawing.

While, as a general rule, "legal" migrant workers are selected based on the high level or scarcity of their skills on the German labor market, the analysis of legislation has exposed several, partly intersecting classification principles in German labor migration regulation. Most important is the preferential admission of those with domestic qualifications and the selection of migrant workers by their country of origin, which is facultative for some skilled and all unskilled workers and which privileges nationals of fellow European or rich industrialized sending countries.

Migrant Classification in France: Skills and Talents ... and Post-Colonial Origin

The emphasis on selectivity in the French *"immigration choisie"* agenda, dating from 2006, prima facie marks the return of a utilitarian migration policy approach. The ministerial statement in the introduction to this chapter highlights policies' role as response to specific sectoral labor demands, with many experts appreciating economic selectivity in French labor migration policy as apt and highly desirable (Saint-Paul 2009; Tribalat 2010). Others critique the unequal treatment of different migrant workers and the precarious, often irregular situation of many among them (Morice 1996; Morice and Potot 2010; Terray 1999). The mapping of the French legal infrastructure for labor migration below relies on data from governmental policy documents, but mainly draws on the comprehensive legal codification of migration issues laid down in the French Foreigners Law (*Ceseda*; République Française 2010), including amendments up to the interviewing period in summer 2010 (appendices). Again, more recent developments are included where relevant.

Focusing on Skill Level and the Resident Labor Market

There is a clear distinction between so-called professional schemes and shortage routes for incoming migrant workers in France. As in Germany, migrants of different skill levels face different selection criteria and rights regimes, with the higher-skilled "professional" entries being treated most benevolently (see French classification map, figure 4.2). Foreigners normally need a work authorization to enter the French labor market. Since the so-called recruitment stop was established in 1974, migrant workers have been admitted via a RLMT, just like in Germany. More specifically, "the company must provide evidence of its failed search for an applicant on the labor market in France (attestation from the Employment Hub for example)." (OFII 2012b) The enforcement of the RLMT certainly contributed to a drop in official annual labor inflows since the 1970s, but might equally have contributed to a large-scale informalization of foreign workers' situation (see chapter 3). Shortage recruitment governs most significant labor entry schemes to date with only a few high-skilled professionals being excluded from the demand-based logic.

Courting High-Skilled Migrant Workers

The generally protective attitude toward the domestic workforce has gradually been lifted for higher-skilled workers since 1997. To facilitate the entry of scientists the Chèvenement Law abolished the RLMT for those carrying out a research project at a French institution. The "scientific" work permit offers

What Makes Migrant Workers "Legal"? | 115

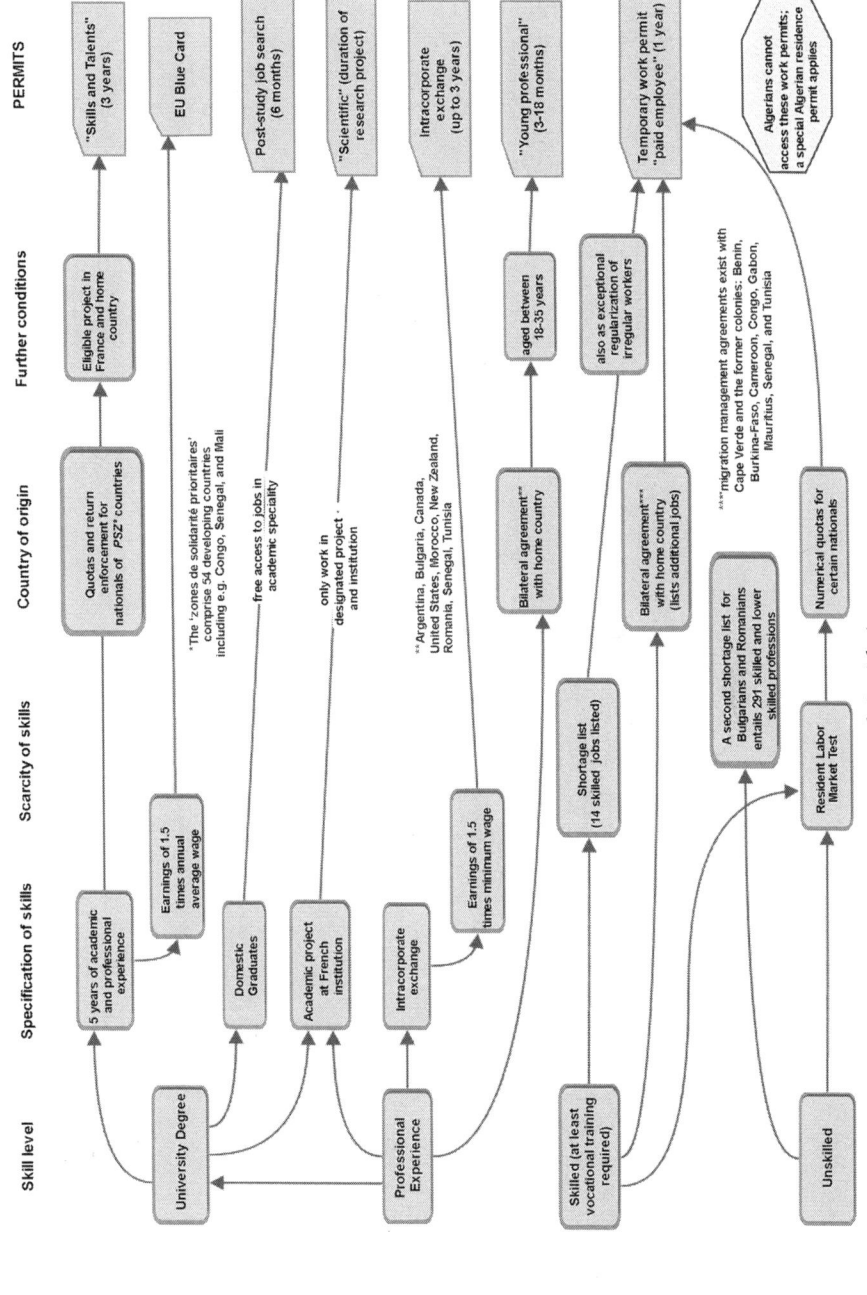

Figure 4.2. Classifications of Labor Migrants in French Legislation

researchers a secure residence for the duration of their project; all while tying them to an academic institution and a fixed-term designated research project of four-year duration at most. Prefectural decision makers were asked to "fast-track" applications of IT specialists in 1998 (Menz 2009: 146).

Even more importantly, 2006 saw the introduction of a renewable three-year permit for "skills and talents." This flagship of French "immigration choisie" provides for prolonged professional stays and even eventual settlement. It is the currently most advantageous permit, (most other permits cover one year of residence or less), is explicitly targeted at highly qualified workers, and includes high-ranking scientists who would otherwise be covered by the less advantageous provisions of the *"carte scientifique"* (Ministère de l'Immigration 2010b). Further, foreign graduates who achieved at least a postgraduate degree in France also encounter facilitated conditions for admission: they can look for a job irrespective of the domestic labor market situation for six months and can obtain a "paid employee" permit if they secure a job offer in the field of their academic specialty (Ministère de l'Immigration 2010b).

Graduate- and postgraduate-level skills serve as a minimum entry requirement to all professional migration routes. Applicants for the "skills and talents" permit, for instance, need a combined total of five years of academic training and/or professional experience in a skilled job to qualify. They must further provide a credible professional project that makes use of their academic education and professional experience, and that also benefits their home country on return (Ministère de l'Immigration 2010b; République Française 2010). Discretion about what counts as an eligible project has triggered some criticism about lack of transparent admission criteria (Ferré 2007). Earning thresholds are used as an additional proxy for high skill levels. Post-study job searchers must earn at least 1.5 times the national minimum wage net in order to obtain a more permanent work permit.

The European Blue Card has recently added further to the "professional routes." It comes with similar selection procedures as the skills and talents permit (focus on graduate skills and professional experience) but stipulates additional earning requirements of 1.5 times the average gross annual salary, or roughly €51,400 in 2011 (Cerna 2013).

France further provides two more temporary professional routes: one for "young professionals" (three to eighteen months) who are in search for initial job experiences abroad, and one for intra-corporate transfers (ICT, up to three years). Both routes enforce strict circularity and prevent longer-term residence. The former denies renewal options and prohibits in-country change of status to more permanent categories when the permit expires. The latter excludes the possibility of accessing long-term residence rights on the basis of the EU Directive (CEU 2003a), even though workers can change their status from "visitor" to "resident" upon application (OFII 2012b). It seems fair to suggest that intra-corporate exchanges do not count as admissions dealing with migrant workers in the first place, as they are missing from the respective annual statistics. Their exemption from the usual duty to sign an integration contract (CAI) further evidences that, just as in Germany and the United Kingdom, employees who are posted within their multinational company are not expected to settle in France. In order to enter, ICTs must provide proof of their professional qualifications and attract a salary of 1.5 times net the national minimum income (approximately €1,500 currently). The young professionals permit offers temporary access to employment in France for individuals aged 18–35 who hold a degree or display relevant work experience and are fluent in French. The reciprocal permit is negotiated with specific countries of origin.[13]

The scrutiny of French labor migration policy highlights a strong judicial concentration on high-, graduate-level skills. A range of different residence and work permits—more differentiated than in the German or British cases—is available and secures the relatively smooth recruitment of professional. Most professional migration routes come with a relatively advantageous set of employment rights and most equally entail multiannual residence rights.

Identifying the Scarcity of Migrants' Skills

While the abundance of different recruitment channels suggests empirical salience of the high-skilled permits discussed, their actual use is very limited compared to other categories of worker inflows (see table 4.2). In the first year of comprehensive operation in 2008, only 183 migrants entered France with a skills and talents permit and numbers remain low to date. Entries of scientists increased from around 1,300 to more than 2,200 annually from 2004 to 2010, but are much less relevant than others. The most important permit in quantitative terms is the "paid employee" permit (*carte salarié*), which gives much more restricted and temporary access to the labor market than the aforementioned permits (one year, renewable). The temporary work permit enables employment in the designated job only, while access to the whole labor market is

Table 4.2. TCN Worker Inflows per Type of Permit in France

	2005	2006	2007	2008	2009	2010
Skills and talents	–	–	5	183	368	317
Scientists	1318	1310	1531	1926	2242	2269
Paid employees	8377	8356	13448	18371	15499	14147
Intra-corporate transfers	–	–	–	1612	2007	2486
Exceptional regularizations through shortage job	2697	2695	1541	1862	2583	n.a.
Algerian residence certificates	31344	31060	26635	26133	25245	24119

Sources: CICI 2011; INSEE 2012, OFII 2011

delayed by two years. Most of the increase in regular labor entries from around 14,100 in 2004 to almost 28,300 in 2008 (Sénat 2010) has been among skilled and unskilled paid employees, whose admissions more than doubled in this period (seasonal workers also contributed to the overall increase).

Selection for skilled and unskilled paid employees focuses on the principle of labor scarcity and mainly draws on the RLMT and shortage lists as key policy tools. Respective admission requires a work contract that respects minimum wages and demands a proof of labor scarcity in the given occupation and region. The default preference of domestic workers and standard operation of the RLMT or shortage lists as means of selecting "legal" migrant workers sharply distinguishes paid employee permits from the high-skilled ones discussed in the subsection above.

Once the RLMT is passed, work authorizations are issued by Departmental Employment Agencies (*Directions Départementales de l'Emploi, du Travail et de la Formation Professionnelle*, or DDETFP) on the basis of what could be best translated as a "mismatch degree" (*taux de tension*) of labor supply and demand in a given profession and a designated region based on data from the *Pôle Emploi*. The labor scarcity assessment is highly institutionalized in a centrally coordinated labor market. As in Germany, employment agencies facilitate the matching of foreign labor supply and demand and can veto paid employee recruitment if unemployment in the sector and/or region is high (*opposabilité de la situation de l'emploi*).

In order to avoid the lengthy RLMT and long-winded institutional involvement, the French administration has waived these procedures for sectors with structural recruitment difficulties. For this purpose two shortage lists—only one of which is accessible to TCN and the other reserved to Bulgarians and Romanians (and since 2013 also to Croatians)—were introduced in 2008. Migrants with a matching skills profile can access the professions detailed on the TCN list without RMLT and obtain a paid employee permit. Both RLMT and shortage lists target the scarcity of skills per sector, profession, and region and seek to ensure that a migrant applicant's profile matches a specific, genuine labor demand.

Since the Hortefeux Laws (2007), shortage lists entail the possibility legalizing employment of already employed unauthorized migrant workers. The TCN shortage list can be used—by discretionary decision of the responsible prefecture—to exceptionally regularize *sans-papiers* who are employed in one of the listed professions with recruitment difficulties (GISTI 2009b). Table 4.2 shows that some two thousand unauthorized workers could make use of this provision—regularization via work permit—on average. We have to bear in mind that most shortage jobs on the TCN list require high qualifications in IT or engineering and do not reflect the employment situation of many unauthorized workers in lower-skilled and lowly paid jobs (see also chapter 3 and policy makers' interpretations in chapters 5–6). Overall, a considerably larger number of migrants in France have been granted regularized statuses—31,775 in 2009 (CICI 2011). Only a small share of regularized migrants seemingly benefit from the exceptional legalization via their employment in a shortage job.

Selecting Newcomers by their Country of (Post-Colonial) Origin

The classification map indicates the prominence of selection by country of origin in French labor migration border drawing. As opposed to the way in which Germany selects workers by origin predominantly in lower-skilled parts of the labor market, France's origin-based classification system also targets the high-skilled migration schemes. Under the pretext of co-development and brain-drain prevention, circular migration schemes dominate the rights regime for nationals from so-called priority solidarity zones (PSZ).[14] In this context, the skills and talents permit can only be issued to individuals from a PSZ country if a bilateral agreement states so. This can be subject to an annual cap, and/or the applicant in question has to agree upfront to relinquish the long-term resident pathway and go back to their country of origin after a maximum stay of six years (GISTI 2009a: 108f.).

Secondly, and maybe most emblematic as a case of selection by origin, the government in Paris has negotiated bilateral migration management agreements mostly, though not exclusively, with former colonies (*accords de gestion des flux migratoires*). France has so far signed nine agreements specifically dealing with labor migration: with Senegal (2006), Gabon, Congo-Brazzaville, and Benin (2007), Tunisia, Mauritius, and Cape-Verde (2008), Burkina-Faso (2009), and Russia (2011). Agreements have been reached but so far not ratified also with Cameroon, Lebanon, and Macedonia according to the official webpage on labor migration by the OFII as of November 2013. As negotiations are ongoing and provisions differ considerably by signatory country, it is hard to keep track of the details of this policy tool; especially since information also varies within administration (the OFII presents different data than the former Immigration Ministry, for instance). There is record of further agreements being under negotiation, inter alia with Mali, Haiti, Nigeria, and Egypt (Carrère and Duval 2009), but none of these have so far been finalized. In any case, the strong focus on former colonies in Sub-Saharan Africa and the Maghreb cannot be denied in French bilateral migration management even if the more recent expansion of agreements to the Balkans and Russia should be noted with interest.

Bilateral agreements contain restrictive provisions with regard to annual quotas for skills and talent permits, thus limiting certain nationals' access to these high-skilled routes. Further, however, some bilateral agreements also include more beneficial specifications. According to official statements, the aim of agreements is "to promote privileged exchanges" with sending countries (OFII 2012b). Most importantly, appendices in most agreements detail "enlarged shortage lists" for nationals of the respective sending country in addition to the generic TCN shortage list. These enlarged lists display a great degree of variation by country of origin in terms of number and skill level of the listed professions. For example, only 9 rather high-skilled additional professions are available to applicants from Gabon and 15 to Congolese, while Tunisians can enter 77 and Senegalese an entire 108 occupations, some of which require a lower set of skills (Ministère de l'Immigration 2010a; OFII 2012a). In return for privileged access to the French labor market for their own nationals, "partner" countries consent to fight irregular flows by enforcing their emigration controls and facilitating repatriation procedures.

Regardless of the critical question of how beneficial migration management agreements really are for the sending countries (more in Carrère 2009; Kunz 2013), the special treatment of former colonies in bilateral agreements evidences not only selection by origin of migrant workers, but by their postcolonial identity. This sets France apart from the German case with its focus on a largely European workforce and its previous guest worker connections. There are also more levels and layers of country of origin selectivity in France than in Germany: the annual quotas for skills and talents permits set in migration management agreements might be restrictive compared to regulation for other TCNs, but they are at the same time more advantageous compared to TCN from the priority solidarity zones whose governments did not yet sign a bilateral agreement with France and who can therefore not access certain permits at all.

To add even further to the layers of country of origin selectivity in French labor migration legislation, thirdly, Algerian nationals cannot access any of the above mentioned high-skilled routes, shortage routes, or exceptional regularization provisions. Since the Evian Agreements of 1962—which ended a bloody independence war with one of the largest and most populous former French colonies—the operation of permits that limit Algerians' liberties are unlawful. Once admitted, Algerian nationals in France cannot be limited to a specific job, region, or sector, or forced to leave after a project has finished, as the specific Algerian Residence Card entails free movement on the French territory and labor market. De facto, however, this de jure beneficial treatment ex-post admission means that Algerians are often excluded and not admitted in the first place. Table 4.2 indicates that Algerian inflows—at around 25,000 in 2009—are still larger than the TCN work routes taken together, but they have been decreasing over the last years.

Lastly, the French shortage list regime displays a clear hierarchy of regions of origin in two ways: it separates EU from non-EU workers in two distinct generic shortage lists and it further distinguishes "privileged" former colonies from others by offering additional "negotiated shortages" as part of specific bilateral migration management agreements. While the latter issue has already been discussed above, the first deserves further attention. The shortage list for EU nationals from Bulgaria and Romania was originally established with 150 professions and includes not only high-qualified but also unskilled jobs[15]. However, the separate list for TCN was established with only thirty-five mostly skilled and high-skilled professions (OFII 2010).[16] In August 2011 the list for TCN workers was further reduced to 14, while the list for EU nationals was extended to 291 professions (OFII 2012b). In effect, access to low-skilled employment—even when defined as shortage sector—is highly curtailed for descendants from most non-EU countries. As further evidence of the differential treatment by origin, the longer EU list grants workers access to the whole French metropolitan territory while the shorter TCN list is further bound to shortages that specific regions pick out of the pool of listed professions.

The overall pattern of migrant worker classification in French labor migration management then is one of conflating selection by high academic and professional skill level and by scarcity of skills with a multilayered selection by country of origin that reflects clearly the country's colonial past. This pattern is also evident in the visual representation of the classification regime in figure 4.2.

Migrant Classification in the United Kingdom: Skills, Points ... and the "Numbers Game"

The points-based system (PBS) has been a core ingredient of New Labour's recipe for attracting labor force from abroad. Since late 2008 it has channeled all labor entries to the United Kingdom, following the view that managed migration buttresses prosperity and growth, as Tony Blair's statement above suggests. The British PBS selects migrant workers according to their anticipated success in the labor market: "points will be scored for attributes which predict a migrant's success in the labor market, and/or control factors, relating to whether someone is likely to comply with the conditions of their leave" (Home Office 2006: 2, pt. 10). In each tier applicants can score points according to their educational attainment, work experience, prospective earnings, English language proficiency, or previous periods of residence, employment or education in the United Kingdom. The required points and the combination of criteria—some mandatory and some optional—needed to score high enough differs across the five tiers. The following analysis concentrates on the work routes laid down in tiers 1, 2, and 3 while disregarding tier 4 students and tier

5 working holidaymakers. The mapping draws on key policy documents from the Home Office, UK Border Agency (UKBA), and the Migration Advisory Committee (MAC). I also consider the restrictive changes[17] to the PBS by the Conservative-led government (appendices).

Distinguishing Workers' Skill Levels

All applicants in the work-related tiers of the PBS need to prove proficient English language skills and sufficient funds to cover their maintenance independently from social benefits. Apart from this commonality, the three tiers regulate labor migration of three distinct skill levels. Each tier features specific selection mechanisms and a different set of rights, leading to a highly differential admission regime structured by skill level (see British classification map, figure 4.3). Let us examine each tier in its own right to discern this differential treatment.

Tier 1 (general) had been initiated as supply-led scheme for high-skilled migrant workers. In its original form, it offered relatively easy access for migrants with a combination of university qualifications and high previous earnings. By virtue of their set of high skills they could enter without a specific job offer without passing a RLMT. The Conservative-Liberal government has diluted this supply-driven approach significantly: the points level required for entry clearance was raised in 2010. Applicants with a bachelor's degree, for instance, now require immensely high annual earnings of more than £75,000 (£40,000 had sufficed before).

Changes to the PBS in April 2011 further restricted tier 1 entry by limiting the circle of potentially successful applicants to investors, entrepreneurs,[18] and persons "with exceptional talent."[19] This comprises "world-leading" scientists and artists with a renowned reputation (Salt 2010). While annual caps will limit tier 1 entry options even further, as I will discuss later, the more demanding qualification requirements were equally designed to force down admissions in the high-skilled route from comparatively elevated levels (up to 15,000 annual newcomers; see table 4.3). Under the original PBS, beneficial treatment also applied to domestic graduates who were granted a job-search visa for two years under tier 1 post-study work provisions within a year of their award, and who could switch to a regular work category if successful. As the post-study work route was eliminated in April 2012 in the context of the government's aim of reducing overall net migration, domestic qualifications are no longer of any advantage in the British labor admission system. The sole exception is PhD graduates from British universities who, since 2013 and thus after the timeframe of this analysis, can search for a job again for one year to find skilled work or become an entrepreneur.

What Makes Migrant Workers "Legal"? | 123

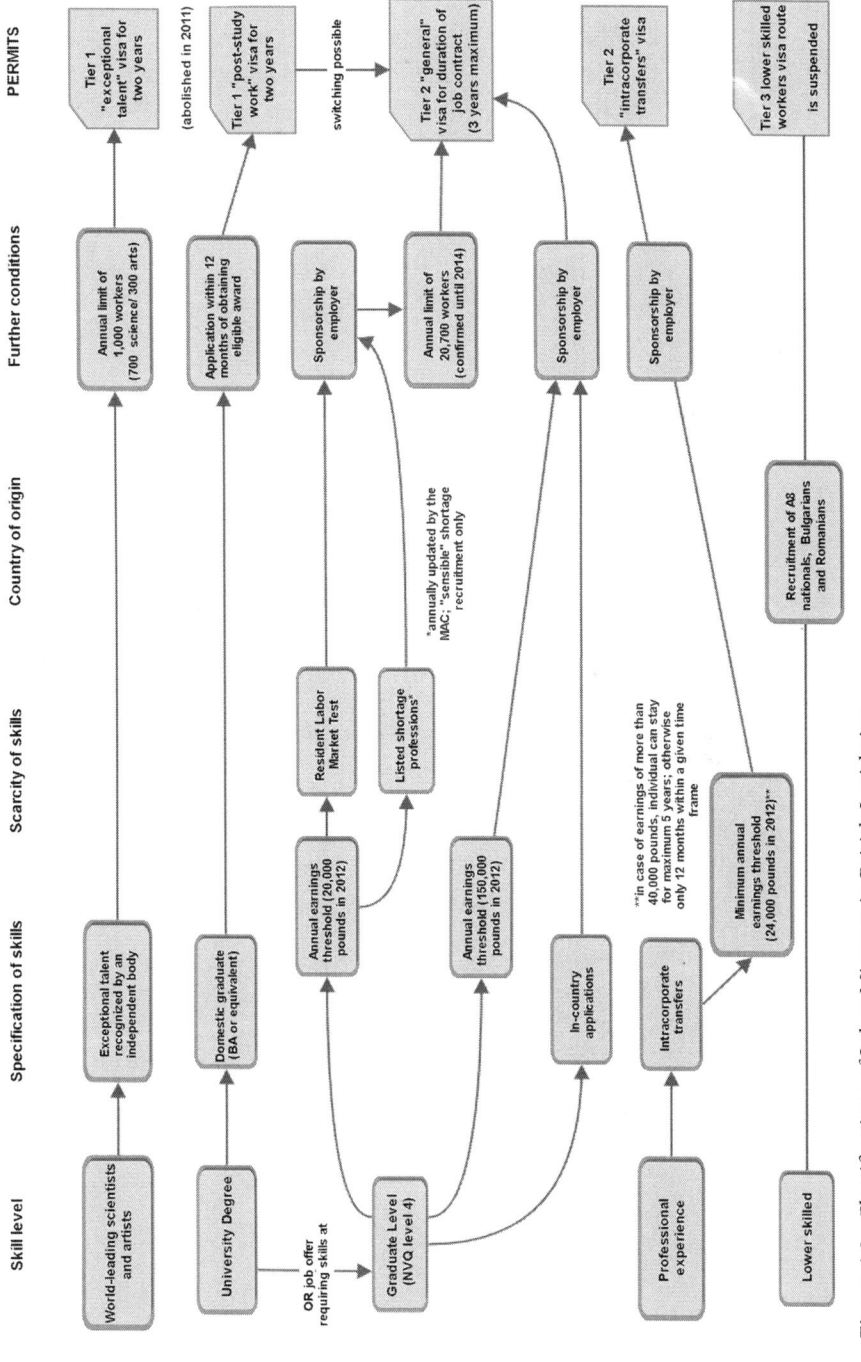

Figure 4.3. Classifications of Labor Migrants in British Legislation

Table 4.3. TCN Worker Inflows per Type of Permit and Entry Route in the U.K.

	2007	2008*	2009	2010*	10/2010–04/2011	2011
Tier 1 (general)	–	2980	15000	12200	*(interim cap at 5400)*	7370 *(re-newals included)*
Tier 1 (exceptional talent)	–	–	–	–		10 *(max. 1000)*
Tier 1 (post-study work)	–	215	3360	3910		3810*
Tier 2 (general)	–	15	8970	14000	*(interim cap at 18700)*	10100 *(max. 20700)*
Tier 2 (ICT)	–	45	14200	21400		21900
*Work permit holders**	64115	54900	5025	240		n.a.

* Launch of PBS in Q2/2008; redesign of PBS with caps and restriction of tier 2 in Q4/2010 and closing of tier 1 (general) to newcomers (renewal is still possible), work permit system prior to Q2/2008 (phased out gradually); post-study work route abolished in 2012

Source: Home Office 2012

Selection by skill level also guides tier 2 admissions of "sponsored skilled workers" (Salt 2010). The New Labour government defined *skilled* as NVQ level 3 qualifications,[20] but David Cameron's administration raised the skill requirements to at least graduate level in April 2011 (NVQ level 4). At the same time, tier 3 for lower-skilled professions was never activated and the coalition government made it clear in 2010 that the suspension of lower-skilled recruitment from third countries would be maintained. This means that, currently, no TCN without a higher education degree or graduate-level professional experience can enter the UK labor market through the PBS. Should tier 3 ever be activated in the future, it is likely to entail more restrictive residence conditions: tiers 1 and 2 open pathways to settlement after five years (long-term residence), but tier 3 applicants would be expected to "return home at the end of their stay in the U.K." (Home Office 2006: 15). As the law currently stands, they would not be able to settle as long-term residents, would not be allowed to switch into other tiers, and would not enjoy family reunion rights either. In short, we find the pattern of granting fewer rights to migrants of lower skill levels confirmed in the British case.

Identifying Trustworthy Migrant Employers

The British classification map evidences that the rights attached to tier 2 visas are less generous than those granted in tier 1. While high-skilled migrants can obtain a leave to remain for two years, tier 2 permits are limited to the duration of their work contract (three years maximum in case of permanent contracts, renewable). More importantly, however, tier 2 visas grant access to a specific job only and tie the migrant worker to a specific designated sponsoring employer. Workers can only switch job or employer with the UK Border Agency's consent, and only start employment with another officially licensed sponsor.

Selection by trustworthiness of the employer is a specific characteristic of the recent British labor migration regime, covering most incoming TCN workers and their employers. Apart from the small circle of tier 1 workers, all others require a sponsorship from a specific employer with a license from the UK Border Agency. This UK-specific mechanism shall ensure the applicant's genuine will and ability to do the designated job, the employer's respect of wage conditions, and their commitment to the RLMT mechanism (Home Office 2006). Any breaches of the labor and migration law by the employer—for instance recruitment with false documents—will be recorded and might eventually lead to the withdrawal of sponsorship licenses. Employer sponsorship puts an unparalleled emphasis on the responsibility of employers as users of foreign workers in the migratory process; neither France nor Germany operate a comparable system, apart from the sponsoring of scientists by academic host institutions.

Identifying the Scarcity of Workers' Skills

As with the other two countries, the United Kingdom operates a RLMT for most skilled entries. Employers have to demonstrate that a graduate level job they want to offer to a migrant could not be filled from the domestic labor pool. Unlike in France and Germany, the British RLMT relies exclusively on employers' attestation rather than being carried out by an Employment Agency or matched with centrally administered labor market data. Both the National Audit Office and the Public Accounts Select Committee—two influential critical observers of government policies and spending—have criticized this mechanism as being prone to inviting non-compliant behavior by employers (House of Commons 2011; National Audit Office 2011). In order to heighten compliance and reinforce the weight of the RLMT as a means of establishing scarce skills, the UK Border Agency has made the acquisition of sponsorship licenses conditional upon employers' genuine use of the RLMT prior to recruitment decisions. Selection by scarcity of skills is thus meant to be enforced with the policy tool of sponsorship licenses.

The scarcity assessment has not only been challenged with regard to skilled workers but also for intracompany exchanges. Policy advisors criticized the frequent use of the ICT route—with more than twenty thousand admissions in 2010 by far the largest admission category (see table 4.3)—and suspected its misuse as welcome circumvention of RLMT or shortage list requirements (MAC 2010a). As a response stricter selection rules have been established for the ICT route in 2011—meaning that many workers who might have been recruited as ICT earlier would now need to fulfill the requirements for standard skilled shortage recruitment (i.e., sponsorship, RLMT, or shortage list). As ICT entry figures for 2011 remained high the MAC has advised the government to survey uses of that route while keeping the cap for tier 2 (general) in place until 2014 (UKBA 2012).

The second major tool for discerning scarce skills before admissions is the annually updated shortage list. Since 2008 an independent group of scientists in the Migration Advisory Committee (MAC), founded as part of the UK Border Agency, has advised the government on recruitment mechanisms and shortage definitions. MAC shortage lists rely on evidence from employer surveys, but also on data and strategic policy papers from the UK Commission for Employment and Skills and the Alliance of Sector Skills Councils. They jointly define skills profiles for tier 2 shortage admissions (for role of the MAC, see Anderson and Ruhs 2010; for a neat account of shortage definitions, see Dench et al. 2006). Among all skills shortages only vacancies for which foreign recruitment seems "sensible" will make it on the list (MAC 2008, 2010b).

The definition of a "sensible" shortage remains notoriously vague. The MAC tries to balance policy objectives such as the prevention of job displacement, protection of British workers, skills policies targeted at the UK resident workforce,[21] or the support of innovation and productivity. This means that while companies are generally supported in their shortage recruitment for utilitarian economic reasons, in some "priority areas for upskilling" employers are supposed to refrain from relying excessively on migrant labor (UKBA 2010). Employers have to demonstrate their efforts in domestic education and training to obtain sponsorship certificates (ibid.). While the Home Office has not yet specified what these efforts should look like and under which conditions penalties could be enforced, we see further instances of disciplining employers in British labor migration regulation. Selection by scarcity of skills and wider policy objectives clearly intersect here, sometimes in a contradictory way, and impede the "employer-led" focus of tier 2 (Home Office 2006).

Since qualification requirements became more demanding, the MAC only lists graduate level jobs as shortages. While the 2010 list still included some NVQ level 3 jobs in food processing (meat cutters), catering (chefs and cooks), or care (care assistants), the 2011 version focuses on higher-skilled jobs such as construction management, several engineering fields, leading cuisine,[22] or senior care assistance (MAC 2010b; UKBA 2011). In its revision of the shortage list, the MAC—directed by government policies—rejects scarcity as a legitimate selection mechanism for TCN migrant workers with less than graduate-level qualifications. From a cultural political economy view, this evidences the political and highly selective character of defining a labor shortage and rendering this definition the basis for legal labor migration.

A third mechanism of scarcity selection, conflated with skill level, concerns earnings thresholds which seem much more important in the UK context than in the other two cases. The specification of skills and relative labor scarcity as extraordinary earning potential is a significant marker of labor migration border drawing in the United Kingdom and significantly determines migrant workers eventual rights. The PBS offers more beneficial admission and residence rights to well-paid migrants. Graduate-level professionals with prospective annual earnings of at least £150,000 can obtain a tier 2 visa without RLMT. Similarly, ICT workers with high annual wages (£40,000 minimum) are granted more advantageous residence rights and can stay for up to five years, while other workers in the ICT category can only live and work in Britain for up to a year. The assumption of higher labor scarcity (and higher tax contributions) of workers with higher earning potential opens them access to more encompassing rights.

Earnings do not just serve as a proxy for exceptionally high and scarce skills in the recruitment of foreign elites. They are also a widely applied minimum entry requirement to the United Kingdom for "normal" workers: ICT need to earn at least £24,000 and tier 2 (general) applicants have to demonstrate earnings of at least £20,000 to score enough points for admission. It is worth noting that the high earnings thresholds, while officially linked to scarcity and economic contribution arguments, is likely to provoke country of origin selectivity in practice: the sought-after well-educated and well-earning workers will more often than not originate from the rich global North.

Selecting Newcomers by their Country of Origin

While the United Kingdom does not operate bilateral recruitment agreements with extra-European countries similar to the French *accords de gestion* or the German *Anwerbeabkommen*, British legislation structures labor migration by origin as well. Similarly to the other two cases, it has been the political will of British policy makers to fill low-skilled gaps with free-moving workers in the enlarged European Union. The suspension of tier 3 for TCN does not coincidentally co-occur with large inflows of Eastern European workers to the British Isles; it has been explained in that very context (Home Office 2005; UKBA 2010). For example, with a view to being relatively independent from further TCN recruitment, Britain currently recruits workers from Bulgaria and Romania to fill low skill gaps in seasonal agriculture and food processing. Border drawing by skill level is de facto conflated with the British liberal approach to EU free movement and supply of lower-skilled workers from these countries. Overall then, the (increasingly) strict qualification rules for tier 2, the suspension of the lower-skilled tier 3, and the exclusive recruitment of EU workers into lower-skilled shortages limit entry options for TCN workers considerably.

This makes the legal access of non-EU workers with lower than graduate-level qualifications to the UK labor market virtually impossible.

The preference of EU workers in lower-skilled shortages specifically excludes individuals from former colonies and Commonwealth countries—typical sending countries, as chapter 3 has shown—from a range of skilled and low-skilled jobs. The fact that they are treated indifferently to any other TCN, much in contrast to France and its bilateral agreement approach to negotiation relationships with former colonies, indicates that the chapter of postcolonialism is closed in the United Kingdom. If anything, we find a pattern of negative discrimination, not least in policy rhetoric. Indeed, it seems that British openness to EU-8 workers with large inflows, very much unlike the more restrictive enlargement approaches in France and Germany, has curtailed the space for TCN labor migration in the United Kingdom. The effects of open borders toward Eastern Europe on entry figures and public opinion seem to have triggered, at least in part, the recent restrictions to the UK's TCN migrant admission regime. Chapter 6 will explore this argument further with data stemming from interviews with decision makers.

Limiting Net Migration with Annual Caps

A characteristic of contemporary UK labor migration policy—and one that chiefly distinguishes the case from Germany and France—is the operation of annual caps, or maximum volumes of net migration. Caps represent deliberate cutoffs of the previously described border-drawing mechanisms based on scarcity and skill level. The cutback of annual net migration figures has been one of the core election campaign topics in 2010, and the Cameron government has implemented annual limits swiftly after a consultation conducted by the MAC (UKBA 2010). An interim cap on tiers 1 and 2 was implemented in autumn 2010.[23] Since April 2011, tier 1 admissions are capped at 1,000 persons "with exceptional talent" and tier 2 is limited to 20,700 entries per year (Home Office 2011).[24] The government has announced that they will keep these limits in place until at least 2014 (UKBA 2012).

Under the cap regime we find evidence, however, that border drawing privileges domestic skills, in-country applications, project-based professional stays, and high investment levels and earnings: the cap does not apply to the (now-closed) post-study work route, ICT workers, investors, and entrepreneurs. Also, tier 2 workers with high earnings of more than £150,000 or those who apply from within the United Kingdom do not count toward the annual migration flows that the Cameron government seeks to limit to "the tens of thousands" (see chapter 3).

Critics highlight the limited scope of the cap in this context: further to the many exceptions in TCN work routes, the cap does not control EU workers,

British emigrates, or repatriates. Moreover, the United Kingdom faces severe practical and legal-humanitarian obstacles to limiting family and student entries. Given these hindrances, some experts have expressed their fear that tier 1 and 2 might be "asked to do too much" for the aim of reducing net immigration to the United Kingdom (British Policy Adviser). Be that as it may, border drawing by annual entry limits has become a dominant feature of the British labor migration system and represents a deliberate cutoff of the otherwise important principles of selecting migrant workers by scarcity and level of their skills profiles.

Comparing Classifications in German, French, and British Labor Migration Management

Our reflections on the value of the border-drawing concept for migration policy analysis in the first chapter have founded a key objective of this book: to map and understand how states classify migrant workers in comparative perspective. The scrutiny of legislation on labor migration in the previous sections has exposed how Germany, France, and the United Kingdom select and classify incoming TCN workers. We are now ready to establish first comparative findings—similarities and differences—with regard to the three legal classification systems (overview in table 4.4). Responses to the question "what is done similarly and what is done differently across legislatures?" also determine the investigative strategy for the subsequent comparative analysis of policy meanings.

Commonalities: Skills and Scarcity as Key Selection Criteria for Migrant Workers

I have identified two significant common principles of migrant classification in legislation across our three cases: selection by skill level and selection by (assumed) labor scarcity. A pattern of skills-based rights differentiation (most benevolent for highly skilled workers) and differential application of the scarcity principle (less relevant for higher skills and tightly enforced for migrants who aim to work in skilled and lower-skilled jobs) emerges from all three cases, even though we also find slight variation in the specific mechanisms involved in scarcity checks.

Firstly, the clear distinction of entry routes by skill level is a marked feature that transcends the single case. Labels and specificities of permits may vary, but all three countries broadly structure the regulatory terrain into the same sets of routes: (1) high-skilled professional routes, including post-study job search and intra-company exchanges; (2) shortage routes and a RLMT route in the skilled realm; and (3) lower-skilled routes that are sometimes inactive (United Kingdom). Legislation in all three countries inscribes a Janus-faced approach that privileges high-skilled workers and imposes much tighter entry channels and residence control for lower-skilled workers, with skilled workers being caught somewhere in the middle. The most beneficial rights regime for the highly skilled can certainly be seen in the German permanent residence permit; but the French multiannual routes (e.g., skills and talents) and the British tier 1 (exceptional talents) also offer more secure residence, easier and more comprehensive labor market access for TCN than other routes. Academic expertise and professional experience are the most common markers of a "high-skilled" worker, but earnings thresholds are also widely used to distinguish particularly scarce high or specific skills.

France and Germany further offer a specific post-study work route to give domestic graduates better labor market access, whereas the United Kingdom has recently abolished this principle of selection by domestic qualification. Governments commonly apply specific ICT routes, which do not count toward long-term labor migration statistics. The relatively easy access as ICT comes at a cost though: permits are strictly temporary, transferees cannot switch into standard migrant worker categories, their permit is fixed-term, and they cannot apply for settlement (France). The legal definition of ICT workers as non-migrants is striking for subsequent analysis. Interestingly, entry figures for high-skilled routes, apart from ICT and post-study work, are consistently low compared to skilled routes, sometimes only attracting a few hundred individuals each year—a specification worth keeping in mind for the contextual anchoring of our findings on the meanings and rationalities policy makers attach to the benevolent treatment of high-skilled workers.

In contrast to the high-skilled domain, skilled and lower-skilled employees are tied to their employer, at least initially, and they can usually only stay for the duration of the work contract. Any change of employers needs to find the consent of employment and migration authorities, a requirement that is certainly most pronounced in the British sponsorship certificate system. Additional labor market protection mechanisms in the guise of shortage lists, RLMT, and bilateral recruitment agreements or country-specific quotas apply across the board. The low-skilled realm displays the highest levels of restriction, as additional labor market protection clauses (Germany) or the complete suspension of the route (United Kingdom) evidence. Overall, and irrespective of nuanced variation in the precise definition of skill levels, the common legal distinction and differential treatment of migrant workers by skill level is a marked comparative finding that deserves further in-depth exploration.

Secondly, labor scarcity serves as a shared guiding principle of admission across legislative contexts, and one that implies similarly customization by skill level targeted. Scarcity of high-skilled workers is taken for granted due to their high academic and professional qualifications and/or earnings, and it is rewarded with relatively smooth and free labor market access and generous rights. Only Germany additionally requires a RLMT for access to the permanent residence permit. Access to skilled jobs, by contrast, generally requires the formal establishment of skills scarcity either via a RLMT or a shortage list, or indeed a combination of both policy tools (Germany). This means that for skilled workers their skills profile and its matching with a specific labor demand is one of the determining factors during the selection process. For lower-skilled jobs the problem of labor scarcity is mostly resolved within the EU context. All countries draw on the enlarged EU labor pool: through liberal EU free movement regulation and simultaneous suspension of TCN recruitment (United Kingdom), with the help of specific shortage lists for EU nationals (France), or in the shape of bilateral agreements (Germany). The strong structuration effect of EU labor mobility on TCN labor admission policies—involving mainly restrictive effects for lower-skilled TCN workers—is a key point to scrutinize in the analysis of expert interviews.

All three countries use similar policy tools to select "scarce" skilled workers. Indeed, our statistical overviews of work inflows have shown that shortage lists and RLMT admissions, by far, are the numerically most significant entry routes. Despite the common application of these policy tools, what scarcity means, how it is established in practice, and which groups of migrants are exempted from the scarcity principle varies. Germany, for instance, combines the shortage list with a RLMT, rather than using them as two separate tools. Legislation excludes only scientists and domestic graduates from the strict double scarcity check. The strong procedural involvement of the Federal Employment Agency and a special labor market protection clause for lower-skilled jobs further evidence comparatively strict scarcity logics in the German case.

France and Germany both display high degrees of institutionalization with regard to labor scarcity checks: labor market institutions are consulted in the RLMT procedures as well as the definition of scarce skills for shortage lists. The picture seems most permissive in the United Kingdom where the RLMT requires an employer attestation instead of an independent check of employment agencies or job center databases. This nuance seems to mirror comparative political economy claims quite neatly: corporatist coordination prevails in French and German labor market governance as opposed to a liberal hands-off strategy in the British LME. Indeed, the straightforward reliance on earning thresholds and migrant workers' qualifications for the identification of scarce skills affords much less institutionalized involvement of employment agencies in Britain than shortage recruitment does in France or Germany.

While this example certainly reflects different traditions of labor market coordination, including different roles of the state in the facilitation of matching global supply and national demand of labor, the apparent liberalism in British RLMT recruitment features some severe limits. Since 2011, UK legislation is much stricter in its definition of shortages, with the MAC list only comprising graduate level jobs. By contrast, France provides some non-graduate jobs on its shortage list for TCN and Germany even offers some (restricted) lower-skilled and untrained positions to migrant workers. Sponsorship certificates are another distinctively British policy tool that seems to refute economic liberalism. These elements of tightly monitored shortage recruitment in the United Kingdom certainly ought to be related to the country's approach to the EU's Eastern enlargement. Openness toward new EU free movers—certainly when measured against the cautious German and French attitudes—meant that most skilled and low-skilled jobs have been almost by default filled with highly mobile Eastern European workers since 2004 (see workforce composition statistics in chapter 3). The normative claims of economic liberalism were certainly not abandoned in British labor migration policies. Rather, the comprehensive application of economic openness rationalities to EU free movement after the Union's Eastern enlargement seems to have fueled a restrictive agenda toward TCN entries. Chapter 6 will support this argument further with insights from interviews.

Differences: Migrant Workers' Origin, EU Labor Mobility, and Numerical Cap Policies

The legal document analysis also exposed striking differences between classification regimes. This is most marked for the selection of migrant workers by their country of origin, a classification principle that varies greatly in relevance and kind. Two features appear striking when considering selection by origin. Firstly, it implies a departure from economic rationalities of border drawing that are predominant in skill level or skills scarcity assessments. Instead, migrant classification by origin stipulates questions of citizenship, historical ties with certain sending countries, or the embeddedness of a country within the EU labor geography. Secondly, selection by origin varies much more across our three cases than selection by skill level and scarcity. While all three countries rely on EU free movement, especially for skilled and lower-skilled shortage recruitment, the privileged treatment of European workers implies varying effects—and supposedly rationalities—with regard to TCN entry options. Indeed, the document analysis has painted fairly national portraits of non-skills-related selection mechanisms.

French migrant classification displays strong post-colonial elements both with regard to Algerian exceptionalism and the wide use of bilateral migration management agreements with former colonies. These tools instigate special treatment of workers from the former French empire and render classification by origin an omnipresent device that cuts across other forms of selectivity in

French labor migration border drawing. Despite a shared colonial history, the United Kingdom does not follow the French example of selecting and excluding workers by their origin from the former empire, even though the strong focus on EU recruitment in lower-skilled job market segments does of course entail restrictions for TCN from former colonies. The different ramifications of colonialism in France and Britain seem to relate to the civic border-drawing assumptions raised in chapter 2. The deeply politicized struggles over French citizenship in post-colonialism seem to be a key ingredient of labor migration policy and border drawing. The pragmatic approach to decolonization and citizenship pursued in the United Kingdom, on the other hand, seems to shape current migration governance, too, as the determined turn toward EU labor recruitment and concurrent restriction of TCN and post-colonial migration indicates. In lack of an important colonial heritage, Germany exclusively selects workers from within the wider European labor geography. The Federal Republic also continues to entertain special relationships with major guest worker sending countries—most importantly Turkey—as well as reciprocal liberal labor mobility agreements with a few hand-picked rich countries.

The role of EU internal labor mobility as a justification for restrictions toward TCN recruitment varies considerably between our three cases. The United Kingdom embraces EU free movement head-on, Germany has favored a strategy of cautious phasing-in of Eastern European free movement and limits most skilled and lower-skilled shortage recruitment to prospective EU member states, and France has set an extensive shortage list for Bulgarians and Romanians in direct opposition to a very restrictive list for TCNs. This variation highlights that the EU labor geography—a shared context for TCN labor migration policy making in the EU—is drawn on rather selectively and for different reasons. The United Kingdom makes ample use of EU flows to fill shortages to afford a suspension of tier 3 for low-skilled TCNs; France explicitly seeks to restrict post-colonial migration by EU free movement in the lower-skilled realm; and Germany pursues a cautious phasing-in of free movement by help of hand-selected bilateral agreements with current and prospective accession candidates. In all cases, the selective preference of EU nationals—and in the German case also EU citizens to be—precludes virtually all entry options for TCN workers of lower skill levels.

A specific feature of the German classification regime is a comparatively strong privileging of domestic skills in admission decisions. Beneficial provisions apply to TCN graduates from German universities and schools in Germany and abroad, thus expanding the logic of earned integration into the realm of Germanic education and culture. Moreover, provisions for *Geduldete* allow some of them to end their semi-legal position and obtain a work-residence permit on the basis of their educational and professional achievements in Germany. This bears features of an earned integration regime, employing the logics

Table 4.4. Comparison of Selectivity in Labor Migration Policies

Selection Principle	Selection Mechanism	Germany	France	United Kingdom
Skill level	Graduate qualifications/ professional experience	permanent residence permit for high-skilled professionals; facilitated entry for scientist and specialist (mainly IT); ICT route; Blue Card	multi-annual permits for graduates and experienced professionals; easy entry for project-based work and scientists; ICT route; Blue Card	tier 1 visa for high-skilled individuals (world-leading academics and artists); tier 2 (general) for graduate level jobs; tier 2 for ICT route
	Earning thresholds as proxy for qualifications	for permanent residence permit for high-skilled workers who are not academics and for Blue Card holders	for ICT and post-study work visa	RLMT waived for tier 2 high earners; longer visa for well-earning ICT; min. wages required for tier 2 (general) and ICT
	Lower skilled access	suspended apart from some bilateral agreements, access mainly for EU-nationals	via RLMT with annual quotas, privileged access EU-2 nationals via specific shortage list	suspension of tier 3, exclusive access for EU-nationals
Origin of skills	Domestic qualifications	post-study work route; work permits accessible to tolerated residents (*Geduldete*) with domestic qualifications	post-study work route; exceptional regularization for irregular workers when employed in professions on TCN shortage list	(abolished in 2011) privileged treatment of in-country applications

Scarcity of skills	Resident Labor Market Test (RLMT)	applies to all entries apart from ICT, scientists and domestically skilled; institutionalized at Federal Employment Agency	applies to all lower-skilled entries; for skilled jobs which are not on shortage lists; institutionalized at regional employment agencies	for all tier 2 (general) entries except in-country applications and high earners; not institutionalized (employers' attestation suffices)
	Shortage Lists	for skilled and unskilled TCN, mainly reserved for EU-8 and EU-2 nationals before full free movement and for nationals of accession candidates (e.g. Croatia)	for higher skilled and skilled TCN (also as exceptional regularization); distinct larger list for EU-2 nationals	for selected graduate professions only; instead use of EU-8 and EU-2 workers' free movement
	Bilateral agreements	with Croatia for skilled shortages; with several EU and European countries for lower skills	predominantly with former colonies (with additional shortage lists and quotas for some permits)	x
Origin	Exceptions by origin	full labor mobility for nationals of some rich countries	no mobility restrictions for Algerians, *if* admitted	x
	Role of EU free movers	preference in lower-skilled and skilled shortages	preference in lower-skilled and skilled shortages	preference in lower-skilled and skilled shortages
	Country-specific quotas	as part of some bilateral agreements, not for high skills	as part of bilateral agreements, for all skill levels	x
Numerical limits	Annual caps	x	x	1,000 in tier 1 (exceptional talents) and 20,700 in tier 2 (general), valid since 2011 and confirmed until 2014

Source: author's analysis based on comparison of classification map

of equivalence between contributions and rights that set the normative contours of the Bismarckian welfare state. The French policy of offering ex-post regularization options to *sans-papiers* workers in shortage jobs could be interpreted in a similar way. The United Kingdom, by contrast, does not show any engagement with irregularity in its labor migration regime, and domestic skills have equally ceased to matter with the abolishment of the post-study work visa in 2012. Presently, migrant irregularity features mostly as a phenomenon to be toughly controlled in the government's discourse. A last striking comparative difference is the operation of annual caps in the United Kingdom. Both France and Germany also define quotas for some permits in bilateral agreements, yet none of these countries limit the number of overall work inflows in order to stay below a numerical ceiling of annual net migration. Chapter 6 will elaborate on the justifications and rationalities of the British cap policy and their effects on overall border drawing.

Conclusion

In this chapter I have mapped the legal infrastructures for labor migration in Germany, France, and the United Kingdom case by case and analyzed them comparatively. This nuanced policy mapping paves the floor for the remainder of the empirical analysis, as it enables us to go on and scrutinize the meanings vested in the classification principles and selection mechanisms discerned here and to reconstruct their embeddedness in economic, social, and civic norms of border drawing. My legal document analysis has exposed mutual significance of selection by skill level and scarcity of skills across our three cases. This indicates that, in line with reflections in chapter 2, economic utilitarianism and competitiveness rationales might indeed play a key role and involve a great deal of commonality in countries' border-drawing rationalities. However, it also suggests that economic utility definitions fall short of accounting for markedly *national* aspects of labor migration management in the social and civic dimensions of policy meanings. The miscellaneous prevalence of selection by origin, the different uses of EU mobility to steer TCN migration in the lower-skilled job market, and the British particularity of setting numerical ceilings to overall migration highlight that negotiations about socio-political concerns take place within otherwise economically determined border-drawing processes. They trigger a greater degree of national variation in labor migration management than shared economic selection mechanisms would otherwise have us assume, and indeed part of the literature suggests.

The empirical insights gained in this chapter sustain a clear division of labor in this book's further endeavor to comprehend similarities and differences in labor migration management. Chapter 5 scrutinizes the meanings attached to a seemingly shared modus of economic border drawing by skill level and labor scarcity. Chapter 6 seeks an explanation for the cross-national differences in admission policies by examining why countries put migrant workers' countries of origin, the skills they acquired in the "host" country, or the political objective of reducing net migration figures onto the center stage of their border-drawing regime, and, further, why this is done in nationally distinct ways.

Notes

1. Translation from German: "The admission of foreign workers is directed by the demands of the German business location, all while considering labor market conditions and the need to fight unemployment effectively."
2. Translation from French: "In order to respond to recruitment needs in specific sectors of the economy, France aims to better organize professional migration and to facilitate foreigners' access to selected professions."
3. While this analysis concentrates on the creation of "legal" migrant worker categories through admission legislation, our border-drawing perspective intrinsically relies on the recognition that—by the very act of defining specific selection criteria and principles—certain TCN workers are purposefully sorted into "illegal" status categories.
4. The analysis concentrates on the main employment routes and excludes detailed consideration of categories such as working holiday makers, self-employed, or permit-free entries of sportspersons, ministers of religion, or cross-border operating journalists.
5. When I use the terms *high skilled, skilled,* and *unskilled* or *lower skilled* I refer to the categorization in legislation and do not mean to transmit any normative claim as to the "actual" skill level of a migrant worker or a job. The distinctions are being problematized as constructed categories in this interpretive policy analysis.
6. *Duldung* in German law refers to the temporary omission of expulsion orders for asylum seekers on German territory who have been rejected as refugees but cannot be expelled due to the unstable situation in their home country, for example. While *Duldung* is not a secure residence status and expulsion can be executed at any time, many *Geduldete* have resided in Germany for several years, go to schools, do training (etc.) and are de facto long-term residents. Some recent policy changes have targeted the improvement of their status, including their access to skilled jobs and secure residence.
7. The MIPEX index acknowledges access to a stable status with the settlement permit and ranks German long-term residence rights among the more favorable worldwide (unlike in its previous ranking). Denizenship in Germany is considered more favorable than in Britain where migrant workers have to rely on temporary permits for longer and face stricter eligibility conditions for an indefinite leave to remain (MIPEX data based on Huddleston and Niessen 2011).
8. These include language teachers, chefs-de-cuisine for specialities, university graduates, IT specialists, graduates of German schools abroad with a university degree or a vocational training, blue collars and skilled specialists in German and German-multinational companies, social workers in foreign families employed by a German service provider, carers for children, ill, or elderly people, intra-corporate exchanges, and project workers in multinational firms (BA 2009b).
9. This analysis does not consider seasonal workers as they are not covered by the conventional definition of migrant worker—someone who stays in a host country for at least twelve subsequent months—applied in this book. This might seem problematic

given high annual recruitment figures of around 290,000 workers since 2007 (BAMF 2011b: 77–80), yet the origin of most seasonal workers from within the EU excludes them from our analytical scope on TCN admissions.
10. The list for unskilled labor shortages comprises seasonal workers, carneys, au pairs, housekeepers, entertainers, and vocational trainees (BA 2009b).
11. Workers recruited by German companies to contribute to a project in Germany for a limited period of time, often in the construction sector (*Werkvertragsarbeitnehmer*).
12. Andorra, Australia, Israel, Japan, Canada, Monaco, New Zealand, San Marino, and the United States
13. Bilateral agreements for young professional exchanges (often including annual caps) have been negotiated with Argentina, Canada, the United States, Gabon, Montenegro, Morocco, New Zealand, Senegal, Serbia, Tunisia, Benin, Cape Verde, Congo, Mauritius, and Russia (OFII 2012b, 2013).
14. The "zones de solidarité prioritaires" comprise fifty-four developing countries including for instance Congo, Senegal, and Mali. French development policy aims to prevent brain drain from these countries (Ministère de l'Immigration 2010b; République Française 2010).
15. The EU list mentions, for example, unskilled or low-skilled jobs such as window cleaners, housekeepers, carers for children and the elderly, caterers and service staff in restaurants, woodcutters, metal workers in industry, coppersmiths, machine tool operators, concrete contractors.
16. The TCN list comprises mostly qualified jobs such as IT specialists, several types of engineers, site managers, or other skilled construction jobs. By contrast, especially jobs in unskilled construction, catering or cleaning—believed to be the most relevant for unauthorized workers—are missing.
17 A workshop of the title "Playing the numbers game" in London on 5 September 2011, organized by Bridget Anderson of COMPAS at the University of Oxford and Bernhard Ryan of the Migration and Law Network at the University of Kent, analyzed these restrictions.
18. Both entrepreneur and investor categories are only sparely used compared to the general tier 1, with roughly 100 to 150 annual entries (Home Office 2012).
19. Those who entered under the old scheme before April 2010 can ask for a renewal.
20. This included, for example, a first or foundation degree, a diploma in higher education, teaching or nursing qualifications, international baccalaureates, two or more A Levels equivalents, four or more AS Levels equivalents, or any other higher education below the degree level (MAC 2008: 71).
21. This relates to the National Skills Strategy of the Department for Business, Innovation and Skills (BIS) of 2009.
22. Chefs must be executive chefs, head chefs, specialty chefs, or sous-chefs with a high pay of more than 28,000 annually (2011 provisions).
23. This limited the total number of non-EU migrant worker inflows to just over 24,000 before April 2011, a cut of 5 percent on 2009 entry figures; 5,400 of the visas were issued in tier 1 and 18,700 in tier 2.
24. A scrutiny of entry figures per route (table 4.3) indicates that recruitment in tier 2 (general) has in fact been much lower than the new annual limits (only 10,100 entries in 2011 as opposed to the 20,700 suggested as a cap). This notional increase of migration scope, however, is due to the simultaneous limitation of other routes. Applicants will be likely to be diverted into the new tier 2 (general) as a consequence of closed schemes (tier 1 general) or stricter requirements in alternative routes (ICT for example).

CHAPTER 5

A "Tool for Growth"?
The Shared Cultural Political Economy of Labor Migration Policies

"There always has to be a balance, meaning different responses for different groups of employees. Well, at the moment … we try to be attractive for the highest qualified and high qualified whilst offering virtually no entry options for unskilled workers." (German Labor Ministry official)

"The way I think of tier 1 [of the points-based system] is that … it greases the engine. They aren't going in there to fill specific roles, but by having those people come here you increase the diversity and quality of the labor market. … Tier 2 workers on the other hand are the cogs within the engine. Sorry about the poor analogy! But they're there for a specific reason." (UK Border Agency official)

The statements from German and British policy makers above reveal a need to respond flexibly to labor demands in different parts of the economy. The previous chapter has identified a shared legal classification of migrant workers by skill level and labor scarcity. Here we go on to seek explanations for cross-national similarities in labor migration management and find a consensus on economic border-drawing norms at the heart of this partial policy convergence.

Economic Imaginaries of Migrant Workers' Skills and Scarcity of Their Labor

The analysis builds on interviews with high-ranking policy makers[1] in Berlin, Paris, and London, including former home secretaries, leading Labor Ministry, Migration Ministry, and Border Agency officials, and trade union and employer representatives. How do policy makers make sense of the selection of migrant workers by skill level and labor scarcity? The theoretical engagement with competition state theory and varieties of capitalism in chapter 2 lets us expect that economic utility drives labor migration policies as part of a competitiveness and innovation strategy more generally. However, studies have also highlighted differences in the labor recruitment strategies of Liberal Market Economies such as the United Kingdom, Coordinated Market Economies such as Germany, or the more state-led French version (Menz 2009, 2010a). This should inform different interpretations of the state's own role in foreign labor recruitment.

The analysis builds on the analytical concept of economic imaginary developed in Cultural Political Economy (Jessop 2009; Jessop and Sum 2006; Sum 2009). The first chapter has specified how this analytical tool enables a critical exploration of meanings entailed in border drawing and highlighted its intellectual links to the interpretive policy analysis approach in this book. I provide a more detailed critical appraisal of Cultural Political Economy (CPE) and its use in labor migration policy analysis elsewhere (Paul 2012a). It suffices summarizing here that, as an analytical tool, "economic imaginary" highlights the selective assemblage of a policy field by examining which parts of the social world are chosen, privileged, and combined in labor migration management.

I identify three economic imaginaries of labor migration from interviews. They operate in similar ways across all three cases studied and thus explain the common selection of workers by skill level and labor scarcity. Economic imaginaries of labor migration are characterized by three key elements: (1) different skill levels targeted in regulation, (2) diverging policy rationales, and (3) diverging spatial reference points for recruitment (synopsis in table 5.1). The privileging of very different economic activities in each imaginary informs a shared economic border-drawing logic in German, French, and British labor migration management. Guided by the three-fold regulatory divide into high-skilled, skilled, and lower-skilled labor migration (see chapter 4), three specific admission strategies emerge. These strategies act upon various combinations of justifications of labor migration and their spatial embedding, and are stipulated vividly (even metaphorically) in policy makers' interpretations of selection principles. In summary:

- Strategy 1 facilitates high-skilled migration in the context of global competitiveness,
- Strategy 2 manages skilled migration in the context of domestic labor shortages,
- Strategy 3 delimits lower skilled admissions in the context of EU labor self-sufficiency.

This chapter unpacks and discusses each economic imaginary of labor migration and the associated recruitment strategy in its own right; using statements from interviewees to illustrate the substance of the empirical data (see statements to follow). Despite the dominance of cross-sectional variation in economic border drawing, the analysis also identifies country specific nuances that confirm regime-typical modes of coordinating labor markets and national economies. Overall, however, the manifestation of three shared economic imaginaries of labor migration and three associated recruitment strategies as explanation for the common classification of migrant workers by skill level and labor scarcity remains unaffected.

Admission Strategy 1: Facilitating High-Skilled Global Labor Competitiveness

The generous treatment of high-skilled migrants crystallizes as a chief common feature of European labor migration management. Chapter 4 has shown that national legislation facilitates recruitment of graduate specialists and professional elites in all three countries, thereby not least mirroring EU-level developments such as the adoption of a Blue Card for high-skilled migrants (CEU 2009). Policy makers contextualize the high-skilled recruitment strategy in a perceived "global" economy and discuss foreign labor admission as a chief tool for promoting and sustaining the national economy's competitiveness. What emerges is an economic imaginary of high-skilled global labor competitiveness in need of public facilitation, in other words, "a tool for growth" (French Migration Ministry official). Notwithstanding the common favorable treatment of high-skilled migrants, we also witness some nuances in the actual operation of high-skilled migration border drawing in nationally variable economic coordination models.

Constructing the Economic Imaginary of High-Skilled Migration

Policy makers in all three countries agree on the main rationales connected to high-skilled labor admissions: these workers serve the national economic interest. With the aim of boosting domestic innovation and economic growth, national policies have a role to play in the "global competition" for the "brightest minds." The basic postulation extensively expressed across cases is that the national economy's success in international competition is inhibited by obstacles to high-skilled migration (original statements S1–6).

We find clear evidence of competition state logics and Schumpeterian innovation targets elaborated on in chapter 2. Supported by metaphors with strong

Statements on Labor Migration and Global Competitiveness

> Statement 1 (S1): "We equally have to acknowledge that today, with an internationalizing economy; we punish ourselves when we build too big obstacles against workers' mobility." (French Migration Ministry official)
>
> S2: "Professional immigration is ... a tool for growth.... We find ourselves in a reasoning of international football, where the big teams recruit in the entire world, and it is these big teams that happen to be in the finals. So ... if you were to limit your immigration options for great foreign professional players, you could not become champion." (French Migration Ministry official)
>
> S3: "I do think at a certain level, however, we are a world economy. And in a world economy, that is where we have tiers 1 and partly 2, there are people who circulate around the whole world economy, so that is not so much the skill needs of our particular economy, it is the way our businesses work.... Global companies operate globally.... And the question is ... whether we want those companies to be active in the U.K. and see the U.K. as a base. Well, my basic answer to that question is: yes!" (British Home Office official)
>
> S4: "Someone ... who works for a certain large U.K. airway manufacturer ... takes the view that if someone in this field comes up then we hire them, not because we need a job, but because if we don't hire them General Electric will, and these people are like gold dust." (British employers' representative)
>
> S5: "One of our primary economic interests is to offer sufficient options and conditions for highly qualified individuals ... in order to be attractive in a global context. This is where we are in competition with others, especially ... with the English-speaking countries." (German Home Office official)
>
> S6: "I think the issue for Germany is simply to remain a technology and innovation location in international competition.... The promotion of high potentials ... is relevant not just for companies, to allow them to sustain their know-how transfer internationally, but also for the entire society." (German employers' representative)

positive connotations such as "greasing the engine," "gold dust," or comparative allusions to international football "champions," policy makers construe and construct openness to high-skilled migration as a matter of competition for scarce global professional elites. The very scarcity of high-skilled elites makes them the target of benevolent admission and right regimes in the competition for the "brightest minds." Their decision to come to France, Germany, or the United Kingdom, rather than going elsewhere, supposedly implies a big advantage for the business location as a whole. Policy makers' deep conviction that, if only just recruited, "talents" and "potentials" will automatically boost national competitiveness, growth, and innovation acts as a largely naturalized mythical figure of reference. High-skilled migrants' huge beneficial impact on the national economy simply seems to be beyond doubt. Affectionate language supports the ongoing "imaginnovation" around the talent term (Thrift 2010). To limit recruitment to the national or EU realm is thought to prompt detrimental effects to the competitive position of the domestic business location: "These days, we live and die by our ability to attract inward investment ... [and] if you are an international business you need the ability to bring people in" (British Employers' representative). Eventually, the ease with which professional elites can migrate into these countries (i.e., legal entry provisions) is perceived as a key driver of international investment in the national business and innovation location. Put frankly by UK employers: a big non-European car builder is unlikely to invest in Britain were they not allowed to bring in the Japanese blue collars "they need" to run an electric cars production line in Derbyshire.

Policy makers moreover highlight the fiscal contribution of high-skilled and highly paid migrant workers. Especially those paid "stellar wages" are associated with benefits for the funding of welfare and social services. High-skilled elites are also believed to promote domestic job creation, as they are likely to attract additional foreign investment. Not surprisingly then, from this viewpoint, statement S6 sees the affluence of the entire German society at stake in high-skilled migrant labor admissions. This strongly recalls what former British Prime Minister Tony Blair has said about labor migration—and meaning predominantly its high-skilled version: "It is essential for our continued prosperity" (Home Office 2005: 5).

Besides its strong focus on economic competitiveness, the main marker of the high-skilled economic imaginary is its genuinely global regulative perspective. Policy makers refer to the "world economy" and global competition, and they highlight that globally operating companies need to be able to recruit in the entire world. This leads to the assumption that, in order to attract and tie these companies to the national business location and thereby secure investment and economic growth, labor admissions must provide easy, flexible, and generous access routes for the globally dispersed professional workforce these companies require. In the words of a French official, these companies have to be able to say: "I recruit who I want ... because this person brings me a bonus in terms of their work, intelligence and innovation. ... We will recruit in France, we will recruit in Europe, we will recruit in the entire world" (French Migration Ministry official). This sets labor migration border drawing in a spatial framework of a global economy without territorial borders. References to the domestic labor market situation are superfluous and inadequate given the strongly perceived need to compete for a highly mobile international labor force on a global scale. Indeed, this is the realm of a "global war for talent" that is believed to have triggered the initial reopening and gradual liberalization of entry routes for high-skilled workers since the late 1990s in our three countries, following the pattern of other high-income economies across the globe (Cerna 2009; Ruhs 2013).

A particularly interesting legal materialization of global competitiveness and mobility aspirations can be observed with respect to intra-corporate transfer (ICT) routes. Both in law and in policy discourse they feature as a matter of global labor markets which do not (have to) correspond to the domestic job situation or indeed the wider EU labor market. We have seen in chapter 4 that exemptions from otherwise default control mechanisms like the resident labor market test or shortage definitions apply for ICT in all three cases. Moreover, even in the British context of annual caps on labor inflows the ICT route is exempted (MAC 2010a: 257ff.)[2], with employers lobbying fiercely to keep it that way (British Employers' representative, confirmed by Border Agency official). Eventually, labor migration policies in our three cases do not treat ICT as migration, but as temporary and global professional movements completely detached from the host country and domestic labor market. The waiving of usual integration measures such as language tests and prevention of access to long-term residence and settlement rights for ICT workers strengthen this claim. In summary then, border drawing for high-skilled, highly mobile employees of multinational companies operates in remarkable disconnection from domestic labor market or societal concerns and is perceived as a matter of competing over scarce global supply of professional skills.

Facilitating Admissions with a Supply-Led Recruitment Strategy

If the assumption of global skills competitiveness dominates interpretations of high-skilled migration, it equally feeds into a specific recruitment strategy. The economic imaginary surrounding the upper skills end of labor migration founds a facilitating role for the state, putting it in charge of creating legal structures that target and attract high-skilled migrants. Selection by high skill level, mostly expressed through qualifications and high prospective wages, is the chief economic border-drawing principle for migrant workers here. In general, high-skilled migration routes follow labor supply principles, rather than stipulating a demand-led logic. This contrasts the economic imaginary of skilled labor migration according to which—as we will see later—migrants can enter in case of domestic shortages only. This supply-driven strategy is certainly most explicit in the British PBS in its initial shape (see chapter 3). The belief at the time was that "the U.K. can't have enough incredibly highly skilled, talented migrant workers, so let's create a route to let them in" (British Border Agency official).

Policy makers cherished the attempt to diversify high-skilled British labor supply with tier 1 of the PBS, with no reference to acute labor market shortages. The introduction of annual caps in tier 1 has partly distorted the supply logic, but the exemption of ICT routes from annual limits retains a partial supply-led approach within tier 2. A French Migration Ministry official similarly argues that high-skilled permits such as "skills and talents," "scientists," or ICT permit do not have to correspond to the domestic labor market, as they will bring a bonus to the economy. Only Germany applies the RLMT to high-skilled applicants, putting more emphasis on domestic labor supply, but regulation equally excludes ICT workers from this check.

Statements on Attracting High-Skilled Migrants with Generous Entitlements

> S7: "The role of residence regulation has to be facilitating to some extent. So, residence legislation is no end in itself but a means to achieve certain objectives. That concerns the mentioned objectives, our interest to recruit high and highest skills. So, we have to design our residence law in a way that does not discourage the Canadian professor to come to Germany because he has some problems with the labor market access for his wife." (German Home Office official)
>
> S8: "Our social protection system and our labor law is indeed a trump card that we can make the most of. It equally protects foreign employees ... and is interesting for the highly qualified." (German Labor Ministry official)
>
> S9: "The skills and talents permit, I think, reflects the interest of the French state, it is about France's attractiveness for highly qualified people ... companies don't check whether it is a permit for skills and talents, or whether it is [something else].... I am not sure that companies identify themselves with one permit or another; it is a tool for them." (French employers' representative)
>
> S10: "I mean we've got to be helpful to those sorts of companies—to the Japanese companies for example, massive inward investment in Britain ... the Japanese production engineers are contributing a lot to the British economy, and therefore, who are you going to exclude [from the annual cap] is very important, that you don't exclude the Japanese production engineer." (British policy advisor)

The regulatory shortcut to growth and competitiveness is paved with attractive regimes for high-skilled migrants and facilitated professional mobility across the globe. Statements S7–10 highlight the perceived importance of "facilitation" and "being helpful" to global companies so that they can recruit the high-skilled professionals they require to remain competitive and innovative. This welcoming strategy has born more global ramifications on European and OECD level, with an increasing number of policy experts and academics internalizing the alleged benefits of liberal high-skilled migration regimes (Cerna 2009; OECD 2009; Ruhs 2013; Zaletel 2006). Their creation of indices to rank countries' openness in that respect marks the emergence of a new subset of the competitiveness "knowledge brand" (Sum 2009) in which countries have to compete on liberal entry regimes. The most advantageous system is currently embodied by the German permanent residence permit. Further, the French multiannual routes for high-skilled foreigners (mainly "skills and talents" permits) and the British tier 1 ("exceptional talents") offer relatively secure residence and easier and more comprehensive labor market access—often without any reference to the resident labor market—than all other work routes. Post-study work routes also count as a tool to attract current and prospective graduates who are welcomed as future specialists in policy makers' narratives.

It is important to qualify that, despite the overwhelmingly positive rhetoric accompanying high-skilled migration; the scope of these favorable regimes is limited in practice. We require a careful recontextualization of the economic imaginary of high-skilled migration, as uttered by policy makers, in actual labor markets. Chapter 4 has shown that states do by no means open up large entry and residence routes when facilitating high-skilled migration. Leaving aside relatively large numbers of ICT workers coming to the United Kingdom—which triggered criticism and a stricter redefinition of the route—the scale of high-skilled labor inflows has remained rather small in all three countries, especially when compared to shortage routes. Low numbers certainly also sustain the treatment of high-skilled migration as a primarily *economic* question that can be disembedded from the usual social and political concerns over migration. Policy makers argue, for instance, that the small number and high qualifications of entries raise public acceptability. Chapter 6 will show that some of these concerns do nonetheless layer the global competitiveness imaginary. Yet, we will also highlight that high-skilled foreign recruitment is affected to a much lesser extent by socio-political filtering mechanisms compared to skilled and lower-skilled entries. Overall then, economic border drawing by skill level remains a chief commonality in comparative labor migration management.

Varieties of High-Skilled Foreign Labor Recruitment? National Nuances

Despite sharing a strategy of facilitating high-skilled labor migration, cases display important nuances when it comes to fine-tuning the legitimization of the recruitment strategy. These nuances mainly speak to the varieties of capitalism (VoC) literature, but also of the political momentum of labor migration regulation, and they are important sources of comparative difference in terms of norms about how economic coordination shall be done. Policy makers in Germany, for example, largely adhere to the idea that regulation needs to welcome workers "with a red carpet" (German Labor Ministry official), and it is through offering highly favorable residence rights that German administrators think they can best provide this red carpet (settlement permit). A self-perception as "enabling facilitator" in line with discursive-institutionalist VoC claims (Schmidt 2002b) surfaces in the debate. Germany's economic border-drawing regime further seems to confirm the claim that high and specific skills typically required by firms in a Coordinated Market Economy rely on institutional support through high levels of social and job security (Estevez-Abe et al. 2001). Some allude to the comparatively advantageous social protection system as a particular strength in the competition for talents (S8). It seems that the cornerstones of the typical German production and labor reproduction system delineated in VoC are being re-tailored to suit high-skilled migrants: not just the typical job and employment security, but also residence security and comparatively generous labor market access for high-skilled workers (see also Huddleston and Niessen 2011) shall generate a supply of high-skilled foreign individuals for German companies.

In contrast to Germany, interview data from France suggests a self-perception of the administration as promoter, rather than just facilitator, of highly skilled recruitment. The skills and talents permit, for example, comes with rhetoric of "splendor" and "shining" (*rayonnement*) of the country and nation as a whole, and refers to the promotion of its role in the world (see Loriaux 2003). Equally, the post-study work visa is considered to be "part of France's attractiveness" as a cosmopolitan labor market (French Migration Ministry official). One expert emphasizes the "emblematic function" of permits and their enchanting names to signal French openness to the world (French Migration Ministry official). An OFII official highlights the administration's role to promote new permits among employers, and to educate them toward a more conscious and embracing use of the created recruitment routes. This explains why the French Employers' representative's quote (S9) construes the skills and talents permit as a tool for *France*, rather than a tool for actual French companies. While German policy makers emphasized their facilitating role in close connection to companies' needs on global markets, the seeming disconnection between government rhetoric and employers' perceptions of regulatory requirements indicates a modus operandi of state-*enhancing* capitalism in French labor migration policies. We witness, at least partially, the attempt of the stereotypical "interventionist leader" (Schmidt 2002b: 204) to shape the market according to an a priori vision of French competitiveness, rather than facilitating companies' demands a posteriori. Labor migration policy in France thus seems to be part of the arrangement which Elisabetta Gualmini and Vivien Schmidt (2013) have described as a vivid "economic patriotism" under Nicolas Sarkozy.

What about the United Kingdom, our emblematic "liberal arbiter" (Schmidt 2002), then? The openness to employers' calls for unlimited high-skilled labor supply under the initial PBS—and indeed the liberal response to Eastern European free movement in 2004—have been interpreted as a typical LME response to labor migration needs (Menz 2009). Yet, chapter 3 has started to show that the introduction of annual caps as ceiling to points-based recruitment in 2010 implied a considerable shift of directions. Interview data confirm that British labor migration management seems to depart from the logics of a Liberal Market Economy, at least partially. The role of tier 1 high-skilled supply to "guild the lily" in the national economy (British Border Agency official) is currently crumbling, with the annual limit of "exceptional talent" entries set at one thousand. In other words, you can apply with the most stellar CV and skills profile, but if you happen to be the 1,001st applicant your qualities as "talent" and alleged booster of national competitiveness will not be rewarded with a positive admission decision. At the same time, however, the exclusion of the comparatively numerous ICT entries from the annual cap points to a hidden continuation of relatively liberal and employer-led professional mobility, as both a leading trade unionist and a chief policy advisor have pointed out in interviews. Statement S4 emphasizes this political wish to maintain the global competitiveness and easy access logic in economic border drawing. The "Japanese production engineer," so the statement goes, must still be able to enter under an otherwise restrictive annual cap. We will come back to the hidden continuation of liberal recruitment in the British case throughout the remainder of this analysis.

Admission Strategy 2: Responding to Skilled Domestic Labor Shortages

Skilled admissions represent by far the largest legal entry route for workers. Roughly 25,000 skilled workers joined the German and 15,000 the French labor market in 2009, while the British PBS has set the tier 2 general recruitment scheme to 20,700 annual entries. In contrast to the high-skilled domain, skilled employees in all three countries encounter stricter entry and residence conditions. These routes are justified in the context of specific skilled labor shortages that need filling. Given this policy rationale, skilled admissions are firmly embedded in the national labor market context. A demand-led recruitment strategy—chiefly relying on resident labor market tests and shortage lists—emerges, with some differences as to the exact operation of domestic labor scarcity assessments between cases. This recruitment strategy has two sides: foreign labor can act as short-term add-on in case of domestic shortages but, at the same time, domestic training and "upskilling" are demanded in order to ensure a heightened independence from migrant labor in the longer term.

Constructing the Economic Imaginary of Skilled Migration

Policy makers consider skilled foreign labor recruitment as a legitimate satisfaction of urging labor demand. We come across a plethora of terms such as *economic need, demand, specific shortage,* and *add-on* in both documents and interviews, all describing the drivers of skilled recruitment and specifying the role of migrant workers accordingly: migrant workers fill labor market gaps and satisfy the "immediate" needs of companies (see S11–15). According to interviewees, Germany needs skilled workers, France wants migrants to satisfy labor market needs and companies' "immediate" needs, and the United Kingdom's tier 2 looks for "cogs in the engine" to fill specific shortages. The rationale of recruitment being the satisfaction of urging labor needs a direct relationship between labor market gaps and legitimate recruitment is created. Policy makers allude to the fine nuance between workers "who bring a bonus" enabling "better growth" (high-skilled) and those who fill an urging shortage (skilled).

Statements on Labor Migration and Domestic Labor Market Shortages

S11: "Why do we need labor migration? Because we need skilled workers (*Fachkräfte*). That means that the labor market is in the centre.... So the main rationale is: labor migration as an add-on where the domestic labor market does not supply enough employees but not where we have enough domestic workers." (German Labor Ministry official)

S12: "We always have this tension a little bit: on the one hand to satisfy the demand of the labor market for workforce, and on the other hand, given the unemployment situation, to steer migration in a way so that the domestic labor market does not bear negative consequences." (German Labor Ministry official)

S13: "The foreign worker is someone who satisfies labor market needs, or who brings a competency with them—a bonus—that will enable better growth. Eventually, everyone benefits. But under no circumstances ... is the foreign workers someone who ruins French jobs." (French Migration Ministry official)

S14: [compares shortage routes to skills and talents route] "Work permits for lower skilled jobs are of particular interest for companies' immediate needs. I don't think that's the same.... It's not the same competition, effectively. People [in shortage routes] compete for jobs on the French labor market." (French employers' representative)

S15: "The way I think of tier 1 is that ... it greases the engine, they aren't going in there to fill specific roles, but by having those people come here you increase the diversity and quality of the labor market.... Tier 2, on the other hand, is the cogs within the engine. Sorry about the poor analogy! But they're there for a specific reason." (British Border Agency official)

Unlike in the global competitiveness imaginary, recruitment of foreign workers is not considered valuable in itself. Recruitment addresses concrete and specific domestic labor market shortages, making labor scarcity the key principle in admissions. Labor migration fulfills a "specific" role in this context: the availability of the right "cogs"—or skills—is essential for the smooth running of the national economy's "engine," to use the metaphorical words of a British Border Agency official. The scarcity rationale links skilled migration directly to the domestic labor market, departing considerably from the vision of a global talent world described with regard to high-skilled admissions. Border drawing for skilled migrant workers is strictly embedded in the national labor market, regardless of the excellence of their qualifications. TCN workers can enter as legitimate "add-ons" only where the domestic labor force cannot satisfy demand. The protection of the domestic labor market—completely disregarded in the first imaginary outlined earlier—prominently enters the stage here: foreign workers must not "ruin French jobs" (S13) and migrants are not welcome "where we have enough domestic workers" (S11), for example.

Migrant workers thus compete from a subordinate position on the domestic labor market rather than being perceived as part of an attractive globally free-floating labor supply. Their allegedly lower professional qualifications also turns skilled migrants into explicit targets of integration policy efforts: governments assume that skilled workers are less mobile and might settle, but their lower qualifications—as compared to the allegedly multilingual cosmopolitan high-skilled elites[3]—also imply that the integration process is no automatism and needs monitoring and facilitation. This explains why integration contracts such as the French *CAI* or language proficiency requirements apply to them but not always to high-skilled workers. Not international excellence and competition, but a specific skills profile and its relationship to the domestic labor market situation form the main reference points in border drawing for skilled workers. They are not seen as beneficial due to surplus skills or competencies they bring to the national economy (as high-skilled entries), but they potentially threaten domestic employment and need to be checked tightly before being able to fulfill labor shortages.

Filling Labor Shortages with a Demand-Led Admission Strategy

The ambiguous position of skilled migrant workers between "beneficial" and "threatening" informs a Janus-faced recruitment strategy of filling shortages in the short term while protecting the domestic workforce and training them to become economically more self-reliant in the longer term. Overall, the handling of skilled shortage recruitment is much more restrictive than of high-skilled routes. Short- and mid-term shortages on the labor market are responded to with temporary and job-specific permits. The permit system reflects a strong economic utility interpretation of migrant labor that can be imported—and indeed expelled—according to changing economic needs. For instance, German government officials describe shortage recruitment as a "flexible and demand-oriented" strategy to *react* to changes in economic demand, the labor market structure, and the economic situation and downscale in times of economic crisis. Shortage routes thus create highly constrained legal work spaces for skilled migrant workers: they are tied to the defined shortage space by fixed-term permits and obligatory links to their employer, and might not have their temporary permits extended if the shortage ceases to exist or domestic unemployment rises during economic downturns. This departs considerably from the longer-term perspectives—even immediate right of settlement—offered to "experts" and "talents" in the former imaginary. A job offer is obligatory and the employment with the specific employer a prerequisite for continued legal residence. Policy makers see the migrant-employer link—most pronounced in the UK's sponsorship approach—as a viable way of monitoring both parties. The confinement of shortage recruitment to certain "key industries and sectors" (German Government representative), specific professions, or labor districts, and the role of "responsible" conduct ascribed to employers as "partners" in migration control (most explicitly highlighted by officials in the British and German Home Offices) further demonstrates the tight monitoring of skilled labor admissions. While within the first imaginary, labor scarcity is assumed by default and informs supply-led recruitment strategies, additional and much more detailed scarcity checks dominate skilled labor recruitment. In the words of a French Employment Agency official, employers need to present "good reasons" to convince employment and border agencies of the inevitability of foreign recruitment. Migrants need a specific vocational training certificate or higher-education award to prove their professional ability to fill the specific shortage described in their job offer. The matching of a migrant's skills profile to a specific shortage in the host labor market—either established through a resident labor market test or in a shortage list—acts as the most important economic selection mechanism for skilled migrant workers.

We find some cross-national variation when it comes to the exact operation of shortage assessments. While all three countries focus on shortages by sector, Germany certainly features the strongest institutional crystallization of establishing regular sectoral scarcity assessments. To define shortage routes and domestic training efforts, the German government has initiated an "alliance on skilled workers" (*Fachkräfteallianz*)[4] in 2009, thus willingly fulfilling the role of a tightly coordinated "sectoral CME" (Kitschelt et al. 1999b). In the United Kingdom, the Migration Advisory Committee (MAC) fulfills a similar role when reporting on shortages. However, the MAC consultation focuses on gathering scientific evidence on shortage occupations and comes with a much less institutionalized and corporative dressing than the German version.

The strong procedural involvement of employment agencies in the resident labor market test in France and Germany, and a special labor market protection clause in the lower-skilled realm in Germany indicate a strict application of the scarcity principle. French regional employment agencies calculate shortages using a centralized database with information on vacancies and skills profiles of unemployed people. By contrast, in the United Kingdom the resident labor market test solely relies on employers' attestations of demand.

Indeed, employers' appraisal of the "flexible" recruitment route opened with the resident labor market test (British Employers' representative) has triggered skepticism about the accuracy of establishing actual shortages and preventing domestic labor replacement (National Audit Office 2011). Given the firm institutional links between labor market policies and foreign demand-led recruitment in their countries, policy makers in France and Germany seem much less concerned about the meaning and effectiveness of the resident labor market test. This might reflect different philosophies of labor market governance and degrees of institutionalization of scarcity assessments in LMEs and CMEs in comparative perspective. Though not the focus of analytical attention here, we assume that the nuances in operating shortage assessments in labor migration governance—as attempts of corporative consensus building in Germany, as scientific consultation and employer attestation in the United Kingdom, and as administrative output of centralized employment agencies in France—highlight marked differences in the labor market coordination of these countries and their effects on foreign labor recruitment strategies.

Filling Longer-Term Shortages through Domestic Training and "Upskilling" Strategies

Policy discourse draws an important boundary between short-term and long-term TCN recruitment by alluding to future aspirations for a "sensitive" domestic skills strategy. The German skills alliance and MAC shortage lists both engage with this long-term labor market strategy explicitly (BMAS 2008a; MAC 2010b). Policy makers see a prospective need to train the domestic workforce and become less "reliant" on migrant workers. While it seems acceptable to recruit skilled workers to fulfill shortages today, employers are asked—and indeed claim themselves to be committed—to develop domestic labor supply strategies for the future at the same time (S16–18).

In Germany and the United Kingdom shortage recruitment is accompanied by the perceived need to train the domestic workforce, but the extent to which this claim is institutionalized varies. German interviewees speak of a "dual strategy" of admitting workers into current economic gaps with the tools mentioned above, and at the same time assessing future demand and investing in specific training. The latter strategy follows the aim of increasing job opportunities for resident workers and closing any gaps self-sufficiently.[5] The corporately structured "skills alliance" is designed to functionally link scarcity assessment, legitimacy of migrant labor imports, and the need to train for prospective self-sufficiency. What seems to drive the strong focus on making the skills alliance work in the German case is the specific demographic decline situation (chapter 3), which neither France nor the United Kingdom seem to perceive to be as crucial.

Statements on Long-Term versus Short-Term Admissions

S16: "One is an issue which is solvable in the long term but not in the short term, which is where there are skills shortages in the U.K., and we've always talked about labor migration policy within a skills framework, because I think it is acceptable to say to the government: there is a skills shortage here, we can't hire someone else, can we have someone from outside the EEA? Now, it might not be acceptable to still be asking that question in ten years' time, if the government says: well, what exactly did you do on skills development in the meantime?—you can't be reliant." (British employers' representative)

S17: [talking about which skilled jobs can 'sensibly' be included on shortage list] "Immigration can be an efficient way of responding to a shortage, but it's often not the only way.... So when we talk to employers, we say: ok, we accept that you have a shortage. We also ask: what are you doing about it? Have you tried to raise wages? Have you tried to train domestic workers? Have you tried to mechanize?" (British policy advisor)

S18: "The task of the [skills] alliance is to consider the following issues: how do supply and demand develop in the medium term on the labor market? How can we sensibly steer education and training? And which jobs can we not fill from the available labor pool but might need to satisfy them with migration?" (German Labor Ministry official)

British policy makers want to incentivize employers to signal shortages "more systematically" to educational institutions and Sector Skills Councils, and to provide more funding for training. The propositions to link allocations of sponsorship certificate to companies' efforts of "upskilling" (UKBA 2010) sustain this claim, but have not yet been specified let alone implemented. In the absence of an encompassing vocational education system, the responsibility for training remains an issue of contestation[6] in the United Kingdom. The Cameron government seems determined to win this tug of war by putting in place additional measures that limit employers' non-EU recruitment options and eventually—or so the hope goes—make them revise their domestic training strategies: the skills level needed in tier 2 (general) has been lifted to graduate only, several notionally less skilled occupations have been removed from the shortage list in 2011, and "priority areas of upskilling" have been announced (UKBA 2010, 2011). Regardless of the practical feasibility or political seriousness of the claimed domestic training efforts, the aspiration in itself demarcates borders in labor migration. If a job is removed from a national shortage list because the government considers nursing or meat cutting a priority area for upskilling domestic workers, the labor market border for newcomers moves with this redefinition regardless of actual shortages. That means that the role of the state in skilled recruitment goes beyond a mechanical facilitation of matching domestic demand and migrant worker supply in response to national shortages: it has a stake—rhetorically at least—in reshaping shortages themselves and ensuring they can be met in a self-sustained manner in the future.

French policy makers debate longer-term shortages with view of the "activation" of domestic workers without much consideration of how that shall be achieved. Even though one representative diagnoses a "co-existence of a high unemployment rate ... and at the same time non-satisfied demands for labor of companies, as there is no evident correlation between these two populations" (French Employers' representative), this does not inform training pledges. We can only make sense of this absence of engagement with the French political economy in a joint review with chapter 6. This will indicate how labor migration policy is not entirely about the recruitment of workers—also due to the very different demographic outlook of population growth—but about "signaling effects" of "desirability" to the resident population (French trade unionist; French policy advisor).

Regardless of variations the economic space of a "shortage" shares some crucial cross-national features in policy making: it is no statistical entity that neutrally expresses current demand and supply for a specific job position to justify TCN recruitment. Rather, the borders of the shortage space are politically demarcated in light of governments' aspirations about the current and future labor market participation of resident vis-à-vis migrant workers. That means that any scarcity assessment—through updated shortage lists, skills alliances, or employer consultations—will not directly translate into migrant admissions. To quote a British policy advisor, "just because there's a shortage doesn't necessarily make an automatic case for immigration" (see also S16–18). The interaction of economic border drawing with domestic employment and skilling agendas indicates trade-offs between domestic and outward-looking economic coordination targets: protectionism of the current and prospective domestic labor force delimits economic utility claims and clearly demarcates the legitimate place for an incoming migrant worker to fill a skilled shortage.

Admission Strategy 3: Securing Low-Skilled Labor Self-Sufficiency in the European Union

Lower-skilled jobs are virtually inaccessible for migrant workers via legal routes. Outside the scope of the shortage imaginary for skilled jobs described above, regulation in all three countries responds to labor scarcity overwhelmingly with a notion of EU labor self-sufficiency. Policy makers assume that domestic and EU labor supply can and shall abundantly fill lower-skilled gaps and do not accept foreign recruitment to be a legitimate strategy in that realm. The common spatial reference to the domestic and EU labor market implies strong sorting effects in labor migration border drawing, crowding out lower-skilled entries from outside the European Union and thereby, ultimately, cementing the vulnerable positions of unauthorized foreign resident workers. At the same time, the (non-)recruitment strategy with respect to foreign workers interacts strongly with domestic labor activation aims. This section illuminates the imaginary of lower skilled EU labor self-sufficiency.

Constructing the Economic Imaginary of Lower-Skilled Migration

The widespread denial of low-skilled labor demand, with the exception of strictly controlled and temporary seasonal work routes, explains restrictive admission routes. The underpinning assumption is that low-skilled labor supply is abundant on the domestic and European labor market and does therefore not require importing from elsewhere to fill positions (see S19–22).

Statements on Labor Migration, Domestic Unemployment, and Activation

> S19: "By no urgent means do we need lower skilled workers.... We have enough resident job seekers who we would like to activate and put into employment." (German Labor Ministry official)
>
> S20: [talking about demand for seasonal agricultural workers] "I do not see that for other sectors. Well, ... unemployment of the lower skilled is still so high that it [recruitment of foreign workers] is politically difficult to imagine." (German Labor Ministry official)
>
> S21: "It's not completely normal that we lack wood-cutters in France, if you wish, this does not demand a high qualification.... We should be able to demand and offer a job to low-skilled unemployed people in France, as a kind of obligation. But we most often find that, unfortunately, that's not what happens, meaning that the individuals under consideration are not capable or willing to do the job." (French Migration Ministry official)
>
> S22: [on some lower skilled shortage list jobs, which have been removed in March 2011] "Why aren't we actually skilling up the unemployed to do some of these jobs? ... There are occupations on the list like butchers and meat cutters, which train up within 12–18 months with less investment. So why aren't we doing that, why are we bringing in labor to do that? ... And actually if that is, if the opportunities are very low skilled labor that anybody could do, then those people then need to go to those jobs.... But I think that over the last so many years there has been so much choice, this is, there's been the choice to stay at home where people are paid more to stay at home than to go to work.... I think there is enough people in this country to fill these positions and I actually think that is something that the Department for Work and Pensions should be addressing in their work." (British policy advisor)

The official regulation puzzle in lower-skilled recruitment differs considerably from both the high-skilled and skilled realm. It is not about how migrant labor import can be managed as legitimate "shortage filler," and it is indeed far from being about raising a country's attractiveness to desired migrant workers. Here, we talk about the best mechanisms to shuffle the notionally amply available domestic and European workforce into given lower-skilled jobs and prevent additional migration from outside the Union. The spatial focus on the domestic and EU labor market is based on national labor market and employment policy considerations.

Several policy makers make a double reference to the domestic unemployed population: as a workforce to be activated—also with penalizing measures if necessary—and as a politically susceptible group to be protected from labor market competition with TCN workers. The first idea emphasizes the responsibility (for some even "obligation") of resident workers to respond to lower-skilled labor shortages. German policy makers perceive "no use for lower-skilled migration" (German Home Office official) and express a clear role for German job seekers to fill positions. A French Employers' representative highlights companies' roles in the administration of the unemployment insurance and stresses their obligation to treat the domestic labor pool with priority. A British policy advisor mentions recruitment difficulties for butchers and meat cutters—at the time of interviewing still part of the shortage list—due to hard working conditions in "cold temperatures" around "chunks of meat." They call for a tightened "work first" activation approach in which job seekers should "pull their socks up" and do the lower-skilled jobs that are available, also under threat of cutting job seekers' allowance. Other policy makers feel that better working and wage conditions should be offered to British workers in sectors like food processing or catering.

The discursive links between lower-skilled shortages and activation targeted at the resident unemployment population inform a discussion about the boundary between "normal" and "abnormal" shortages and highlight the fluidity of "legitimate" foreign labor admissions. The matching of empirical labor demand with legal provisions fluctuates in a grey area between the skilled shortage imaginary and the lower-skilled self-sufficiency imaginary: while woodcutting might be a shortage job today, and thus form part of the shortage imaginary, the political aspiration might be to move it into the self-sufficiency realm. Annually changing shortage definitions in the British case further prove the point. Policy makers moreover consider the public—and electorate—to be sensitive to unemployment and hence most skeptical of foreign labor recruitment on lower skill levels. Chapter 6 will show that this political calculus has played an especially crucial part in the 2010 UK general elections, but it also shapes labor migration border drawing elsewhere.

Domestic workforce protection and activation targets inform a spatial concentration on recruitment from within the EU labor market. Even if policy makers indicate protectionist targets with regard to their own national labor force, EU integration and the imperative of free movement requires any labor protective measure for nationals from one member state to treat equally all other EU nationals as well. EU free movement thus becomes a prime normative reference point for lower-skilled labor needs. This logic departs from the skilled shortage imaginary where current skilled shortages were accepted as legitimate grounds for recruitment beyond the European Union as well. Whether EU labor supply operates on a basis of liberal free movement (United Kingdom) or via more cautiously controlled routes for new member-state nationals (Germany and France), policy makers across our three cases entirely reject the notion of lower-skilled labor need from outside the European Union. What we find in the realm of low-skilled labor migration then is an intermeshing of EU citizenship as a political border with domestic activation and unemployment concerns as a social border that, in their interaction, illegitimize any existing economic rationale of (formal) foreign labor recruitment and heavily curtail entry options for TCN workers.

Limiting Non-EU Admissions with a "European" Admissions Strategy

The notion of abundant EU labor supply led governments to put into practice mechanisms to recruit lower-skilled workers exclusively from within the European Union. Nationals from new member states—who have been temporarily excluded from full EU free movement—are recruited with preference into lower-skilled shortages. Our legal mapping (chapter 4) has shown that both France and Germany focus on Bulgarians and Romanians as temporarily restricted EU movers in bilateral shortage agreements. Certainly, emerging opportunities for new EU member-state nationals to work in lower-skilled sectors varied massively between the liberal free movement approach in the United Kingdom, the relatively encompassing shortage list in France, and a strict control of few selected lower-skilled shortage routes and bilateral agreements in Germany. Alas, the border-drawing effect for TCN workers has been similar (and will be when free movement is fulfilled): the preference of EU workers has reduced their entry options to high-skilled and some selected skilled routes. Indeed, a policy advisor highlights the strong dependence on Polish workers within the food-processing sector, for instance, and argues that companies would struggle enormously to fill these jobs if EU free movement were limited. The liberal use of the EU labor pool is thus largely seen as beneficial for the British economy.

The relative absence of statements on the EU labor pool debate in French interviews was striking. Only one policy maker refers to EU free movement as a regulatory context specifically. Regulation paints a different picture, though: the special shortage list for Bulgarians and Romanians indicates an institutionalized beneficial treatment of Europeans just as elsewhere. Some policy makers address potential future labor needs from outside the European Union. They frame this expectation in light of ageing European populations—a particular fear in Germany. Moreover, German policy makers in particular expect decreasing wage differentials and migration push-and-pull factors between the new EU states and the EU-15 to trigger prospective labor demand from elsewhere. In case the question "why pick asparagus in Germany?" (S27) should arise for Eastern Europeans, policy makers seemingly want to keep the backdoor of controlled, utilitarian, and strictly bilateral recruitment open.

Statements on Building on EU Labor Self-sufficiency

> S23: "Forget about the bilateral agreements. With the implementation of full free movement, bilateral agreements will vanish, I'd say. Now, it might take a bit longer with Croatia until they are member and enjoy free movement, but it otherwise does not play any role." (German Labor Ministry official)
>
> S24: "Well, we have to see whether there will be lower skilled demands at some point, but that will now partly be equalised by the prospective free movement of workers from Bulgaria and Romania in 2014. So, in that respect, I think we will not have extraordinarily huge demands in the near future." (German employers' representative)
>
> S25: [talking about the lower skilled shortage list for Bulgarians and Romanians in comparison to the skilled shortage list for TCNs] "Well, the issue is a bit different. Because for EU nationals from enlargement countries the idea has actually been to use the European labor force, so it [the shortage list for Romanians and Bulgarians] covers virtually all professions." (French employers' representative)
>
> S26: "I do believe that the EU can provide most of the shortages, and I also believe that even within the U.K., if there are serious shortages, for example of plumbers, then the solution is to train up more plumbers in the U.K. and certainly from within the EU as a whole. And that would be my first priority for trying to balance the labor market problems that exist." (British Home Office official)
>
> S27: "Our experience shows ... that the experience of countries coming into the EU is that they grow very fast up to the European norm, and then slow back to trend. In that light, then push factors for young Polish and Lithuanian people in particular because those are big countries, are going to be much lower. Why get on a flight to come to England, if you can get a job that's just as good and doesn't pay a lot less around the corner. Why pick asparagus in Germany is an equally good question!" (British employers' representative)

Comparative mapping indicated that Germany already extends the imagined EU labor pool to accession candidates, notably in the bilateral recruitment of Croatian care workers. This is interpreted as a pre-accession "simulation of free movement" in which wage and qualification differentials are cushioned to prevent negative effects on the German labor market. Similar considerations shaped the decision to apply transitional limits to free movement to the EU-8 and put workers from the Eastern Europe in an in-between position between the skilled shortage imaginary and self-sufficiency claims: while they were treated more favorably than newly incoming TCN workers with easier access to lower-skilled shortages, they were not yet enjoying free movement and equal labor market access. We have discussed the emerging "complex stratification" of migrant rights and statuses—with most non-EU residents actually enjoying prior labor market access over EU accession country nationals—elsewhere (Carmel and Paul 2013b).

The common legal classification of EU vs. non-EU workers in the low-skilled realm seems to diverge in accordance with the labor geographies under scrutiny (chapter 3). Similarly to the discursive non-engagement with prospective training efforts to steer labor supply in the previous section, French policy makers concentrate on the role of post-colonial (unauthorized) flows and the informal labor market to frame the meaning of lower-skilled recruitment. The strong correlations between low-skilled migrant work, irregularity of employment, and post-colonial migrant descent in the French case explain this position. Some even doubt the economic and demographic necessity of European low-skilled recruitment, arguing that the large share of mostly post-colonial migrants forms a substantial and sufficient—yet often irregular—resident labor pool.

For some observers, therefore, professional migration schemes in France embody "l'affichage d'un volonté politique" (French trade unionist).[7] The strong focus on high-skilled and skilled shortage entries in documents[8] and interviews is accompanied by a silence on the economic context of shortages. Critics thus argue that the third economic imaginary rhetorically disguises tensions in the real economy and further marginalizes a large unauthorized migrant workforce (Anderson 2010b, 2013; Morice 1996; Morice and Potot 2010). It seems that the distinctly post-colonial labor geography—of which the United Kingdom disposed itself earlier and more pragmatically and which Germany lacks completely—and ongoing politicized debates about including unauthorized resident workers (Barron et al. 2011) significantly shape border drawing in France. Chapter 6 explores these socio-political logics—and their effects on migrant admissions—in more detail.

Apart from the political wish to integrate *Geduldete* in the labor market prior to new TCN recruitment, unauthorized migrant labor is absent from the German debate. Unlike in France, interviewees do not perceive any influential external "migration pressure" due to a lack of colonial links and geographical distance to the peripheries of Europe. They argue that this creates a "relatively unencumbered" situation for policy makers (German Labor Ministry official) and legitimizes a utilitarian recruitment approach without a sense of obligation to a historical dependent. Given that Germany's unauthorized migrant laborers were often Eastern European, mostly Poles to be precise, experts had expected a silent legalization of large chunks of unauthorized employment with the arrival of comprehensive free movement in 2011. With the expansion of the European Union, the "problem" of unauthorized labor is perceived to largely disappear for Germany.

Economic-utilitarian and political border-drawing principles seemingly coincide quite smoothly in the German case, very much in contrast to France and the United Kingdom, whose labor migration directly and indirectly engages with colonial history and migration. From that perspective, the absence of references to irregular migrant workers or post-colonial flows from British interviewees' narratives is striking, especially given the comparative relevance of irregular migrant employment in the United Kingdom (chapter 3). Only one trade union representative mentioned "irregular workers," but tellingly asked us to keep their comments on the matter off the record. The absence of post-colonialism, unauthorized migration and informal labor market segments from the British debate will be analyzed in the subsequent chapter. Overall, it seems that references to the norms inscribed in different citizenship models, but also the empirical composition of distinct labor geographies, create distinct contexts for lower-skilled labor migration management (more in Paul 2011, 2013). They play a chief role in explaining cross-national policy variation.

Conclusion: A Common Cultural Political Economy of Labor Migration

The operation of similar policy tools—at least with respect to selection by skill level and scarcity of skills—in European countries' labor migration management does no longer seem surprising once we have exposed the great degree of similar narratives and rationalities dominating the economic border-drawing domain. Policies in Germany, France, and the United Kingdom commonly follow a three-fold division of labor migration by skill level—high skilled, skilled, lower skilled—and operate admissions on the basis of accrued assumptions about the specific meaning and legitimacy of each skill category in the national economy.

In the first economic imaginary, policy makers construe high-skilled labor migration as part of a genuinely global economy and frame foreign labor supply as a tool to remain competitive. To attract high-skilled elites with permeable border regimes and generous statuses allegedly brings a bonus to the national business location. This strongly connects to arguments of "competition state" and emphasizes Schumpeterian innovation logics, very much as political economists would suggest (chapter 2). The economic imaginary of skilled national labor shortages, secondly, conceives of foreign labor recruitment as a legitimate satisfaction of urging labor demand, but also specifies clear limitations of demand-led admissions. In order to prevent domestic labor substitution, legislation strongly embeds migrant employment in the domestic labor market. The shortage space is moreover demarcated in light of political aspirations for the current and future labor market participation of resident workers. Thirdly, the economic imaginary of lower skilled EU labor self-sufficiency assumes abundant supply of lower-skilled labor on the domestic and European labor market and, therefore, illegitimizes recruitment from third countries. Policy makers highlight resident workers' responsibility to fill lower-skilled shortages and link activation and employment policy targets to this role interpretation. Whether this strict official border drawing operates as actual exclusion of non-EU workforce or whether it remains on the programmatic level of policies and sustains (tolerated) informal and unauthorized work and residence (as in Boswell and Geddes's concept of "malintegrated" policies, 2011) is a question beyond the empirical scope of this book. However, the engagement with socio-political border-drawing mechanisms in the next chapter will highlight that unauthorized workers and residents are of great salience as potential "hidden" targets of labor migration policies.

What does cross-national similarity in economic border drawing imply for our comparative analysis? Firstly, the fact that these three shared economic imaginaries and recruitment strategies emerge—with some nuances—in all three cases is striking in itself. They seem to mark the emergence of labor migration management as part of a wider Euro-capitalism project in which countries as different as France, Germany, and the United Kingdom indicate considerable levels of convergence and draw on a common labor market to a considerable extent. Secondly, we have to reappraise the explanatory scope of regime literature in the light of common economic border drawing. We find only limited applicability of competition and innovation state logics in that context. While competitiveness targets are certainly pronounced in the first economic imaginary for high-skilled migration, they collapse in the latter two and speak of highly fragmented economic realities (Paul 2012a).

Findings partially confirm varieties of capitalism accounts, especially those taking a more critical view on discursive underpinnings of economic governance models (Schmidt 2002b; also Hay and Wincott 2012). This is especially true of both the notion of "enabling" facilitation and corporatist coordination in German, and the state-led "dirigiste" promotion of permits in French labor

162 | *The Political Economy of Border Drawing*

Table 5.1. Three Shared Economic Imaginaries of Labor Migration Policies

	High-skilled global labor competitiveness	Skilled domestic labor shortages	Lower skilled EU labor self-sufficiency
Skill level target	High-skilled, very scarce skills, globally mobile skills; post-study work options for graduates	Skilled workers in 'scarce' professions, up-skilling efforts in national workforce	Low and unskilled; skilled where not in scarce supply; assumed 'vast' domestic and EU labor supply
Policy rationales	Support economic competitiveness and attractiveness of national business location; support innovation and growth; secure fiscal benefits through high earning migrants	Secure short-term economic productivity in shortage situations; boost domestic labor supply longer term to prevent reliance on migrants	Secure domestic/EU labor supply; lower reliance on migrants; activate domestic unemployed; manage and contain informal labor market
Spatial focus	Globally mobile labor pool and globally operating companies; 'world economy' dis-embedded from national labor market	Global supply in case of domestic shortages; sometimes in bilateral recruitment only or EU worker preference; embedded in current and prospective national labor market	Reliance on EU and domestic workers to fill shortages; priority of domestic employment and activation policies; ignorance towards global unauthorized labor supply
Recruitment strategy	Global supply-led recruitment in competition for 'brightest minds'; global 'war for talent'; highly generous admission and residence regimes	Selective demand-led recruitment as 'add-on' to domestic shortages; fine-tuned identification of shortage jobs in which migrants are then contained; state-led labor market command and control in promotion of domestic up-skilling	Exclusivity of EU and domestic supply to fill shortages; activation and 'matching' by state; strictly controlled bilateral agreements with third countries in exceptional cases; fight against unauthorized work and residence
Metaphors used to describe policy aims	*Discourse of 'talents' and 'high potentials' signifies innovation capacity; 'gold dust' signifies scarce skills and magical quality of some migrants to boost innovation and growth; 'greasing the engine'; rolling out 'red carpet' with generous treatment*	*Discourse of 'economic need', 'demand', 'specific shortage' and 'add-on' signifies demand-led focus; concrete space for migrants as 'cogs in the engine' with specific and contained role; discourse on 'reliance' signifies future self-sufficiency aspirations*	*Use of attributes like 'amply' and 'enough' signifies abundance of domestic/EU labor supply; reference to 'duty' and 'obligation' of domestic unemployed to 'pull socks up' ascribes responsive role to them with regard to achieving labor self-sufficiency*

Source: author's analysis of semi-structured interviews and policy documents

migration discourse. As this book's afterword indicates, more recent policy reforms in Germany have seemingly even deepened the typical path of the coordinated market economy. However, the restrictive British approach with enforced reliance on annual admission limits points to severe difficulty of the institutionalist capitalist regimes literature to make labor migration policy intelligible—unlike of course otherwise stated by Georg Menz (2009), who could plausibly not resist reading the British case of labor migration management as prime example of a liberal market economy at his time of writing (a more detailed argument on recent policy changes is provided in Paul 2014). In order to explain the apparent oscillation of UK policies between epitomized economic openness and tough border control (the latter having been strengthened even more since the end of this book's research span in autumn 2013), we now turn to the non-economic drivers of labor migration management and examine their interactions with our three economic imaginaries in multidimensional border-drawing processes.

Notes

1. To ensure confidentiality and anonymity, direct statements are labeled as to disclose only interviewees' national context and generic institutional affiliation. Interviewees are not distinguished by rank (i.e., home secretary vs. senior officials in Home Office) or specific organization (i.e., precise Employers' association or department within Ministry). See documents section for more details.
2. A British trade union representative criticizes that ICT migrant workers are not perceived as migrants but as components of a globally mobile talent pool to be offered "free routes" without any reference to the resident pool of labor in the United Kingdom, or indeed concerns about potential crowding-out effects.
3. A German Labor Ministry official argues that a high-skilled job serves as proxy for anticipated successful integration.
4. This brings together some government resorts—such as Labor, Economy, Education, Home Affairs—the Länder, trade unions, Employers' associations, Chambers of Crafts and of Commerce, some companies and board members, and researchers.
5. Germany applied this approach for the so-called Green Card, when money went into IT training courses alongside the recruitment of TCN IT specialists (German Home Office official).
6. Employer representatives and Sector Skills Council officials call for government funding instead. See Durrant (forthcoming) on the paradoxes of British skills policies.
7. Announcement of a political intention without actual consequences.
8. Comité interministériel de contrôle de l'immigration 2011a; Ministère de l'Immigration 2010c.

CHAPTER 6

"Poles Don't Even Play Cricket!"
Embedding Labor Migration Policies in National Socio-Cultural Norms

"Concerning TCN we don't experience, how shall I put it, any concrete pressure at our external borders.... We have no colonies that are still on our back historically; I'd say we are relatively unencumbered in that respect." (German Labor Ministry official)

"[*Immigration choisie*] does not speak to those who will come; it speaks to those who have been here for two generations. The legal texts won't apply to them, but nonetheless speak to them.... And immediately we talk about the banlieues, we talk about terrorism,... because all gets mixed up." (French trade unionist)

"The incoming [Conservative-LibDem] government thought it needed to be tough on migration, and so they tried to find anywhere that they could show that they were offering tighter regulation." (British Home Office official)

The cultural political economy of labor migration only goes halfway in explaining the classifications of migrant workers identified in chapter 4. Indeed, the analysis of interview data so far falls short of accounting for variegated patterns of selecting TCN workers by their origin, by domestically acquired skills, by anticipated welfare or socio-cultural cohesion effects, or with annual caps. The astonishment of a Jamaican resident at the fact that the incoming Polish workers "don't even play cricket" (narrative related by a British trade unionist) is only one of the ways in which economic border-drawing logics are challenged. Much more than having their economic rationales contested from the outside or by underground practices, labor migration policies include socio-cultural norms at their very heart and form specific arrangements of economic, social, and civic border drawing.

The introductory statements point toward considerable nuances in the way in which post-colonial relations, experiences of migration "pressure," or electoral migration control promises shape labor migration policies. Unlike their relatively homogeneous economically driven counterparts, social, and civic border drawing mechanisms and rationales are much more heterogeneous across the three cases under scrutiny here. The decision to organize this last analytical chapter by case rather than by crosscutting theme (as in the previous chapter) is hence not coincidental. The shift of attention away from shared border-drawing mechanisms and norms toward manifest national differences in migrant classifications forms the core empirical argument of this book: a shared cultural political economy of labor migration that predominantly selects "legal" migrant workers by the level and scarcity of their skills is compounded by social and civic border-drawing rationalities that expose country-specific struggles between openness and closure. While seemingly straightforward economic rationalities are challenged in all three countries, they are challenged from different directions, to different degrees, and with different implications for migrants.

In this chapter I identify and analyze key reference themes that policy makers employ in interviews when justifying limits to economic border-drawing mechanisms, such as the operation of annual caps or the deliberate selection of TCN workers by origin. This allows us to eventually pin down the complex interactions between economic, social, and civic border-drawing principles in the definition of "legal" labor migration as well as rights and statuses of legal migrant workers.

Bismarckian "Earned" Migration and Germany's European Geopolitics

German policy makers widely internalize the argument that in order to remain competitive the national economy needs workers of specific skill levels and profiles to fill labor shortages. The demographic shrinking scenario seems to lend sufficient credibly to demand-led TCN labor recruitment of a rather technocratic and utilitarian kind. However, further policy rationales are mapped onto utilitarian recruitment in the social and civic realms of border drawing. In the German case, this particularly concerns the special treatment of migrants with domestically acquired skills, nationals from certain rich countries, and preferential shortage recruitment of workers from prospective EU member states. If the recruitment of demographically required skills under the labels of global competitiveness or national labor shortages were the sole rationale of labor migration policies, surely workers' origin or the origin of their qualifications should not matter. The fact that they do is justified by policy makers in interviews with reference to three key policy visions:

(1) a model of "earned" migration that dovetails and explicitly utilizes the Bismarckian logic of socio-economic integration and relative status maintenance via successful labor market participation,

(2) a strong promotion and geographical expansion of the European project through economic and labor market integration within the EU and with accession candidates,

(3) and the persistence of ethnic recruitment hierarchies as a means of cushioning adverse social and cultural cohesion effects.

"Earned" Migration for Some: Mainstreaming Bismarckian Inclusion Logics

Interviewees widely point to the seemingly natural links between the rationales of economic labor migration management and the German "way of doing welfare" (Sainsbury 2006). Indeed, the Bismarckian welfare state serves as a hub for the discrimination between wanted and unwanted migrant workers. This concerns two regulatory areas: the anticipation of socio-economic integration prospects of newcomers at the point of first admission, and the ex-post "earned" admission of residents in unauthorized positions into legal statuses. Interview data and legislation indicate that the Bismarckian welfare state underpins, just as chapter 2 has suggested, policies in both categories with its contribution-rights-equivalence and status maintenance logics.

Within the first economic imaginary we discussed earlier in this book the status maintaining and relatively generous German welfare state is seen as "trump card" (German Labor Ministry official) in the process of courting especially high-skilled professionals. Interviewees further recognize the German welfare system as a key reference point when assessing the economic and social inclusion capacities of a migrant worker *before* admission. The prerequisite of a binding job offer, for instance, is not just an economic selection mechanism within demand-led shortage recruitment, but German interviewees frequently link it to anticipated integration success (S1–2).

Following this pattern of anticipating earned migration, the highest potential is ascribed to high-skilled migrant workers who are seen to "deserve" the beneficial rights regime offered by the settlement permit. Interviewees perceive high professional skill levels among respective workers as guarantor for quasi automatic and successful labor market inclusion. Eventually, the status maintenance principle of contribution-based welfare provision in the Bismarckian welfare state will prompt high levels of social inclusion for high-paid and high-contributing professionals as well. Although a similar "automatic integration" argument is brought forward with respect to high-skilled migrants' immediate family reunion rights and their exemption from language proficiency requirements, some policy makers castigate this vision as unrealistic and unfair toward other migrant groups in Germany (German

Statements on "Earned" Migration and Labor Market Participation

> Statement 1 (S1): [talking about job offer requirement as selection mechanism] "I mean, work is the utmost and first priority and essential also with regard to integration capacities." (German Labor Ministry official)
>
> S2: "Indeed, work is one of the most crucial paths to integration. This is why it is always underpinning labor migration management." (German employers representative)
>
> S3: "The philosophy of Minister X [former Labor and Social Affairs Minister] was that those who have been here many years should be able to stay and not be restricted in their labor market access.... Because if they stay it makes sense in terms of humanitarian and labor market policy concerns to say: if they are willing to integrate in the labor market, they should have an option to do so, and who succeeds in maintaining their own living should have a residence rights perspective. Especially since we will need workers." (German Labor Ministry official)

Federal Migration Office official, German policy advisor). Irrespective of that critique, the logic of societal integration via labor market participation constitutes an omnipresent subtext in German labor migration governance co-shaping the selection and classification of "legal" migrant workers.

The functional link between work and equivalent social and residence rights also accounts for the comparative weight of domestically acquired skills in German regulation. In recognition of their already demonstrated professional and educational integration, *Bildungsinländer*[1] can access the labor market without RLMT or shortage assessment: "Achieving a German educational degree means a demonstration of your integration capacities" (German Home Office official). Hence, selection by origin of qualifications does not just shield the German VET system against foreign competition; it is also part of a socio-civic integration imaginary in which domestic skills acquisition opens a viable pathway toward socio-economic inclusion (more detailed analysis in Kaiser and Paul 2011).

As statement S3 indicates, the narrative of earned migration also matters with regard to ex-post regularizations of foreign residents. Most importantly, the retrospective acknowledgement of education and employment achievements as integration success structures the—meager but available—access to more stable residence rights for *Geduldete*. Policy makers overwhelmingly request a settlement perspective for semi-legal residents who have acquired a German qualification or worked and contributed to social insurance consecutively for two years. They share the opinion that those who are successfully integrated in the labor market should benefit in terms of residence rights, not least with regard to the perceived need of skilled workers for demographic reasons. In the case of *Geduldete,* eventually, an otherwise quite restricted group of migrant-residents is cautiously drawn into the logic of the national skilled shortages imaginary and can thereby improve their residence status. However, research shows that these paths to "legality" are burdensome and often unpromising for "rightless" undocumented migrants in Germany, unless—and this is often not the case—they manage to mobilize, gain public support, and "voice" their concerns at politically salient moments and in targeted ways (Schwenken 2006, forthcoming).

All this boils down to a German discursive obsession with work (and VET training is considered a relevant part of it) as the prime pathway to obtaining—and "deserving"—all thinkable other sets of rights. Most striking is probably the notion that proven labor market or educational integration by semi-legal residents can trump formal lack of legal status. The analysis of the German case shows that the Bismarckian welfare state can serve as a veritable linchpin in labor admission policies. The equivalence between social insurance contributions and welfare entitlements is strongly utilized to create a pathway of socio-economic integration for migrants both ex-ante and ex-post their initial entry, with earned migration and earned integration coexisting. Certainly, not only in Germany is work seen as a prime pathway for migrants to obtaining—and "deserving"—other sets of rights. Yet, a comparison with the French case in particular will demonstrate that in the German case Bismarckian entitlement and status differentiation logics coincide more smoothly with economically selective labor admission policies—just as Diane Sainsbury (2006) claims (more in Paul 2012b).

The central role of Bismarckian entitlement logics as means of selecting legal migrant workers bears at least three implications for border drawing in the German case. Firstly, ex-post labor admissions of some residents adversely affect new TCN admissions: *Geduldete* and new applicants might compete for the same shortage jobs in which case preference is given to residents even where "just" *geduldet*. Their domestic skills acquisition and work experience incorporates even unauthorized foreign residents into the domestic labor pool, thereby limiting entry options below the high-skilled level for all other TCN workers. Detention and migration control policies are traded off with labor migration and integration policies; the skilled national labor shortage perception can trump other concerns and even pave pathways to social inclusion and formal residence.

Secondly, the design of admission policies alongside migrants' anticipated or actually demonstrated social insurance contributions sharply departs from the guest worker mentality that governed policies until recently. Most interviewees directly refer to this heritage when contextualizing current policies, speaking of "lessons learned" and the need to anticipate and utilize dominant pathways of inclusion and settlement in the selection of suitable migrant workers. Lastly, and connected to the above, we witness a colonization of the German citizenship model with notions of earned integration. On the one hand, anticipated integration through work and social insurance contribution is pivotal for first entry and admission in an earned migration scheme. On the other hand, several interviewees highlight that work has also become the most dominant domain of societal inclusion for ethnic Germans (see Kaiser and Paul 2011). Eventually, the policy legacy of ethnic selectivity is recontextualized in a socio-economic border-drawing logic according to which skill level, labor scarcity, anticipated welfare contribution, and socio-economic integration outlook matter more than consanguinity.

Continuous Raison d'État: Labor Migration Policy as European Geopolitics

Despite transitional drawbacks on encompassing EU citizenship and free movement for nationals of accession country, selectivity by European descent continues to be crucial in German labor migration regulation. This is justified by interviewees with references to EU free movement and the vision of a geographically expandable European labor pool. Certainly this vision powerfully structures the economic imaginary of lower skilled EU labor self-sufficiency (chapter 5), just as in the other two cases. Yet there is a considerable German tweak to this. Interview data suggests that migrants' classification by wider European origin pursues an influential policy imperative of maintaining and increasing Germany's geopolitical rootedness in the expanding European economy and labor market. With trade interests further underpinning this normative support of the European project, the historical Europeanness of German labor recruitment lives on in the present as a veritable raison d'état.

Statements on Ideational Scope and Limits of European Labor Market Integration

> S4: "Well, forget about bilateral agreements! They had grown historically.... Recruitment agreements will then [once free movement is established] no longer be interesting in terms of the legal provisions for foreign workers, but as an issue of EU-wide job placement.... This is eventually no longer a matter of migration, but a regular placement issue.... [A future focus is] that we don't just have free movement but actually practice it. Well, the Brits offered a nice example, wanting to send the Portuguese back home and stuff. Now, quite a big mentality change still lies ahead of us in order to become Europeans. This is why migration from third countries is just not topical for me." (German Labor Ministry official)
>
> S5: "Concerning TCN we don't experience—how shall I put it?—any specific pressure at our external borders.... We have no colonies that are still on our back historically; I'd say we are relatively unencumbered in that respect." (German Labor Ministry official)

Interviewees in the German Labor Ministry, for instance, recall the deliberate extension of the EU reference labor market to accession candidates as a chief strategy that has piloted free movement with these countries all whilst controlling TCN labor flows. Moreover, frequent ideational references in interviews to "our" obligation to become "true" Europeans before envisaging other foreign labor recruitment options (see S4–5, in representation of similar statements by other interviewees) carve out the Eurocentric contours of German policy design. This focuses on creating more synergies between the EU internal workforce (extended to accession candidates), the needs of the national economies, and identity formation processes among European workers, employers, and politicians alike. German labor migration policy does not merely refer to EU free movement as a natural barrier to TCN admissions in the third economic imaginary, but, unlike France and the United Kingdom, also contextualizes contemporary TCN recruitment within the *prospect* of free movement by means of selective recruitment agreements with accession candidates.

Impulses of labor market protection within the European Union are criticized, and interviewees highlight the necessity to advance a genuine European identity with regard to internal labor exchanges. This discourse might seem hypocritical in a context where transitional limitations were imposed on Eastern Europeans post 2004 and levels of EU-8 migration remained low, especially compared to Britain. This caution might indeed explain a more relaxed attitude to EU free movement: in light of relatively small entry figures, German policy makers do not seem to perceive similar "pressures" on public services, which underpins the British closure reaction. Indeed the very notion of "pressure" does not feature in any of the German interviews at all.[2]

As evidenced in chapter 3 the European origin of many of Germany's foreign workers, with one of the highest contemporary shares of fellow EU workers in the EU-15 (Eurostat 2011a), is entrenched in past policies. Categorized as a colonial "have-not" in the citizenship regime literature (Howard 2009) Germany can seemingly afford a relatively straightforward and rather uncontested Eurocentrism in labor migration policies (S5). Conceiving of no struggles over national belonging related to a former Empire—and not least finally featuring a geographical position without external EU borders—interviewed policy makers feel free to apply an ethno-utilitarian approach in which, some highly-skilled migrant workers apart, a worker's origin from within wider Europe becomes the default admission criterion.

Peo Hansen and Stefan Jonsson's (2012: 1035) historical account of German motivations for joining the European project in the 1950s suggests yet another interpretation: "Although a non-imperial state, West Germany ... showed itself very eager to reap imperial benefits via other means—that is, via European integration." Just as in the early days of the Union, by integrating in a European economy, labor market and polity German policy makers pursue geopolitical goals in contemporary migration management. Indeed, economic openness toward EU neighboring countries and accession candidates features not only as an economic tool for labor supply and trade relations, but as a vital security strategy. With specific reference to the example of a bilateral agreement with Turkey (Bundesrepublik Deutschland 1980), interviewees highlight the geopolitical significance of labor migration policies. Long before the "Islamic State" troubles the region, they allude to Turkey as a buffer zone to the Middle East within NATO and claim that beneficial treatment with regard to labor admissions has to be understood in this geopolitical context (German policy advisor).

In the absence of prevailing post-colonial ties and a decreasing relevance of ethnic German selectivity, the German instinctive response to labor shortages seems to be just what it has been in the past: to turn to its geographical backyards before recruiting from elsewhere. While common German descent has lost its importance in civic border drawing, the positive discrimination of workers from the European Union and wider Europe is a prevailing pattern of selection by origin. It solidifies reduced entry options for most non-European TCN, especially those not fortunate enough to fulfill the requirements for high-skilled admissions, and suggests that an ethnocentric model of belonging has not been abandoned but expanded to include nationals of the enlarging European Union and part of its immediate neighborhood.

Socio-Cultural Cohesion Concerns: Ethnic Recruitment through the Backdoor

The definition of economically useful and socio-culturally "acceptable" migrant workers might not always coincide, not even in the realms of high-skilled migration. Some German policy makers—interestingly enough all affiliated with the Home Office—evoke ethno-cultural recruitment hierarchies that reach beyond the usual European boundaries of belonging. They justify why nationals of some rich countries[3] are treated more favorably than other TCN (chapter 4) as follows: easier access builds on the anticipated higher integration capacities of these nationals and their expected willingness to return to their countries of origin.

Interviewees introduce a reasoning of cultural otherness when contrasting "unobtrusive" Japanese with migrant communities whose customs, values, and beliefs supposedly cause more concern (S7). This specific policy maker depicts especially Turkish and Arab communities as sources of trouble and relates alleged "problems" to their low educational attainment, but also to their particular cultural and religious practices. This discussion mirrors Germany's ongoing struggle to integrate a large, predominantly Turkish, second- and third-generation resident population emerging from unexpected guest worker

Statements on Hierarchies of Socially and Culturally Acceptable Migrant Workers

> S6: [asked why privileged labor market access is given to some OECD nationals] "Well, the reason for this simply is that we did not have any problems with these nationals in terms of residence provisions in the past thirty, forty years. We don't have any return issues with New Zealand, Australia, or especially the US. That is quite different for many [other] countries.... Under the heading of residence provisions we simply don't experience any problems with Japan. Hence we can be quite generous." (German Home Office official)
>
> S7: "The Japanese come for economic reasons. They are also valuable for our country in terms of trade relations.... We don't have any integration problems with them. Indeed, they remain Japanese, but are unobtrusive. I would not know of any problems we ever had with Japanese people, causing riots, destroying windows, or walking around in headgears that we have a problem with, or building flamboyant Shinto temples. The Japanese are no problem. But their numbers are quite limited as well." (German Home Office official)

settlement. While former guest workers of European origin (mainly Italians and Greeks) are drawn into policy makers' vision of an integrating EU workforce, descendants of Turkish guest workers fall behind nationals of richer (or what could also be viewed as culturally more similar) nations in recruitment hierarchies. Where these workers cannot present high-flying professional skills portfolios, they predominantly surface as objects of migration control and integration efforts.

Japanese workers seem more acceptable precisely because they are fewer in number, especially compared to Turks who still form the major migrant group in Germany (chapter 3). This addresses otherwise silenced (especially in the Labor- and Economy-related divisions of government) social cohesion concerns. For a leading Home Office official, the question of social cohesion is pressing not least because racist tendencies in the "German" population might develop into wider-spread social unrest that does not only target incoming workers but also the settled and often German-born resident population. The recent scandalous unearthing of racially motivated killings effectuated throughout the 2000s by the right-extremist cell NSU seems to confirm this fear in a miserable way.

Lastly, economic utility and social acceptance interact in both directions, as the emphasis of trade relations with Japan by one policy maker shows. A migrant's origin closely relates not only to their anticipated integration potential and socio-cultural acceptability, but also their likelihood to fit into the global labor and knowledge exchange model tailored within the first economic imaginary. The focus on competitiveness in the high-skilled realm of legal labor migration is thus likely to reinforce the division into a rich global North and a poorer South. The preference of domestic skills exacerbates this dynamic, for who, on average, is able to access a university education in Germany or attend a German school abroad and will subsequently benefit from labor market access? In 2011 the German Academic Exchange Service counted more than a quarter of a million foreign students at German universities for the first time, with the main nationalities being Chinese, Russian, Bulgarian, Polish, and Austrian (DAAD 2012).

In addition, the embeddedness of most German recruitment within a European labor pool and the country's lack of colonial heritage create a comparatively weak incident to "deal with" perceived obligations toward extra-EU sending countries (see S6–7) or indeed "poverty migration from Africa" (German Home Office official). The analysis of France and the United Kingdom will show that post-colonial legacies of labor migration set very different tones for the selection of migrant workers by origin.

Managing Post-Colonialism, Irregular Workers, and EU Integration in France

French labor migration policy mapping found that post-colonial relationships structure entry routes, especially with bilateral migration management agreements and special provisions for Algerian nationals. Unlike in Germany, country of origin selectivity does not only apply for skilled and lower-skilled routes, but quotas for particular sending countries operate within the high-skilled routes as well. Interviewees predominantly contextualize selection by origin in a post-colonial setting. According to interview data, the promotion of economic selectivity in *immigration choisie* and the operation of by-origin admission schemes evidence the political attempt to manage and recast post-colonial labor routes and to renegotiate an inclusive Republican citizenship model:

> (1) In combination with country-specific admission conditions for workers from former colonies, the *"immigration choisie"* agenda signals a general disinclination to accommodate and integrate a large post-colonial resident population, with a tendency of overwriting inclusive civic citizenship norms.

> (2) Policies utilize EU free movement and differential shortage recruitment to manage and contain unauthorized *sans papiers* workers in the French labor market, with most of these workers again originating from former colonies. Cautious regularizations are accompanied by tough control rhetoric and entry restrictions elsewhere due to a perceived lock-in in a policy (and electoral) discourse of "zero immigration."

"Immigration Choisie" *as Post-Colonial Population Management*

Post-colonial relationships are omnipresent in French regulation as well as interviewees' accounts of policy. Most notably, French bilateral agreements serve different functions and rhetorical underpinnings than those used in Germany. The latter have been interpreted as cautious political and economic deepening of the European project. By contrast, interviewees construe the French *accords de gestion* as policy tools that control the resident population, including those with unauthorized status, and restructure post-colonial relationships.

Statements S8–11 are representative of the discursive layers within this debate, and equally mirror the strong political contestation over post-colonial relationships, which is in stark contrast to the United Kingdom, as the next section will show. The first statement (S8) offers a wider contextualization of migration policies within French colonial history and current foreign policy. It indicates that struggles over the legitimate role of post-colonial descendants in the country's labor market, welfare state, and society are ongoing and thus underpin a large part of the contemporary French labor migration management approach.

Statements on Post-Colonial Population Management and Labor Migration Selectivity

> S8: "France ... sees itself as a former empire, which possessed grandeur and has lost its grandeur.... And so it happens that migrants are, to a considerable part, nationals from our old colonies. Eventually, there is this connotation of a somewhat ambiguous figure of a migrant who is, at the same time, the one we colonized and who tried to resist, who wanted his independence, and the one who now comes here and steals our work, steals our women, steals our bread, steals our social security system, steals everything." (French policy advisor)
>
> S9: "Well, the only country that we would love to come to an agreement with is Mali, as this is the country that generates most illegal flows in France. It is the only country so far with which we have not been able to compromise." (French Migration Ministry official)
>
> S10: "The government says: we have to limit family migration which ... grants labor market access, but is not 'chosen' migration in terms of our labor market needs. That means that we might have people here who are not qualified, ... at least their qualifications are not selected according to employers' needs." (French employers' representative)
>
> S11: [talking about "*immigration professionnelle*" agenda] "When stating 'but we need these people and all', what is also implied is that those who we do not need, they can go back home. And the main target, or increasingly so, ... are citizens.... We talk of 'citizens' because these are people on the pathway to becoming French!" (French trade unionist)

The government officially promotes the *accords de gestion* as codevelopment tools that enable close economic and political cooperation with sending countries that are developing countries, many of which former French colonies (Le Président de la République and Le Premier Ministre 2009). French development aid to these countries does not come for free, but it is contingent on their commitment to facilitate repatriation of their nationals, and to strictly control their borders and avoid unauthorized entries to France. This control rationale is explicit in the remark of one official who highlights the necessity to negotiate an agreement with Mali as one of the biggest sources of undocumented migration (S9).

This means that labor admission policies on the one hand, and control targets with regard to current and prospective unauthorized residents from former colonies on the other hand are strongly conflated in *"immigration choisie."* Critiques argue that bilateral agreements thus represent a continuation of French colonial domination with other means (French trade unionist, French policy advisor), a claim that has recently been elaborated in a critical historical analysis of wider European policy making as well (P. Hansen and Jonsson 2011).

With regard to bilateral migration management agreements, several policy makers further argue that labor admission policies are no genuine recruitment tools in response to economic demands or shortages but control tools that target the post-colonial resident population (S10–11).

Research on so-called migration partnerships has shown how policy agendas of economic recruitment, migration control, trade, and development policies are being conflated; mostly of course with a dominance of the richer labor receiving countries in the global North (Kuntz 2013). In France, policy targets of increasing "selected" labor inflows and simultaneously reducing family entries are not coincidentally coupled in "partnership" agreements with former colonies. Several interviewees argue that discourses of economic selectivity carry signaling functions vis-à-vis post-colonial residents, especially family members: they have not been "chosen" according to economic needs and are hence not desired. Several interviewees see family reunion rights and traditionally inclusive settlement and citizenship paths as being symbolically revoked with the promotion of economic selectivity by skill level and labor scarcity in contemporary French labor migration management. The official guideline of limiting family entries while boosting professional migration as well as concomitant cutbacks of the right of other migrant groups (asylum seekers and family members mainly) further evidence this claim (chapter 4).

The statement by a trade unionist at the beginning of this chapter indicates that post-colonial population management is being further conflated with public order and social cohesion issues in the context of the 2005 *banlieue* riots, but also terrorism and international conflicts. The intermeshing of economic selectivity and post-colonial migration management imposes economic *and* ethno-cultural hierarchies of migrant worker acceptability. We find in this a continuation of the historical pattern of selecting guest workers "à la carte" (Spire 2005). Indeed, the increased conditionality of TCN admissions with regard to professional skills and the specifically targeted control of some nationals in bilateral agreements establishes a policy logic that delegitimizes the position of lower-skilled workers from former colonies as legitimate workers on the French labor market, often with the consequence of pushing them into irregularity and precariousness (Morice 1996; Morice and Potot 2010). With the former colonies happening to be in (Muslim) North Africa and (black) Sub-Saharan Africa, ethno-cultural sorting effects are inherent to French by-origin recruitment.

The amalgamation of post-colonial population management and "choosing" migrant workers on economic utility grounds is further supported in French integration policies. Not dissimilarly to the German debate, integration prospects for high-skilled workers are considered to be extraordinarily high. While "ordinary" migrant workers and their family members need to proof their willingness and capacity to assimilate (signing of *CAI*, language classes) and their integration progress is subsequently monitored, policy makers believe that high-skilled individuals "will integrate without difficulties in our country" even where they don't speak French initially (French Migration Ministry official). Migrants with high professional qualifications are welcome not just for the economic benefits their recruitment is believed to bring to the French national economy. They are also considered as easy to integrate new members of the French society. This is very much in contrast to the treatment of other migrant residents and citizens of post-colonial descent whose economic utility and societal integration potential are questioned (chapter 3).

In light of this differential treatment it might seem hypocritical when leading French policy makers officially resent the "selective mechanisms" of a points-based system as a serious violation of "Republican equity principles" (French Migration Ministry official). The ongoing political debate about the legitimacy of selecting migrant workers by economic utility and origin thus mirrors both France's difficulty "to be in harmony with its Republican logic" (French trade unionist) and its uneasiness in overwriting inclusive civic citizenship norms.

Shortage Lists and Cautious Regularizations: Managing the Irregular Workforce

A second main theme in French socio-civic border drawing concerns the governance of the unauthorized workforce, again overwhelmingly of post-colonial origin (chapter 3), through shortage recruitment and exceptional regularizations. This might be most obvious in the operation of two different shortage lists for EU workers and TCN migrants. Remember that the former list admits individuals into more than 290 professions of all skill levels, also lower ones, but the latter has been limited to 14 exclusively higher skilled jobs. Policy makers rhetorically draw on the different economic imaginaries discussed in chapter 5 to forge a regulatory containment of unauthorized migrant labor: it cannot be legalized in the lower-skilled segments of the labor market in which EU-internal self-sufficiency applies. Within this logic we observe an affirmative rhetoric around phasing-in free movement for new member-state nationals in the context of shortage lists. Initial fears over the substitution effects of EU-8 migration for domestic workers, severe enough to have informed transitional restrictions for Eastern European mobility, have seemingly vanished: "We no longer roll on the ground[4] when thinking of the Polish plumber" (French Migration Ministry official). Instead, the perception of EU workers as part of "us" seemingly triumphs as their gradual integration is considered "*logique*" and free movement represents an increasingly uncontested part of European market making (French Migration Office official). As in Germany, the lower-skilled EU labor self-sufficiency imaginary is hence underpinned by a political imperative of actively forging a veritable European labor market.

The de jure preference of EU workers in low-skilled labor market segments, precisely those segments de factor often catered with inform TCN workers, further works to contain the irregular workforce. The regulatory concern with high-skilled professions on the TCN shortage list has been criticized as an "administrative joke" (French policy advisor). This criticism relates not so much to strenuous entry conditions for newcomers—it is certainly hard for migrants from the global South the fulfill qualification requirements for the fourteen high-skilled professions—but refers to the salience of irregularity in the French case (see chapter 3).

The simultaneous courting of high-skilled TCN workers *and* relying on EU workers for lower-skilled jobs challenges traditional labor ties with former colonies and labor market realities. Indeed, when rumors about potential case-by-case regularization surfaced in 2007, especially NGO advocates and trade unionists had hoped for an encompassing list that reflects the often low-skilled and low-pay employment conditions of many unauthorized TCN workers in France: "As if in the high circles of power they did not know what everybody knows, that numerous *sans-papiers* in France are employed on the most ingrate construction sites, as dishwashers in restaurant kitchens, or to clean car parks in the night" (Carrère 2008, translation from French: R.P.).

Statements on Managing the Irregular Workforce

> S12: "Well, we recognize that there should be a regularization of a certain number of irregular workers who have been in France for a certain time, generally 5 years, under the condition that they have a preceding work contract, that they will have a new contract for the future, and under the condition that their employer has respected social rights [*le droit social*].... We tend not to forget if someone has breached social rights norms.... Our principle is that we can adapt to realities, and the reality is that the labor force is partly a foreign labor force, even in irregular situation, but ... we do not accept social dumping." (French Migration Ministry official)
>
> S13: [talking about unauthorized workers and links to "*immigration choisie*" approach] "In this context, we enter sectors that are not at all 'high potential.' We enter the cleaning sector, we enter difficult professions filled by the migration population. It has always been like that; since the first [migration] waves in the 1960s it was about filling positions that no-one wanted to take, in kitchens, in cleaning, in jobs that are rarely full time.... Eventually, the policy of attractiveness in terms of professional migration is actually challenged by the regularization policies for *sans-papiers*." (French Employment Agency official)
>
> S14: "Part of the discourse is about demonstrating to the French: 'we manage, we won't have a big regularization, ... we will attract the qualified workforce we need.' Because if you explain to the French that the workforce you need and ... that you will legalize, are kitchen-assistants, masons and construction workers ... , the French will say to themselves: 'well, ... you have told me for decades that migration is dangerous, that migrants steal our jobs; and at the same time these people already work in these sectors for years, they keep these sectors going ... and that we need to regularize them; what is this mess?'" (French policy advisor)

Critical readings therefore suggest that the French labor shortage recruitment strategy, with its emphasis on EU free movers, contradicts labor market realities, therefore contains lower-skilled migrant workers in precarious unauthorized work and residence situations, and eventually sustains cheap labor availabilities (Anderson 2010; Morice 1996; Morice and Potot 2010; Terray 1999).

It should have become clear from the above that in French shortage regularization policies the borders between inclusion and exclusion are ambiguous and partly contradictory. On a positive note, a notion of "earned" integration surfaces in this context, just as in Germany. Policy makers feel that someone who integrated into the labor market under certain conditions deserves a secure residence status, thus justifying the policy tool of exceptional regularization via shortage lists jobs (S12).

The quest against migrant irregularity hence interacts with the economic imaginary of national skilled labor shortages, creating the potential of releasing merited "illegal" skilled workers from the insecure work and resident spaces to which they are otherwise confined. However, ex-post regularizations come with significant limits. They operate on a strict case-by-case basis and are subject to the discretion of local government. This means that the economic utility logic does not make a general case for regularization, but that ex-post shortage recruitment of unauthorized workers remains a highly arbitrary and politically filtered endeavor. As such, it represents another layer in a highly asymmetric post-colonial migration management "partnership": while sending countries ought to agree to enable repatriation and control emigration, France reserves itself plenty of room for maneuver and discretion in the selective admission of migrant workers from its former colonies (see also P. Hansen and Jonsson 2011).

Further, any employment to be regularized has to abide by French *droit social,* the social norms regulating working hours, wages, and other labor rights. Unlike the United Kingdom, but similarly to Germany, France legally distinguishes between unauthorized migrant residence and informal migrant employment. In a comparatively strong political tradition of protecting workers' rights and preventing "social dumping," French migration control has tended to be tougher on informal sub-standard employment than on unauthorized residence. This means that the Bismarckian welfare state can trigger inclusive effects for those paying social insurance contributions in work, even where their residence is irregular. Yet, and once more, the *droit social* clause triggers uneven effects for workers of different skill levels: as in Germany, the often unrealistic prerequisite of law-abiding employment is likely to render those at the lower skill, lower pay, and more precarious ends of the labor market ineligible for regularizations. Distinction by skill level hence strongly continues to shape the treatment of unauthorized workers. Critiques argue that ex-post shortage regularization is no genuine escape from irregularity, but has the potential to confine the often post-colonial unauthorized working population to low-skilled jobs in precarious spaces of both the labor market and society (French policy advisor; Morice and Potot 2010).

Regularization policies are further contextualized in what interviewees describe as a historical path-dependency on "zero immigration." Some argue that the liberalization of admissions since 2006 has been "hard to communicate" in France even when highly skilled workers were targeted (French Migration Office official). Policy makers perceive a historical lock-in in rhetoric of closure and control since the 1970s and argue that this has rendered both active recruitment and regularization practices politically incredible (see S12–14). The notional misrecognition of informal labor market realities in shortage recruitment practices is explained in this context. Regardless of more liberal implementation practices, the official message sent out to the French population, for decades now, has been: we don't need foreign workers, especially not in lower-skilled segments of the labor market (S13).

While employers and policy makers might recognize that domestic unemployment and labor shortages in lower-skilled jobs continue to coexist and render recruitment necessary (French Employers' representative), this reality is being disguised by the current admission policy approach. Government officials confirm that the creation of a "public immigration policy" and the policy rhetoric of "management" are partly fueled by the intent of claiming back territory from the Front National with symbolic policies (French Migration Ministry official; see chapter 3). Electoral politics seem to entail severe limits for merely economically driven labor migration border drawing, even where the policy labels of "*immigration professionnelle*" and "*immigration choisie*" suggest otherwise. Against the backdrop of an incessantly relevant irregular labor pool from which many shortage jobs could be readily filled, the genuine economic intentions and effects of a "professional immigration" policy seem questionable.

Overall then, the socio-civic signaling and classification effects of *immigration choisie* toward post-colonial residents, unauthorized workers, and, not to forget: the French electorate, seriously curb the economic logics of labor migration border drawing. Instead of "just" signaling openness to workers who hold specific skill levels and profiles, both the regulatory arrangement and policy justifications by interviewees highlight non-openness to all other flows. More than that, resident workers who hold seemingly suitable skills profiles might be rejected due to their origin. The lack of a severe demographic "pressure" scenario comparable to Germany further substantiates the claim that demand of workers serves, partially at least, as a window dressing for other governance aims in France—that is, post-colonial population and management of a large unauthorized migrant workforce.

Managing Desired and Adverse Effects of EU Mobility in Post-Colonial Britain

Unlike the other two countries, the United Kingdom does not select TCN workers by origin directly in bilateral agreements. However, the current design of the PBS and overwhelming reliance on the EU labor pool features important by-origin classification effects. Far from just mirroring a common self-sufficiency claim across our three cases in the lower-skilled labor market segments, the dedication of the New Labour government to virtually unlimited EU free movement from 2004 has shaped virtually all subsequent TCN admission decisions. Contemporary British labor migration border drawing has been forged in the context of high numbers of Eastern European inflows, comparatively high net migration figures,[5] and a strong saliency of the topic in the 2010 general elections. Border-drawing mechanisms and justifications in the socio-civic realms fall into three closely related categories:

(1) The promotion of EU free movement is seen to justify restrictions for TCN workers. It further gradually substitutes post-colonial labor ties and represents a continuation of silent detachment from the former Empire.

(2) At the same time, the preference of EU free movers in skilled and lower-skilled jobs is contested as adverse effects on public services are associated with high entry figures.

(3) The lack of control over EU entries, lastly, justifies even more restrictions for TCN workers. Annual caps, most importantly, are seen as an attempt to appease a seemingly hostile public opinion and create a perception of control. Eventually, economic border drawing in the United Kingdom strongly intersects with the perceived "pressure" on public services caused by substantial EU inflows, and respective electoral "responses" to public opinion since 2010.

Desired EU Mobility Effects: (Silently) Substituting Post-Colonial Labor Ties

In sharp contrast to the French case, British policy makers do not express labor selectivity in terms of post-colonial population control. The role of post-imperial obligations is astonishingly absent from British legislation and interviewees' narratives alike. This, however, does not preclude that the preference of EU mobility over traditional patterns of Commonwealth-internal recruitment features by-origin classification effects for TCN workers. High levels of EU labor mobility, especially from Poland, have started to re-compose the foreign workforce in the United Kingdom. As chapter 3 has shown the level of work permits issued to TCN stagnated at around 140,000 in the early 2000s and declined to around 120,000 in 2008. During a similar time span, the number of EU nationals on the UK labor market doubled to more than 1,300,000 in 2009 (Eurostat 2011; Salt 2009). Studies have shown that workers from former colonies are indeed being substituted by Eastern Europeans in sectors such as hospitality and catering (McDowell et al. 2009).

Some policy makers interpret Britain's liberal EU free movement approach as a deliberate attempt to invalidate post-colonial labor ties featuring "all sorts of unspoken levels of … racism" (S16). Obligations toward Commonwealth nationals have been a subject of parliamentary debate, with some Labour MPs perceiving the liberal approach toward EU-8 mobility as an illegitimate break with pre-established models of national belonging (House of Commons 2011). The endearing narrative of the Jamaican cricket supporter, which gave the present chapter its title, contests both the economy drive behind EU recruitment and the sheer disregard of cultural bonds with fellow Commonwealth nationals in the contemporary British migration management approach.

According to Linda McDowell (2009) and the above-cited policy maker, "whiteness" seemingly re-emerges as a marker of privilege for migrants in the contemporary British context. The question of whether post-colonial migration control is the genuine target or a by-product cannot be answered to satisfaction here, as too few interviewees engaged with this claim. The more important insight from a comparative interpretive policy analysis angle, however, is that even though policies seem to entail significant (restrictive) implications for migrant workers from former colonies in particular, racial or ethno-cultural implications are silenced in policy discourse and legislation itself.

Statements on Post-Colonial Detachment and EU Mobility

> S15: "I had a wonderful discussion a few years ago with a black workers group in one of our big unions, and he was talking about EU-8 migration, and they said what does this mean for the Commonwealth.... And this old Jamaican bloke says, about the Poles, he said 'they don't share lots of aspects of our culture,' and he got really worked up, and he said 'they don't even play cricket!' (*laughs*) 'What are we doing bringing people into the country who don't even play cricket?!'" (British trade unionist)
>
> S16: "Most of the people in our Empire were brown and black.... There is this element within the last government's policy of relying on EU-8 workers rather than bringing in more people from overseas, when most of those people from overseas are going to be brown and black, basically. So there is all sorts of unspoken levels of racism, basically." (British trade unionist)

Statements S15–16 represent a rather exceptional, albeit vocal and pointed, take on the meanings of post-colonialism within current migration policy making. The absence of a wider debate on these issues matters especially in comparison to France, where the engagement with post-colonial belonging as a meaningful part of labor migration policies has led to the design of policy tools that deliberately select (and un-select) non-EU migrant workers by origin. From an IPA perspective then, the interaction of labor migration management and economically driven EU free movement in the United Kingdom binds the realm of available policy meanings as to exclude any normative claims related to post-colonial belonging or citizenship despite the considerable relevance of these issues in practice (chapter 3). The general lack of a political discussion about the normative principles of British post-colonial citizenship—very much in contrast to the highly politicized French case—further confirms Adrian Favell's (2001: 99) description of the British integration philosophy as "a thoroughly functionalist teleology." Policy making seems to stick to pragmatic, evolutionary responses to emerging integration problems.

We further need to bear in mind that classification by skill level and by origin interact, also in the British case: higher professional qualifications de jure render an individual migrant more independent from their country of origin. Indeed, a high-skilled tier 1 worker from a former British colony—even if "brown and black"—does not face the same restrictive admission practices as their lower-skilled worker compatriots. Eventually any ethnicized recruitment effect, as it is suggested here, is likely to apply unevenly across migrant workers' skill levels.

Adverse EU Mobility Effects: Limiting "Pressure" on Public Services

A majority of interviewees further suggests that high levels of post-2004 EU mobility, and especially the fear of "pressure" on the social infrastructure, have provoked the recent retreat to control-biased labor migration policies. Adverse EU free movement effects, potentially amplified by the economic crisis since 2009, play a crucial role in policy makers' justifications for recent restrictions to tier 1 and 2 admissions as well as for the introduction of annual caps in 2010–2011. This justification demonstrates the limited reach of the economic benefits argument around EU free movement when it meets societal concerns and the restrictive structural consequences of perceived adverse effects of EU mobility for labor migration management.

More precisely, the control impulse is believed to have led to a redesign of the initially liberal approach to EU migration and, by extension, has formed an argumentative basis for further limiting TCN routes. Despite the positive fiscal effects of EU free movement (Dustmann et al. 2010), which all interviewees mention appreciatively, concern about EU-8 migrants' impact on the public infrastructure and its funding has grown.

Statements on EU Mobility as "Pressure" on Public Services

> S17: "Where there was an effect which I think took a while to appreciate, was on the public services side, and that's behind some of the decisions about Bulgaria and Romania.... Things like education funding for schools flowing through six to twelve months later, things to do with health.... If you've got Peterborough—I'm sorry to say Peterborough because everybody uses Peterborough—a town in East Anglia, you've suddenly got a lot of pressure on local services and not a lot of cash around." (British employers' representative)
>
> S18: "It also had adverse side effects, so in the East of England, for instance, Norwich, let's say, East Anglia. They considered themselves to be swamped by Polish people and all this coming and going with impacts on the local infrastructure." (UK Border Agency official)

Statements S17–18 portray to a scenario of pressure due to unexpectedly high EU-8 mobility to Britain. "Adverse effects" of an otherwise economically beneficial approach to EU mobility are construed especially for schooling and housing. Some rely on sheer quantities to convey the pressure scenario, while others also highlight qualitative elements such as foreign pupils' insufficient language proficiency. EU mobility then seems to inform wider concerns about socio-cultural cohesion, integration capacities—as in "being swamped by Polish people"—on the British population. This is in contrast, of course, to the EU's vision of free movement and equal treatment as a right of any EU national anywhere on the Union's territory; a right that cannot be curbed by integration requirements. In an immediate response to the surfacing of pressure perceptions, the New Labour government, in 2007, imposed stricter entry conditions on Bulgarians and Romanians.

Caveats to EU mobility apart, the perception of pressure on public services has predominantly echoed in TCN labor migration management. Be it the closure of the sector-based recruitment scheme for lower skilled jobs to all TCN in 2005, the change to qualification requirements (from vocational training to graduate level only) for a tier 2 permit in 2011, or the suspension of tier 3: the notion of migration pressure—though mainly caused by sudden and high increases of EU-internal migrations to the United Kingdom—has severely limited employers' scope for labor recruitment from outside the EU. This means that the liberal treatment of EU free movers has provoked a double control backlash against TCN workers: firstly, when the promotion of unlimited EU-8 flows coincided with the decision to completely suspend low-skilled TCN migration; and a second time when the scenario of pressure on the public infrastructure due to EU-8 migration has been diverted to TCN entries since 2010.

Public Opinion, Electoral Politics, and Symbolic Control

The perceived adverse effects of EU free movement stood at the cradle of the recent revival of control-biased labor migration policies in 2010. Policy makers overwhelmingly agree upon the relevance of the Conservative Party's electoral promise to cut back net migration rates "to the tens of thousands" when justifying the recent restrictions (see S19–21). A senior policy advisor suggests, for example, that the change of government in 2010 has brought about a major ideational shift in labor migration policies, with the pendulum swinging back, once more, from economic laissez-faire to tough controls and the reduction of migrant entries "by hook or by crook" (S19).

Most interviewees seem skeptical of the extent to which caps on labor entry routes are currently seized as the main tool to bring down overall net migration. Numerical limits apply mainly to tiers 1 and 2 (general), while the ICT route, entrepreneurs, working holidaymakers, but also student and family reunion routes have so far[6] been excluded. Net migration rates also imply British emigration rates and EU free mover entries, both of which cannot be controlled by government policies. A report by the Migration Advisory Committee (MAC 2010a) on the design of annual caps has highlighted that tiers 1 and 2 account for only 11 percent of entries or around 50,000 newcomers in 2009.

Statements on Public Opinion, Electoral Politics, and Symbolic Migration Control

> S19: "The Labour government very strongly believed in the economic benefits of labor immigration.... Now of course, with the numbers going up drastically, and with public opinion really being very strongly in favour of reducing immigration, to the end of the Labour government they really had to do something.... So when Blunkett said 'no limit,' the Tories immediately said 'the points-based system without a limit is pointless.'... So the concern now is all about numbers ... it's really about bringing overall net migration down, by hook or by crook." (British policy advisor)
>
> S20: [talking about economic utility of labor migration for Britain] "I think there's still an acceptance that that's correct and the government remains committed to attracting the brightest and the best. But, the country just doesn't have confidence that we're running the system in the way that they expect it to be run. So we also need to control numbers, in this case by limiting numbers.... The two can go together, it just means that you need to be more selective about the people who come in." (UK Border Agency official)
>
> S21: [talking about government's aim to cut back net migrants inflows to the "tens of thousands"] "They probably should have excluded EU-8 workers from their definition of migrants.... Polish workers tend to resent being referred to as migrants, they're just EU workers exercising their freedom. Unfortunately, the great unwashed public out there who have tendencies towards racism doesn't really pay that much attention to whether people are from within or outside the EU. So it probably wouldn't have helped them in terms of gaining votes, even if it would have made targets easier to actually achieve." (British trade unionist)

With overall non-EU inflows amounting to around 292,000 in 2009, it is difficult to imagine how the government's target of cutting net migration to "the tens of thousands" can be reached even if tier 1 and 2 were cut back to zero. The inclusion of EU nationals in the calculation of annual net migration challenges the EU mobility paradigm and creates a false impression of controllability of EU entries—probably in response to the perceived pressure scenario and increasingly hostile public opinion (S21). High levels of student and, to a lesser degree, family migration to the United Kingdom have also seemed less controllable (chapter 3). Taken together, the lack of control over some flows aggravates the need to cut back TCN labor flows even more in order to fulfill the "tens of thousands" landmark.

Some suggest that *actual* control might not be intended where public opinion is the prime target. A business representative points to the symbolic function of migration control that, irrespective of actual control leavers, makes "people feel" that migration is "well managed" (similar statement by a British policy advisor). While the third expert quoted (S21) seems confident that increased entry selectivity can reconcile economic growth objectives in labor migration policies and control aims, others are more skeptical about the virtues of "playing the numbers game."[7]

Most interviewees express some concern about putting high hurdles up against high-skilled and skilled labor migration in order to make up for the lack of control over other routes. They expect paradoxical effects when the public might not distinguish between EU and non-EU entries (S21) and might even be more willing to welcome skilled TCN workers than the Eastern European "agricultural guys in Lincolnshire" (British policy advisor). Even a Home Office official doesn't "believe that there is a substantial public concern about [TCN] migration people working for KPMG." Paradoxically, the annual caps on tiers 1 and 2 affect precisely these migrant workers most. Interviewees utter concern about potential detrimental effects of annual caps for business and the international competitiveness of the UK market location (cf., House of Commons 2011). Not only does the diverted control reaction—from EU free movers toward the controllable population of TCN workers—curtail the economic logics of global high-skilled labor competitiveness and skilled labor shortages described in chapter 5, it also sustains a deep policy paradox: control and reduction of net migration is notionally required to appease the public opinion, but control leavers are only available for the skilled and high-skilled segments of labor migration that are considered "useful" for economic growth and that "the public" allegedly does not even mind so much. The government seems stuck between either accepting negative consequences for the British economy[8] or letting go of the annual cap policy.

In all this, the sheer absence of consideration for the situation of unauthorized migrant workers is stunning. This is especially noticeable in comparison to France and Germany where, irrespective of much lower estimated levels of irregularity (chapter 3), the issue has gained a role on the center stage of labor migration policies—for better or worse—and triggered some cautious regulatory responses such as exceptional regularizations. The regulatory disconnection between labor migration and the fight against irregular migration as well as politicians' silence on the matter confirm the pattern of "willful negligence" (Wilkinson and Craig 2011) we have already come across in chapter 3. The UK case confirms assumptions about the bigger picture: as long as unauthorized workers "constitute key cogs in the EU's so hotly coveted flexible labor market" (P. Hansen 2010), "more barbwire," tough border control, annual caps, and creation of a "hostile environment"[9] for unauthorized migrants fulfill the job of sustaining exploitability and marginalization among Britain's large unauthorized workforce.

From a theoretical stance, the return to controlling borders and numbers in recent British migration policy history reflects some policy continuity. It seems that alongside the initial unlimited embracement of EU accession free movement in 2004, New Labour's decision to introduce a PBS with a welcoming undertone has broken uneasily with the control primacy in British migration policy that governed most of the second half of the twentieth century. The stereotypical trade-off between favorable anti-discrimination legislation and a sturdy border control dogma is confirmed in recent comparative studies (Huddleston and Niessen 2011). Overall then, the coalition government's recent reaffirmation of the core value of "immigration control"[10] signals the persistence of an "untouchable" and "inflexibly sacred" core of the British integration philosophy even a decade after Favell's (2001) original analysis.

Conclusion: National Socio-Cultural Filters for Economic Border Drawing

We have moved beyond the realm of shared economic border drawing and observed a lot of diversity of policy objectives and justifications within the social and civic dimensions. The analysis in this present chapter has shown that variegated societal policy contexts and migration legacies inform diverse socio-civic border-drawing rationalities in Germany, France, and the United Kingdom. This variety in border-drawing norms accounts for the nationally diverse classifications of migrant workers by origin, by domestically acquired skills, by anticipated integration and assimilation capacities, or with annual caps (table 6.1). Much more than in chapter 5, national context matters as an explanatory factor for policy variation in this chapter. In passing, this also reinforces the intricate value of a case-oriented comparative research design, namely the ability to explain more complex patterns of variation than variable-oriented studies (e.g., Della Porta 2008; Hantrais 1999).

The essential role of policy context might be most obvious in the example of the EU mobility regime as a structuring device for nationally distinct labor migration policies. While EU free movement plays the same chief role within the economic imaginary of EU labor self-sufficiency in lower-skilled segments as a natural(ized) barrier to TCN recruitment across all three cases (chapter 5), its specific part in socio-civic border drawing varies considerably. Germany's pan-European approach in most of its labor migration management—exemplified in specific shortage lists for nationals of accession candidate countries and those originating from the larger EU neighborhood—is part of a raison d'état of furthering the European project as a whole. This Eurocentric approach is directly linked to its position as colonial have-not (chapter 2). By contrast, French shortage recruitment explicitly contrasts EU-2 nationals—who are allowed to work in lower-skilled jobs—and unauthorized workers from former colonies who can only apply for regularization in higher-skilled shortage jobs, despite the fact that they often already cater the lower-skilled shortages into which France now keenly recruits Bulgarians and Romanians. Detachment from pre-established post-colonial labor ties was only one effect of EU mobility in the British case. The comparatively liberal approach to free movement after the Union's Eastern enlargement in 2004 has also entailed "adverse" affects and public hostility against levels of migration. Paradoxically then, high EU mobility stood at the cradle of restrictions toward TCN workers in the form of tougher entry requirements and the introduction of annual caps on tiers 1 and 2 (on these dynamics see also Paul 2013).

What does cross-national variation in social and civic border drawing add to our multidimensional comparative analysis of labor migration management? The interaction of a cross-nationally shared normative framework for economic border drawing with three diverse socio-civic classification schemes produces country-specific legality arrangements for migrant workers. As the shared utilitarian economic rationality is re-embedded in non-economic and distinctly national norms of belonging, the seemingly dominant economic selection criteria (skill level and scarcity of migrant workers' qualifications) are mitigated by social and cultural visions of legality. Overall then, migrant labor admission regimes come in complex flavors that mix a common utilitarian taste with nationally specific hints of sticky colonial histories, past migration experiences, societal cohesion norms and wider geopolitical agendas. Dominant dynamics of border drawing in each case can be summarized as follows:

In Germany, the perceived dire labor demands of the CME—especially of higher skill levels—are catered with entry mechanisms that anticipate the socio-economic integration logics of the Bismarckian welfare state. The Eurocentric geopolitics restricts the pool of potential benefiters of socio-economically "earned" migration to the wider boundaries of the prospective European Union and its immediate neighborhood.

French *immigration choisie* policies seek to establish economic selection principles as guiding logics in migrant admissions to signal desirability and undesirability far beyond the realm of work. The amalgamation of border drawing by economic utility and by origin from former colonies evidences the ongoing attempt of dissolving an inclusive post-colonial Republican citizenship model through labor migration management.

In the United Kingdom, social cohesion concerns, electoral politics, and tough border control aims—fueled by high levels of Eastern European mobility—seem to have muted the stereotypical economic openness to labor migration of a LME after the 2010 government change. The return to tough control, however, coincides with a glaring silence on continued post-colonial residence and migration. The official ignorance of the huge pool of unauthorized migrant workers in Britain further suggests that LME logics of cheap and flexible labor recruitment continue underground.

Overall then, the nationally distinct social and civic border-drawing logics interact with shared economic imaginaries of labor migration in unique ways. These unique interactions determine where the exact demarcation line between desired and undesired, acceptable and unacceptable, legal and illegal labor migration runs. They result in complex (but structured!) arrangements of migrant legality, which are at the same time (1) rationalized with a shared vision of economic competitiveness that often seems to be beyond contestation *and* (2) combined with socio-cultural clarifications of the exact conditions under and extent to which economic logics such as "shortage recruitment" or "skills supply" may, in fact, rule.

With economic explanations largely dominating the terrain of labor migration policy analysis hitherto (Caviedes 2010; Devitt 2012; Kolb 2010; Laubenthal 2012; Menz 2009, 2010a; Menz and Caviedes 2010b; to a lesser extent: Ruhs 2013), the ways in which the heterogeneity of social and civic-cultural border drawing shapes overall regulatory patterns and interacts with economic policy drivers have, thus forth, been frankly under the radar in most research. While the mentioned accounts would certainly acknowledge the limits to lower-skilled migration in socio-political policy rationales, they fail to clarify that social and civic border-drawing dynamics consistently challenge even the "best and brightest" narrative of labor migration that they so widely buy into. Here, the annual cap to "world-leading" specialists in the United Kingdom and "skills and talents" from Senegal or Gabon in France are just the most glaring examples. Received wisdom about tertiary qualifications and professional experience driving competitiveness and therefore provoking liberal reception in Western European economies proves to be empirically only partially valid. The biggest blind spot of orthodox labor migration policy analyses is potentially the continuation of ethnic admission hierarchies that, as the preceding analysis has brought to the fore, are mapped onto economic border-drawing principles.

Surprisingly often—at least when observed from the economy-drive perspective that has dominated many analyses hitherto—answers to the question which migrants can enter as "legal" workers are: "those who are economically useful *and* from countries X and Y" or "those filling a shortage *but not* originating from a former colony." The coexistence of similarities and differences in the norms and mechanisms guiding labor migration management is by no means a sign of chaos, but is part of a highly structured system that accentuates policy commonalities of the EU common market within the economic dimension *but* combines them with nationally specific migration control objectives in the social and civic dimensions of border drawing. When set against the ideal-typical benchmarks developed in chapter 2, border-drawing dynamics thus expose the relevance of and interactions between capitalist coordination systems, welfare state, and citizenship regimes in German, French, and British labor migration management and, eventually, inform a critical reappraisal of the value that regime theories can bring to the pursuit of comparative constitutive explanation.

Table 6.1. The Embedding of Labor Migration Policies in National Societal Contexts

Reference Points	Germany	France	United Kingdom
Welfare state	anticipation of socio-economic integration pathways in Bismarckian welfare state; ex-post civic integration for semi-legal residents is 'earned' through socio-economic integration	not emphasized but social contribution logics apply in legislation; ex-post admission of unauthorized workers as 'earned' integration; regularizations respect 'droit social'	surfaces as perceived adverse effects of EU-8 mobility ('pressure' on public services)
Citizenship model	'earned' socio-economic integration in labor migration overwrites ethnic belonging	labor migration policy as management of migrant resident population on pathway to citizenship; overriding of inclusive civic citizenship with economic selectivity logic	not emphasized; seemingly pragmatic and depoliticized approach to citizenship; silent gradual overwriting of inclusive norms with economic and numerical selectivity
Migration history	'lessons learned' from guest worker period justify anticipation of migrant workers' socio-economic integration potential; absence of colonial past	colonial ties structure selection by origin; bilateral agreements with former colonies as migration control and expulsion policy; high politicization	early 'post-colonial downsizing' and pragmatic laissez-faire approach to EU entries result in far-reaching detachment from post-colonial labor ties
Integration model	Bismarckian social integration via work; stratification by cultural proximity of different migrant groups	'earned' integration layers assimilation approach with economic definitions of 'success'	social cohesion and public order objectives justify tough border control focus (rhetorically, at least)
EU mobility regime	cautious piloting bilaterally; EU mobility as default labor market condition; geopolitics of furthering European project; integration in EU labor market and economy	differential shortage lists for TCN and EU nationals used to manage and contain unauthorized workers and their labor market positions	by far highest EU-8 migration as detachment from post-colonial labor ties; perceived adverse effects of liberal EU mobility approach justify restrictions for TCN routes
Electoral politics	not emphasized, apart from discussion of migrants' socio-cultural integration potential	historical rhetorical 'lock-in' in zero migration approach result in symbolic control politics	annual caps as electoral response to adverse EU mobility effects; symbolic control politics
Others	'demographic pressure' scenario justifies economically-driven labor recruitment	high levels of politicization of citizenship and unauthorized migrant workers' rights	2010 general elections as context for ideational policy shift; by far highest TCN and EU entries

Source: author's analysis of semi-structured interviews and policy documents

Notes

1. TCN with domestic qualifications, i.e., university or VET certificate or equivalent domestic work experience.
2. This discourse changed more recently in 2012–2013 when especially numbers of Roma free movers from the EU-2 started to pick up and questions of housing, schooling, and unemployment benefits for these newcomers started being discussed more fiercely—and with xenophobic undertones in parts of the public. An update interview with a policy maker in the Labor Ministry in September 2013 exposed that the management of "poverty migration" from Bulgaria and Romania was becoming a new focus of German migrant integration policies, even though limits of financial support for the affected municipalities were highlighted.
3. Andorra, Australia, Israel, Japan, Canada, Monaco, New Zealand, San Marino, and the United States.
4. The French expression "*se rouler par terre*" is usually translated as "to roll on the ground laughing," however, the textual context of this statement suggests that interviewee intended an ironic comment on previous fears about "invasions" of Polish plumbers in France and actual low levels of entries after the 2008 end to transitional limitations here.
5. 182,000 in 2009 as compared to 71,000 in France and a negative net balance of –13,000 in Germany (Huddleston and Niessen 2011).
6. A consultation on student and family routes in 2011 looked into possibilities of restricting these, too.
7. A workshop of the same title—held in London on 5 September 2011 and organized by COMPAS at the University of Oxford and the Migration and Law Network at the University of Kent—critically reappraised the Coalition's migration policy. Business, NGO, trade union, and research representatives largely castigated the "numbers game" as unsustainable and factually unachievable propaganda that plays with public opinion while putting social cohesion, economic growth, and the UK's international reputation at risk.
8. The same applies to the British university system where sponsorship agreements and tight residence controls are believed to discourage foreign students from coming to the United Kingdom and have already caused major clashes with Higher Education Institutions (*The Guardian* 2012).
9. This terminology was employed by the UK Border Agency Interim chief executive, Jonathan Sedgwick, and the head of its Immigration Group, Michael Coats, in their oral evidence to the Public Accounts Select Committee (House of Commons 2011).
10. In this context, comparatively strong notions of public interest, public order, and management of perceived migration "pressure" underpin labor migrant admissions in the United Kingdom, as the policy tool of annual caps suggest. Indeed, the British debate frequently applies the term *control* while German and French interviewees and policy documents use vocabulary of *management* or *steering* instead (German: *Steuerung*, French: *gestion*).

Conclusion
Border Drawing, Policy Analysis, and the Governance of Mobility in Europe

Certainly, our policy analysis has been limited to labor migration management, and even then only in three European countries. Here, however, we should step back from the fine brushstrokes on the canvas and contemplate the larger picture. Without giving in to the temptation of generalizing findings from a small-n study in one policy domain, the empirical material indicates some key dynamics and effects of border-drawing processes in Europe more generally speaking. The mechanisms and norms by which "legal" migrant workers are singled out among all potential foreign nationals—including those who already reside and potentially without authorization—have considerable implications for our understanding of what is at stake in European socioeconomic governance processes more broadly. As they are arranged and given weight in particular ways in any one policy, the variable labor migration tales that we met in the introduction of the book jointly contain the "legal" space for migrant workers and their employers. Border drawing offers an analytical approach to public policy governance precisely because it grants access to the various normative foundations of policies, the classification mechanisms by which even competing claims can be arranged, and the structural conditions under which the overall arrangement of migrant worker legality emerges. The added value of the border-drawing perspective is highlighted in this long-owed discussion, with particular focus on implications for policy analysis more broadly speaking and the societal effects of the state's sorting work—especially for migrants' unequal access to mobility rights. This conclusion also offers a tentative reappraisal of our border-drawing analysis vis-à-vis more recent migration policy developments in Britain, France, and Germany in times of economic crisis.

Border Drawing as Policy Analysis

The book's key claim is that the distinction of "legal" from "illegal" migrant workers is at the very heart of labor migration management and thus requires interpretive analytical attention. In ontological alignment with the IPA tradition, I problematized particularly those parts of the migration policy literature that examine the effectiveness or reach of a specific border-drawing regime at the expense of unraveling the sources of its inherent normative claims. Having granted more attention to the normative foundations of border drawing and its structural embeddedness in national settings with this book, it is time to summarize our findings and reflect on what border-drawing dynamics imply for policy analysis more broadly.

Border Drawing and the Creation of "Structured Complexity"

Our empirical analysis throws light on both the complexity of migration as a governance terrain and the powerful mechanisms that seek to structure policy complexity through labor migration management. With due reference to the intellectual foundations laid by Pierre Bourdieu and later Ngai-Ling Sum and Bob Jessop in chapter 1, policies can be understood as tools for designing orderliness in otherwise incomprehensively complex social settings which always involve multiple "reasonable" tales on any one subject of governance. Policies do not find truth among competing tales; they derive order, hierarchies, and relations among coexisting norms and tales through classification processes. Our example of labor migration management has demonstrated amply just in how highly fine-tuned and variable manners policies define legal migrant workers. Legislation analyzed in this book draws on a range of different—and often competing—normative frameworks and remedies this complexity precisely by creating highly selective classification regimes that combine diverse admission criteria, policy tools, and permits in very specific ways. To be sure, scholars have well highlighted the contradictions between drivers for openness and those demanding closure in migration policies before and insisted in the fine-grained character of policy responses (Boswell 2007; Boswell and Geddes 2011; Carmel and Paul 2010; Hollifield 1992; Mau et al. 2012; Ruhs 2013). Border drawing goes beyond merely acknowledging these contradictions by showing just how states manage them through policy making, on what grounds specific normative frameworks gain or lose importance, and with what effect for the structuration of the overall labor migration terrain. Rather than taking any contemporary policy for granted, border drawing forces us to examine how order is achieved in the first place, what is chosen to matter and what isn't in policy, how conflicting agendas are combined and managed, and with what consequences for those governed through policies.

Our detailed empirical mapping of migrant classifications in each country exposed, for instance, that migrants with high skills and scarce skills are courted in all three cases. Their easier entry is justified with assumptions about their economic utility and their positive role in promoting competitiveness. So far, this is no news for existent accounts. Yet, if you happen to be Senegalese in France, your nuclear technology doctorate may not be sufficient for admission, as a bilateral agreement limits entries. If you are unfortunate enough to be the 20,701st applicant in tier 2 general of the British PBS, your specific engineering skills might match a shortage route profile, but your application will nonetheless be in vain with the annual volume already being reached. Borders are experienced by migrant workers as often-unpredictable intersections of economic utility, their origin, their ethno-cultural background, or simply their number on a waiting list. Rather than painting black-and-white pictures of migrant worker legality, border drawing seeks to expose and explain the empirical multiplicity of classifications, "legitimate" entry definitions, and associated statuses and rights as legality arrangements.

More important than the multiplicity of normative frameworks, from a border-drawing perspective, is the acknowledgement that the product of fine-tuned migration management is neither chaos nor irreducible contingency. In a complex empirical field with various coexisting policy tales—remember our introductory news stories—multidimensional border drawing offers a crucial means for creating "structured complexity" (Jessop 2009; also see Sum and Jessop 2013). While a large array of sometimes contradictory normative claims resonates in British, French, and German policies, these norms are deliberately contained in very specific places, combined in specific ways, or silenced for the sake of emphasizing competing norms in specific segments of the policy. The complexity of the social world and its various meanings in a given policy field is structured, channeled, and contained through border drawing.

A prime example of "structured complexity" surfaces in the economic imaginaries discussed in chapter 5. We have shown that the cultural political economy of labor migration features a division into three distinct imaginaries—all with very different foci and spatial frameworks for state intervention. This three-fold division allows government to structure labor admissions in a way that can pursue, simultaneously, contradictory objectives and reconcile otherwise conflicting agendas. Through the very division of legal entry routes by skill level, a neo-liberal competitiveness agenda can, for instance, coexist quite happily with domestic labor market protectionism. The magic is done, quite simply in this case, by limiting the legitimacy of economic utility claims for skilled and lower-skilled workers and, instead, highlighting societal concerns for those groups. It gets more complicated, of course, when high-skilled competitiveness is further chosen not to matter as justification for legal entry of migrant workers of specific origin or for the economically useful but unlucky 1,001st world-leading talent who applies for a visa in a capped admissions regime.

By dividing entry routes and various permits according to specific normative foundations, policies solidify visions of how the social world should be structured and why. Policy analyses that ignore the creation and imposition of "structured complexity"—or symbolic orders and classifications in Bourdieu's terminology—rather overlook one of the most influential instances of state power: to decide in a collectively binding fashion what "makes sense" and what doesn't, what can legitimately count as "meaningful" in what context and what cannot, and to justify beyond recognition as arbitrary choice just why no better way of regulating a policy field is thinkable until further notice.

Border Drawing and the Management of Policy Context

Border-drawing processes hinge on policy makers' decisions about which mechanisms and logics are to be selected as means of distinction between the various objects of governance, what should guide the sorting of "the good into the pot; the bad into the crop" and why. The book's analysis has showcased that a sound and empirically founded understanding of context is essential for any investigation in that respect. In European labor migration management, this predominantly concerns the context of EU mobility regulation (see introduction). The structuring impact of this shared context on member-state policies is most obvious in the notion of abundant EU labor supply, which is used to justify the restrictive treatment of lower-skilled labor migration of non-EU workers unanimously across our three cases. The influence of the common market context on labor recruitment policies is such that even historically emerged labor movement patterns—say of post-colonial character—are now challenged by the dominance of EU mobility, especially so in lower-skilled job markets. Policy tools such as the resident labor market test and shortage lists are crucial in establishing a preference of EU workers before admitting any TCN. In short, labor migration management is bounded by the context of EU mobility, especially so in an enlarged European Union with higher levels of mobility.

Contextualization in the supranational mobility regime, however, is by no means passively received in member states, but used in selective—and nationally distinct—ways and in pursuit of specific ideas about how to best govern the foreign workforce. We have shown, for instance, that EU mobility works as justification of restrictive TCN admission policies for low-skilled labor, but is strikingly ignored when considering high-skilled migrant workers, domestic graduates, or intra-corporate transferees. The context of EU mobility is chosen not to matter for high-skilled workers. Further, the preference for Eastern Europeans in response to skilled and lower-skilled labor shortages coexists with specific migration control agendas with national flavors. This is evident in the French Janus-faced shortage list regime for TCN and EU-2 workers, explained by policy makers as attempt to use Bulgarians and Romanians as substitute labor supply in precisely the jobs that unauthorized residents from former colonies already perform in France. The strategic decision to draw on EU free movers rather than regularizing those who fulfill the same jobs, sometimes since many years, serves as a migration and resident population management tool. This dynamic could only be grasped of course, because the post-colonial context of French labor migration management was an integral part of the analysis.

The British case is indicative of the opposite dynamic: the sheer lack of references to blatantly obvious factors in the wider policy context is of equal interest in interpretive border-drawing analysis. The very absence of post-colonial belonging from the British policy debate has been taken as a hint that historical labor ties with former colonies are no longer ascribed a legitimate role as a source of policy meaning in the selective admission of foreign workers; the imperial context—though continuing to matter de facto in British migration and settlement patterns—is deliberately silenced in favor of an economically driven classification regime that predominantly relies on EU mobility (of course, the analysis has shown how that approach has fallen back onto policy makers' feet when "adverse effects" of liberal EU mobility were experienced).

Eventually, definitions of legal and illegal migrant workers in legislation embody and impose political decisions about the role that specific contextual factors should play. This reiterates the need for careful interpretive reconstruction of meanings *in their context* (e.g., Wagenaar 2011). A lack of contextualizing the analysis of the French shortage list regime, for instance, in a labor market setting that widely employs unauthorized migrant workers from former colonies would have overlooked the strong post-colonial undertone of the migration control agenda underneath the fig leaf of economic utility arguments. The focus on specific contextual factors and negation of others, the emphasis of some aspects of the wider policy environment but ignorance of others, the positive or negative reference to a specific contextual factor: all these are part of the border-drawing game and its normative vision of just how to relate things to one another in a complex social world. In labor migration management, policies' treatment of contexts such as EU mobility, post-colonialism, demographic change, or historical migration experiences, plays a chief part in explaining variation across Britain, France, and Germany. What migrant legality means, exactly, is clearly also forged in each country's attempt to govern policy contexts.

Border Drawing and the Governance of Mobility in Europe

The border-drawing framework suggests that by classifying migrant workers into variable positions of legality, states stratify their statuses and engage in powerful sorting activities even or especially where territorial entry control cannot be achieved. It is time then to reflect on the societal effects of legality arrangements in policies on those sorted out: migrants and mobile workers in Europe. We do so by considering the distribution patterns of mobility rights and assess their implications for migrant workers on the basis of our empirical findings.

Skills-Based Mobility Privileges and the Limits of Economic Reasoning

The strict division of labor migration routes by skill level makes labor mobility a matter of skills-specific privileges in Europe. In a nutshell, the higher or more specialized the formal qualification of a given migrant worker, the more benevolent the entry routes and rights granted. While this correlation does not predestine every individual applicant—their entry options are mitigated in bilateral agreements with quotas or through an annual cap as we have seen—the common tendency of conditioning rights with regard to skill level is overwhelming. An impressively large comparison of forty-six middle- and high-income countries confirms the trade-off between openness in admission policies and rights granted as a more encompassing tendency in labor migration policy worldwide (Ruhs 2013).

The fine-tuned targeting of high and specific skills ascribes a role of globally mobile skills entrepreneurs to legal migrant workers and, in return, offers to them often quite benevolent rights—such as the German settlement permit or the French multiannual permits. Mobility rights—or rather, privileges—for newcomers are increasingly linked to their ability to act as skills entrepreneurs in high-end European labor market segments. In a similar manner, even though slightly more controlled, skilled migrant workers are supposed to barter their skills profile flexibly in response to urging labor market demands. The analysis has shown that the reach of the economic utility and competitiveness claims as justifications of legality is by no means universal. Criticism of utilitarian policy approaches apart (see Carmel 2011), the flip side of the skills-oriented governance of migration is that whoever does not, or is not allowed to, live up to these skill-entrepreneurial expectations faces much more restrictive and temporary access options and a more limited sets of rights. This mainly concerns lower-skilled workers of course, for whom economic utility arguments are chosen not to matter in admission policies, notwithstanding their role as economically useful irregular workers in practice.

Yet, the point of border drawing is to show that this skills trade-off is not functionally given but created through policies which are strongly shaped by the context of EU mobility and competition-focused market making. Irrespective of the national nuances highlighted throughout, and indeed irrespective of the European Union's lack of comprehensive regulatory authority in the field of foreign labor admissions, we witness the emergence of a common cultural political economy of labor migration in Western Europe. Skills-based migration is enabled and promoted with reference to competitiveness aims while lower-skilled TCN mobility (and indeed residence) is crowded out with the argument of EU labor self-sufficiency. Policies examined here suggest that the unified and enlarged EU mobility space reduces mobility opportunities for TCN workers of lower skill level, potential newcomers, and low-skilled worker-residents alike, all while expanding the so-called competition state for hand-selected high-skilled and skilled workers.

This regulatory division bears powerful societal effects within host countries. Most importantly perhaps, the assumption of low-skilled self-sufficiency within the EU labor market continues to contradict economic realities of unauthorized work and migration. But rather than acknowledging these, skills-based migration leaves very meager regularization outlooks for irregular workers who already reside and labor in host economies. Their outlook for having their utility—which they arguably prove in their daily work—recognized in official law is grim indeed and even worsened in approaches such as "*immigration choisie*," tightened skills requirements, or hand-picked integration of skilled "*Geduldete*." In the meantime, the border-drawing perspective reminds us that while TCN migrant workers are not necessarily kept outside physically, their labeling as *illegal* in policies tends to solidify the so-often marginalized and exploitable positions they assume (Anderson 2010; P. Hansen 2010; Morice 1996; Schwenken 2006).

Origin-Based Privileges and the Limits of EU Mobility Claims

The selection of legal migrant workers as skills entrepreneurs in labor admission policies further bears ethnicized effects, some quite explicit and some more indirect, whose implications reach far beyond host societies. We find instances of outspoken exclusion of non-European workers in Germany, where decreasing migrant skill level implies increasing selection of workers by (largely European) country of origin. The same is true of France's numerical and temporal restriction of admissions from former colonies that are developing countries under the banner of brain-drain avoidance. Skills-based labor migration management begs the question of who, exactly, is and should be able to act as mobile skills entrepreneur. The unequal distribution of wealth and access to education and training across the globe is likely to produce more chances for skills-based mobility of doctors, engineers, or geometricians among the knowledge-based economies of the North—maybe now with the exception of countries such as India—while it will immobilize the biggest share of the world's population. Re-occurring refugee dramas off the shores of the Italian island of Lampedusa, with several hundred victims of a shipwrecked boat in October 2013 for instance, are the repeated shameful indications of the desperate tracks that poor and persecuted individuals seek in response to the illegalization of their mobility. But even where sufficiently trained (by definition of legislation) medical or engineering staff is available in the poorer regions of the world, moral issues with brain drain arise immediately and are actively confronted in labor migration management (take the French "*zones de solitarité prioritaires*" for instance; see chapters 4–6). Either way, for the time being, skills-based migration into Western Europe remains a privilege for a few and is certainly less impartial to non-economic markers of distinction (race, religion, ethnicity and so on), by intention or as side-effect, than most labor migration analyses are able or ready to show (e.g., Menz 2009; Menz and Caviedes 2010b; Ruhs 2013).

The rise of a Eurocentric framework for admissions is of particular relevance in this context, especially for France and the United Kingdom, whose migration history since the Second World War has been much less "European" than Germany's. Recall the cynical comment of a French policy adviser that the shortage list policy—offering high-skilled engineering positions to Malians for instance—leads ad absurdum the irregular labor market reality of Malian kitchen assistants and cleaners. Replacement effects are also observed in Britain, where post-colonial workers are increasingly substituted with EU free movers in lower-skilled segments of the labor market, whether unintended or deliberate we could not establish here.

The claim of Eurocentrism as an—so far rather overlooked—element of contemporary labor migration management connects to scholarly work that stresses instances of ethno-cultural selectivity in the governance of foreign workers in Europe (for Germany: Schönwälder 2004; for France: Spire 2005). Some argue that racial and ethnic classification logics have been inherent to EU enlargement policies. As "labor markets have looked East" (Favell 2008b: 704), the ethnic composition of the foreign workforce has started to change drastically on the continent. Peo Hansen and Sandy Brian Hager (2010) suggest that this is no coincidence; rather, ethnic selection hierarchies speak of the making of EU citizenship in amalgamation of economic utility considerations *plus* an ethnicized Judeo-Christian notion of belonging. Together, they work to neutralize and institutionalize both the utilitarian admission of high-skilled TCN labor *and* the ever-increasing restrictions for non-Christian and potentially "black and brown" (as in the words of a UK trade union official; see chapter 4) migrations from the global South.

All tales of economic utility apart, labor migration policies in Europe certainly inform a strong sense of distinction between "us," EU nationals, and "them," non-EU workers. Yet, the bifurcation of labor migration and EU mobility is contested from several angles. Firstly, the embeddedness of border drawing in distinct migratory contexts has stressed that the "other" category of the "TCN worker" is far from homogeneous and that empirical implications of the EU/TCN bifurcation vary across cases. These contingencies matter as the national management of relationships with sending countries informs different origin-based admission hierarchies with distinct privileges or disadvantages for migrants from certain countries in our three cases. While part of the French admission regime targets post-colonial residents from Algeria, Morocco, Tunisia, or Senegal specifically, Britain "deals with" "bogus Indian IT workers," "Jamaican chicken shop owners," or Chinese students,[1] and Germany is mainly concerned with settled Turkish minorities.

I certainly do not claim novel insights when acknowledging that who counts as a target of labor migration management depends on migration legacies and relationships with sending countries. Yet the predominant focus on economic drivers of labor admissions in policy analysis (i.e., Devitt 2012; Laubenthal 2012; Menz 2009; Menz and Caviedes 2010) tends to gloss over, rather than carefully unpack, these persistent sources of variation. A medium-n study would be required to verify whether similar migration experiences—say with regard to imperial legacies in Spain, Portugal, Belgium, or the Netherlands—inform similar border-drawing arrangements by skill and post-colonial origin elsewhere.

Secondly, both the benevolent treatment of some non-Europeans, predominantly those from rich OECD nations, and persistent contestations of EU mobility in public debate obscure the EU-TCN divide. Those non-EU nationals whose countries of origin seem to feature more proximities culturally or economically speaking (Japanese, Canadians and US-Americans in Germany for instance) are actively drawn into the realm of "us" by more permissive regulation.

Certainly, the EU and member states have increasingly neutralized a dichotomous migration and mobility regime in their policy making.[2] But we should not be easily seduced in buying into this framework as a "fact" beyond need for analytical scrutiny. Be it in the shape of highly debated "adverse effects" of EU-8 migration on Britain's public infrastructure, public concern about "the many Poles that come here to do the care work night and day,"[3] even in the self-proclaimed Eurocentric Germany, or the decision to grant some rich OECD nationals easier labor market access than workers from acceding EU countries: the limits of contemporary EU mobility are written on the wall.

Continuous struggles about mobility and social rights attached to EU citizenship and residence (Carmel and Paul 2013a; Favell and R. Hansen 2002; P. Hansen and Hager 2010; Recchi and Triandafyllidou 2010) sustain worries that the common labor market not only leads to an intensified bifurcation of EU free movers and TCN workers, but that the arguments around economic utility, scarcity, and self-sufficiency so widely applied in the neat classification of legal migrant workers from outside the EU backfire on public perceptions of fellow EU nationals. To put it bluntly: German, French, and British voters might not distinguish between EU and non-EU migrants when economic recession hits and threatens "their" jobs. A study of the British Migration Observatory (2011) evidences exactly that, when British respondents utter concern about Polish workers while welcoming Chinese students and Japanese engineers.

It might be in moments of perceived crisis that the instability of politically designed (b)orders—even where they enjoy a status of facticity—becomes most obvious (Jessop 2009). As complexity and tensions between tales can never be conquered once and for all, policies big and small, noticed and unnoticed, will go on to draw and redraw the boundaries of "legality" in the public realm. These ever-shifting normative foundations will continue to have considerable consequences for the parameters within which the lives and relations of those governed by them unfold, and will thus keep interpretive policy analysts busy. Our final assessment of policy developments since the end of the core research period of this study, which covered legislation between 2004 and 2011 (see appendices), pays tribute to the shifting grounds of border-drawing actions in the labor migration domain.

Border-Drawing vis-à-vis Recent Policy Developments

Policies will stay in the business of drawing and redrawing the boundaries of legality in the public realm. As a platform for fierce debates about economic and social governance norms, the economic crisis of the late 2000s and early 2010s provides a particularly useful, albeit undesirable, test for ability of the border-drawing concept to capture policy shifts across time. It offers a lens for discussing more recent policy developments in our three cases and thus informs a tentative reappraisal of the border-drawing dynamics found in this book.

If nothing else, the crisis—unfolding in the aftermath of the subprime mortgage crisis in the United States in 2008 and subsequent defaults of financial institutions across the globe, and amplified by ongoing public-debt crises in the Eurozone—has provided a context for policy reform. While research in the early days of the crisis expected persistent labor migration demands and policies (e.g., Castles 2011), others have identified restrictive tendencies across destination countries in the rich world, with governments "attempting to make new immigration more difficult, protect labor markets for native born workers, clamp down on migrants in irregular situations and encourage ... return" (Kuptsch 2012: 19). Resident labor market tests automatically reduce legal entry options for TCN when domestic and EU unemployment rose, and shortage checks have been extended to more jobs and higher skill levels. Sharply increasing movements of crisis-struck Southern Europeans to a still seemingly well-off German labor market, for example, might mitigate openness toward non-EU entries. Yet, if anything, the border-drawing approach developed in this book warns us against one-dimensional assumptions that link economic development with a country's migration policy in any functional way.

More recent policy developments in the three West-European countries at center stage in this book indicate that the weights in border drawing have shifted considerably in some cases, but continue to vest a highly divergent arrangement of meanings in labor migration management. While the United Kingdom has redrawn borders to labor migrants in much more restrictive ways since 2010 in exactly the way described above, French policy makers have made no substantial changes to formal policies at all (stricter application of existing rules is possible of course), and Germany has chosen to relax its rules further in 2013 despite rising levels of EU mobility. In what ways do these recent divergent trends deepen or nuance the overall picture of border-drawing dynamics depicted in this book then?

To reduce the current British policies of restricting entry options for newcomers, toughening controls of residents, and enforcing removals to an economic crisis response would be misleading. Migrant workers were not even the key targets with the "tens of thousands" agenda instigated by the new Conservative Home Secretary Theresa May after the change of government in 2010 (chapters 3–4). Rather, it seemed obvious to experts and policy makers that, given the lack of control over other types of flows, the goal of reducing net migration could only be achieved if labor entries swallowed the lion's share of the reduction goal. So Britain restricted entry for tier 2 skilled migrants in 2011, 2012, and 2013. For example, the qualification and English requirements were increased for skilled workers, the shortage list was reduced to include only graduate level jobs, an earning threshold of £35,000 will apply to skilled workers outside the shortage route from 2016 onward, ICT entries are controlled more tightly, and a cooling-off period of one year has been introduced for all tier 2 visa applicants whose current visa expires and who seek renewal.

These measures indicate that the logic of numerical border drawing in Britain—bringing net migration down "by hook or by crook" (Member of the Migration Advisory Committee, interviewed in 2011)—thus leaps more and more into the economic rationality of demand-led recruitment. While the economic imaginary of "domestic labor market shortages" still exists in British policy making, its realm has been increasingly curtailed as conditions for its legitimized reign have become stricter. This gradual hollowing-out of the economic rationality of the original points-based system exposes the complex normative foundations of border drawing impressively: not once did the Conservative government change the terminology of policies introduced under New Labour rule; but by redefining what *shortage, skill,* and *qualification* mean policy makers were able to withdraw liberal migration provisions behind a fig leaf of still satisfying economic demands. The migrant whose diploma and earnings sufficed to be welcomed as "skilled worker" in Britain in 2009 but is now rejected as not quite skilled or affluent enough will of course feel the consequences of this redrawing of borders between legal and illegal labor migration most severely.

Irrespective of the generally restrictive tendency of British policies since 2010, a good deal of normative support for the high-skilled global competitiveness framework survives amidst the nominal cap philosophy: recruitment of MBA graduates was recently facilitated, student entrepreneurs are now exempted from many of the above-mentioned restrictions, and "the rules for businesses with respect to the advertising of highly paid or PhD jobs were relaxed" (OECD 2012: 144).

If the UK case shows how economic border-drawing rationalities are hollowed out but not completely thrown overboard in the attempt to stick to predefined nominal limits of net migration, the German case highlights that cultural norms of belonging continue to play a role in the subtext of an increasingly liberal and economy-based labor migration approach. Germany developed its labor migration policy further in almost the contrary direction compared to the United Kingdom since 2010. The EU Blue Card has been enacted on 1 August 2012 and the approximately eight thousand high-skilled newcomers in its first year were celebrated as a success in terms of the country's attractiveness. Take-up of this route thus surmounts that of the pre-existing permanent residence permit (*Niederlassungserlaubnis*) with only some hundred successful applications per year by far.

More important than the Blue Card, however, has been the recent liberalization of the decree that regulates employment of incoming foreigners (*Beschäftigungsverordnung*; BMAS 2013). Having taken effect in July 2013, this law has eased entry requirements for migrant workers who do not hold an academic qualification, but attain a vocational training of at least two years duration of an equivalent level to a German VET certificate and who can fulfill jobs on a newly established "white list" (*Positivliste*) of structural workforce shortages. While the Federal Employment Agency still has to consent to recruitment, the previously obligatory resident labor market test for skilled workers is now waived. The same logic applies, for the first time in this form, to access to vocational training itself. Non-European adolescents can now compete on job-training contracts openly with national and EU applicants. However, the Federal Employment Agency can limit VET entries numerically and by country of origin (note the continuation of potentially ethnic recruitment hierarchies in the subtext here) on the grounds of regional labor market dynamics and integration potential.

The German developments equal an expansion of the high-skilled competitiveness logic (chapter 5) to skilled non-academic realms of migrant recruitment and trickle into the German stronghold of qualified vocational training.

While skilled foreign labor admission still pursues strong demand-oriented logics—an offer for a job or a VET training contract remains a basic requirement—the previously clear subordination to resident and EU workers is gone and supply-oriented arguments gain credit. As the OECD notes in its most recent Migration Outlook (2013: 152): "In an attempt to create a reservoir of highly qualified manpower with domestic qualifications, Germany is developing a comprehensive strategy to recruit foreign students to German vocational and university-level programmes and encourage them to stay after graduation." We seem to witness a partial blending of the economic imaginary of "skilled domestic labor shortages"—which always bore a *temporary* demand focus in policy makers' justifications in chapter 5—with the "global competitiveness" imaginary and its longer-term skills-supply focus. The emerging blend targets the sustenance of high-skilled *and* skilled labor competitiveness in the longer run.

Two contextual drivers surface in the current discussion and might go some way in explaining this German deviation from its own cautious strategy in the past as well as the rather restrictive labor migration approaches across most of the rich industrial nations in response to the crisis (OECD 2012, 2013)—and maybe in starkest opposition to the recent developments in Britain. On the one hand, the demographic decline argument is rehearsed more strongly than ever as a context that goes beyond the crisis and remained largely untouched by it. Policy makers and business alike now demand policy to look beyond short-term demand-driven shortage calculations and respond to the longer-term structural needs of the national economy by recruiting people earlier (at the stage of VET training), supporting their German language training better, focusing on skilled supply more than demand, cutting red tape in diploma-recognition procedures, and signaling openness with more effort and PR campaigns such as a multilingual web portal (update interview with Labor Ministry official in September 2013, first interview held in December 2009). Demographic change seems to go some way in explaining the otherwise surprising statement of the same policy maker that Germany "wants to attract perpetually *more* labor migration in future perspective."

On the other hand, research has shown that the German economy and labor market lived through the financial and economic crisis much better so far than most of the other EU countries and left especially foreign workers largely unaffected (Kim 2010; Hüfner and Klein 2012). The relatively optimistic economic atmosphere in Germany—unlike in most of its EU neighbors—has arguably kept anti-immigrant voices at bay to some extent. In all this new and seemingly intensifying German openness toward labor migration—which would probably not have been thought possible amidst the "reluctant country of immigration" discussions by most migration scholars even a decade ago—routes for migrant workers without skilled job training, academic diplomas, or a VET contract in Germany are always entirely shut now. Past provisions for agricultural seasonal workers, carney assistants, etc., have been phased out and are only accessible to workers from Bulgaria, Romania, and Croatia. Here we meet the familiar—and it seems intensified—notion of a self-sufficient EU workforce that can self-cater for all lower-skilled labor demands (chapter 5). The only exceptions at the moment are made for care workers from Tunisia, Serbia, Bosnia, and Turkey for whom targeted recruitment is organized together with the German development agency GIZ (*Deutsche Gesellschaft für Internationale Zusammenarbeit*). This recent turn to linking development work, foreign affairs, and the soothing of labor demands at home (especially in the growing care sector in an ageing society) might constitute another chapter in Germany's legality arrangement for migrant workers by both skill *and* origin. But again, economic openness toward migration should neither be hastily taken for smooth social integration (Kim 2010) nor all-embracing welcome of workers from all ethno-cultural backgrounds. Moreover, should entry figures increase in Germany's further liberalized model as they did in the United Kingdom in the late 1990s and after the EU's Eastern enlargement, socio-political norms of border drawing might regain influence and lead to similar counter reactions to perceived "adverse effects" of economically liberal labor migration.

Labor migration management has not changed its outfit much in the French case since 2011. Besides the ratification of some more migration management agreements—chiefly in the realm of youth mobility—entry conditions remained more or less stable. Business is as usual in Paris: "the economic crisis as we experience it has not altered the policy directions established in 2006" (Ministère de l'Intérieur 2013). Unlike their British and German homologues, French policy makers seem to see no need to control more or to liberalize further their approach to labor migration. With the economic recession and unemployment having hit France harder than Germany, no comparable demographic crisis scenario as on the Eastern shores of the Rhine, but also no equally strongly perceived migration control crisis as in Britain, President François Hollande and the French government may simply feel that there are more relevant policy scenes to attend to. The pressure to revise the economically liberal aspects of French labor migration policy may rise, of course, with each electoral success of the anti-immigrant Front National.

Policy disparity during the economic crisis leads EU migration policy advisers to somewhat disappointed recognitions: "The absence of converging needs and objectives does not create conditions conducive to the proper development of a common EU policy" (Pascouau 2013: 5). From a border-drawing perspective, this should not come as a surprise. As long as the EU model of mobility, citizenship, and migration works as not much more than a least-common denominator adjacent to the common market project and is stripped off any basic consensus on social and civic norms in Europe—including a concept of mobility that surmounts economic utilitarianism—member states will continue to remedy the tensions of a globalized liberal market with their social, cultural, and political beliefs in distinctly *national* arrangements of migrant worker legality. They want to retain the power to define the extent to which foreign labor admissions are in line with what competitive corporations need, especially when these needs may conflict with social or cultural cohesion aims. Irrespective of the overlaps created in a uniting EU policy context that treats labor migration as merely economic adjacent to the European competitiveness project: member states are likely to cling further to the ultimate power to define and recast "legality" in order to sort the "good into the pot" and "the bad into the crop" on their territories. Precisely because the pursuit of member states' visions on how to best order *social* relations is at stake in the European market-making project, the fine-tuned border-drawing activities toward migrant workers unpacked in this book remain the focal point of *national* state intervention.

Notes

1. Statements from a UK Border Agency official in an interview.
2. Indeed, this study internalized this distinction by reducing the scope of research to the governance of TCN entries, but aimed to avoid its reification in a contextualized policy analysis (see introduction).
3. Statement of a German policy advisor in interview.

Documents and Interviews

Germany

Key Policy

Bundesrepublik Deutschland. 2004. "Gesetz zur Steuerung und Begrenzung der Zuwanderung und zur Regelung des Aufenthalts und der Integration von Unionsbürgern und Ausländern." (Zuwanderungsgesetz), Berlin, Bundesgesetzblatt.

Further Guidelines and Specifications

Bundesrepublik Deutschland. 1980. "Beschluss Nummer 1/80 des Assoziierungsrats EWG-Türkei über die Entwicklung der Assoziation." (Part of Association Agreement between the European Communities and Turkey), Bonn.
———. 2008. "Gesetz zur Arbeitsmarktadäquaten Steuerung der Zuwanderung Hochqualifizierter und zur Änderung weiterer aufenthaltsrechtlicher Regelungen." (Arbeitsmigrationssteuerungsgesetz), Bonn, Bundesgesetzblatt.
Bundesministerium für Arbeit und Soziales (BMAS). 2008a. "Beitrag der Arbeitsmigration zur Sicherung der Fachkräftebasis in Deutschland." (Aktionsprogramm der Bundesregierung), Berlin.
———. 2008b. "Zweite Verordnung zur Änderung der Beschäftigungsverordnung." Berlin.
Bundesministerium des Innern (BMI). 2004. "Aufenthaltsverordnung (aus der Verordnung zur Durchführung des Zuwanderungsgesetzes 2004)," (Aufenthv), Bonn, Bundesgesetzblatt.
Bundesministerium für Wirtschaft und Arbeit (BMWA). 2004. "Verordnung über die Zulassung von neueinreisenden Ausländern zur Ausübung einer Beschäftigung." (Beschäftigungsverordnung—Beschv), Bonn, Bundesgesetzblatt.
Bundesagentur für Arbeit (BA). 2009a. "Beschäftigung ausländischer Arbeitnehmer aus Staaten außerhalb der Europäischen Union im Rahmen von Werkverträgen in der Bundesrepublik Deutschland (Voraussetzungen, Zulassungsverfahren)." Nürnberg.
———. 2009b. "Beschäftigung ausländischer Arbeitnehmer in Deutschland—Fragen, Antworten sowie Tipps für Arbeitnehmer und Arbeitgeber (Merkblatt 7)." Nürnberg.
———. 2009c. "Vermittlung von Haushaltshilfen in Haushalte mit Pflegebedürftigen nach Deutschland—Hinweise für Arbeitgeber." Nürnberg.
Unabhängige Kommission Zuwanderung. 2001. "Zuwanderung Gestalten—Integration Fördern, Bericht der Unabhängigen Kommission 'Zuwanderung.'" Berlin.

France

Key Policy

République Française. 2010. "Code de l'entrée et du séjour des étrangers et du droit d'asile." (Ceseda). Paris.

Further Guidelines and Specifications

Comité Interministériel de Contrôle de l'Immigration (CICI). 2011. "Les orientations de la politique de l'immigration et de l'intégration." Rapport au Parlement. Paris.
Le Président de la République and Le Premier Ministre. 2009. "Lettre de mission du Président de la République et du Premier Ministre à Eric Besson, Ministre de l'Immigration, de l'Intégration, de l'Identité Nationale et du Développement Solidaire." Paris.
Ministère de l'Immigration. 2010a. "Amendments to the Migration Management Agreement with Senegal from 23 September 2006." Paris.
———. 2010b. "L'immigration professionnelle—Professional immigration." (powerpoint presentation from the public relations department), Paris.
———. "Les mesures organizant l'immigration professionnelle." Paris.
Office de l'Immigration et de l'Intégration (OFII). 2010. "Pour la promotion de l'immigration professionnelle." Retrieved 25 March 2011, from http://www.immigration-professionnelle.gouv.fr.
———. 2011. "Rapport d'activités 2010." Paris.
Sénat de la République Française. 2010. "Questionnaire Parlementaire de la Commission des Finances." (Parliamentary questions concerning the budget 2010), Paris.
GISTI. 2009a. "Guide de l'entrée et du séjour des étrangers en France." Paris, Éditions La Découverte.
———. 2009b. "L'admission exceptionnelle au séjour par le travail dite « régularisation par le travail »." Paris.

United Kingdom

Key Policy

Home Office. 2006. "A points-based system: Making migration work for Britain." London.
Migration Advisory Committee (2010a): "Limits on migration: Limits on Tier 1 and Tier 2 for 2011/12 and Supporting Policies." London.

Further Guidelines and Specification

Home Office. 2005. "Controlling our borders: Making migration work for Britain. Five year strategy for asylum and immigration." London.
———. 2011b. "Tier 1 and 2 immigration rules, settlement and asylum—Written Ministerial statement." London.
Migration Advisory Committee (MAC). 2008. "Skilled, shortage, sensitive: The recommended shortage occupation lists for the UK and Scotland." London.
———. 2010a. *Limits on migration: Limits on Tier 1 and Tier 2 for 2011/12 and supporting policies.* London.
———. 2010b. "Skilled, shortage, sensitive: Review of methodology of shortage occupation lists." London.

National Audit Office (NAO). 2011. "Immigration: The points-based system—Work-routes." (Report by Comptroller and Auditor General to the House of Commons), London.
UK Border Agency (UKBA). 2010. "Limits on non-EU economic migration: A consultation." London.
———. 2011a. "Sponsoring migrants under the points-based system." (Information and Policy Guidelines Online for Employers), retrieved 5 May 2011, from http://www.ukba.homeoffice.gov.uk.
———. 2011b. "Tier 2 shortage occupation list." Government-approved version: 16 March 2011, London.

Interviews*

Germany

GER1: Migration expert at German Trade Union Association (*Deutscher Gewerkschaftsbund, DGB*), 1 December 2009, Berlin
GER2: Official at Government High Representative for Migration (*Bundesbeauftragte für Migration und Flüchtlinge*), 1 December 2009, Berlin
GER3: Senior Labour Ministry official (*Bundesministerium für Arbeit und Soziales*), 2 December 2009, Berlin
GER4: Member of Expert Commission on Migration (*Unabhängige Kommission "Zuwanderung"*), 4 December 2009, Berlin
GER5 and GER6: Labour Ministry officials, 7 December 2009, Bonn
GER7 and GER8: Migration experts at German Employers' Association (*Bundesvereinigung der Deutschen Arbeitgeberverbände, BDA*) 14 December 2009, Berlin
GER9: Former Home Secretary (*Bundesministerium des Innern*), 14 December 2009, Berlin
GER10: Senior Home Office official, 15 December 2009, Berlin

France

FRA1: Senior official at Migration Ministry (*Ministère de l' Immigration, de l' Intégration, de l'Identité Nationale et du Développement Solidaire*), 19 April 2010, Paris
FRA2: Official at Employment Administration Office (*Direction Départementale du Travail, de l'Emploi, et de la Formation Professionnelle*), 21 April 2010, Paris
FRA3: Migration expert at Trade Union (Confédération Française Démocratique du Travail, CFDT), 23 April 2010, Paris
FRA4: Policy advisor at migration advocacy organization (*GISTI*), 28 April 2010, Paris
FRA5: National Migration Office official (*Office Française de l'Immigration et de l'Intégration, OFII*), 29 April 2010, Paris
FRA6: Senior official at Migration Ministry, 3 May 2010, Paris
FRA7: Migration expert at Employers' Association (*Mouvement des Entreprises de France, Medef*), 5 May 2010, Paris

United Kingdom

UK1: Migration expert at Employers' Association (*Confederation of British Industry, CBI*), 4 November 2010, London
UK2: Migration expert at Trade Union Congress (*TUC*), 4 November 2010, London

UK3: Representative of high skills–focused Sector Skills Council, 5 November 2010, London
UK4: Policy advisor at Migration Advisory Committee, 5 November 2010, London
UK5: UK Border Agency official, 17 November 2010, London
UK6: Representative of low skills–focused Sector Skills Council, 13 December 2010, York
UK7: Policy advisor at Migration Advisory Committee, 8 April 2011, London
UK8: Former Home Secretary, Home Office, 11 May 2011, London

*All interviewees generously gave their written or taped informed consent to be part of this research. Alongside the anonymized transcripts, consent forms are stored with the author to evidence the authenticity of data. However, to respect the anonymity and confidentiality of informants' identity and the often controversial and sensitive insights they shared, all directly quoted statements in the text have not been coded numerically and have been ascribed to rather generic categories of policy makers (e.g., Home Office official, labor ministry official, employer representative, trade unionist, policy advisor). The author hopes to have thus struck an acceptable balance between the competing research ethics of transparency, credibility and informant protection. As with the core insights on labor migration policies advocated in this book, border drawing can structure and manage, but never fully conquer, the uncomfortable tensions between competing norms.

References

Alesina, A. and E. L. Glaeser. 2004. *Fighting poverty in the US and Europe: A world of difference*. Oxford: Oxford University Press.
Amable, B. 2003. *The diversity of modern capitalism*. Oxford: Oxford University Press.
Ambrosini, M. 2001. "The role of immigrants in the Italian labour market." *International Migration* 39(3): 61–83.
Anderson, B. 2010a. "British jobs for British workers? Understanding demand for migrant workers in a recession." *The Whitehead Journal of Diplomacy and International Relations* 11(1): 103–114.
———. 2010b. "Migration, immigration controls and the fashioning of precarious workers." *Work, Employment & Society* 24(2): 300–317.
———. 2013. *Us and Them? The dangerous politics of immigration control*. Oxford: Oxford University Press.
Anderson, B. and M. Ruhs. 2010. "Introduction," in Ruhs and Anderson (eds), *Who needs migrant workers? Labour shortages, immigration, and public policy*. Oxford: Oxford University Press, 1–14.
Arts, W. and J. Gelissen. 2002. "Three worlds of welfare capitalism or more? A state-of-the-art report." *Journal of European Social Policy* 12(2): 137–158.
Aubusson de Carvalay, B. 2008. "Les démographes se doutent mais les politiques savent." *Plein Droit* 77(June): 10–14.
Baldaccini, A., E. Guild and H. Toner (eds.). 2007. *Whose freedom, security and justice? EU immigration and asylum law and policy*. Oxford and Portland, OR: Hart Publishing.
Baldaccini, A. and H. Toner. 2007. "The Hague: An overview of five years of EC immigration and asylum law," in A. Baldaccini, E. Guild, and H. Toner (eds), *Whose freedom, security and justice? EU immigration and asylum law and policy*. Oxford and Portland, OR: Hart Publishing, 1–22.
Banting, K. 2000. "Looking in three directions: migration and the European welfare state in comparative perspective," in M. Bommes and A. Geddes (eds), *Immigration and welfare: challenging the borders of the welfare state*. London: Routledge, 13–33.
Barron, P., et al. 2011. *On bosse ici, on reste ici! La grève des sans-papiers: une aventure inedited*. Paris: Éditions La Découverte.
Bauböck, R., et al. 2006. "Migrants' citizenship: Legal status, rights and political participation," in R. Penninx, M. Berger and K. Kraal (eds), *The dynamics of international migration and settlement in Europe: A state of the art*. Amsterdam: Amsterdam University Press, 65–98.
Bauman, Z. 2004. *Wasted lives: Modernity and its outcasts*. Cambridge: Polity Press.
Berg, L. and A. Spehar. 2013. "Swimming against the tide: Why Sweden supports increased labor mobility from within and from outside the EU." *Policy Studies* 34(2): 142–161.
Bevir, M. and R. Rhodes 2003. *Interpreting British governance*. London: Routledge.

Bienefeld, M. 2007. "Suppressing the double movement to secure the dictatorship of finance," in Bugra, A. and K. Agartan (eds), *Reading Karl Polanyi for the Twenty-First Century. Market Economy as a Political Project*. Basingstoke: Palgrave Macmillan, 13–31.

Blaney, D. L. and N. Inayatullah. 2010. "Undressing the wound of wealth: Political economy as a cultural project," in J. Best and M. Paterson (eds), *Cultural Political Economy*. London: Routledge, 29–47.

Bloch, A. 2008. "Refugees in the U.K. labour market: The conflict between economic integration and policy-led labour market restriction." *Journal of Social Policy* 37(1): 21–36.

Bloch, A. and L. Schuster. 2002. "Asylum and welfare: Contemporary debates." *Critical Social Policy* 22(3): 393–414.

Blyth, M. 2003. "Same as it never was: Temporality and typology in the varieties of capitalism." *Comparative European Politics* 1(2): 215–225.

Bommes, M. 2000. "National welfare state, biography and migration: Labour migrants, ethnic Germans, and the re-ascription of welfare state membership," in M. Bommes and A. Geddes (eds), *Immigration and welfare: Challenging the border of the welfare state*. London: Routledge, 90–108.

Bommes, M. and A. Geddes. 2000a. "Conclusion: Defining and redefining the community of legitimate welfare receivers," in Bommes and Geddes (eds), *Immigration and welfare: Challenging the borders of the welfare state*. London: Routledge, 248–253.

———. 2000b. "Introduction: Immigration and the welfare state," in Bommes and Geddes (eds), *Immigration and welfare: Challenging the borders of the welfare state*. London Routledge, 1–12.

Bonifazi, C. 2000. "European migration policy: Questions from Italy," in R. King and G. Lazaridis (eds), *Eldorado or fortress? Migration in Southern Europe*. Basingstoke: Macmillan, 233–252.

Bonoli, G. 1997. "Classifying welfare states: A two-dimension approach." *Journal of Social Policy* 26(03): 351–372.

Borjas, G. J. 1994. "The economics of immigration." *Journal of Economic Literature* 32(4): 1667–1717.

———. 1999. "Immigration and welfare magnets." *Journal of Labor Economics* 17(4): 607–637.

Boswell, C. 2003. "The 'external dimension' of EU immigration and asylum policy." *International Affairs* 79(3): 619–638.

———. 2007. "Theorizing migration policy: Is there a third way?" *International Migration Review* 41(1): 75–100.

———. 2008. "Evasion, reinterpretation and decoupling: European commission responses to the 'External dimension' of immigration and asylum." *West European Politics* 31(3): 491–512.

Boswell, C. and A. Geddes. 2011. *Migration and mobility in the European Union*. Basingstoke: Palgrave Macmillan.

Boswell, C. and T. Straubhaar. 2004. "The illegal employment of foreign workers: An overview." *Intereconomics* 39(1): 4–8.

Bourdieu, P. 1989. "Social space and symbolic power." *Sociological Theory* 7(1): 14–25.

———. 1991. *Language and symbolic power*. Cambridge: Polity Press.

———. 1998. *Practical reason*. Cambridge: Polity Press.

Brass, T. 2004. "Medieval working practices? British agriculture and the return of the gang master." *Journal of Peasant Studies* 31(2): 313–340.

Brochmann, G. 1999. "Controlling immigration in Europe," in Brochmann and T. Hammar (eds), *Mechanisms of immigration control*. Oxford: Berg, 297–334.

Brubaker, R. 1989. *Immigration and the politics of citizenship in Europe and North America*. Lanham, MD: University Press of America.
——. 1992. *Citizenship and nationhood in France and Germany*. Cambridge, MA: Harvard University Press.
——. 2001. "The return of assimilation? Changing perspectives on immigration and its sequels in France, Germany, and the United States." *Ethnic and Racial Studies* 24(4): 531–548.
Bundesamt für Migration und Flüchtlinge (BAMF). 2009a. *Ausländerzahlen 2009*. Nürnberg.
——. 2009b. *Grunddaten der Zuwandererbevölkerung in Deutschland*. Nürnberg.
——. 2011a. *Migrationsbericht 2009*. Nürnberg.
——. 2011b. *Migrationsbericht 2010*. Nürnberg.
——. 2011. *Bundesregierung beschließt Erleichterungen bei der Zuwanderung ausländischer Fachkräfte*. http://www.bmi.bund.de (accessed 23 October 2012).
Bundesministerium für Arbeit und Soziales (BMAS). 2013. *Verordnung über die Zulassung von neueinreisenden Ausländern zur Ausübung einer Beschäftigung* (Beschäftigungsverordnung—BeschV). 6 June 2013. Bonn.
Campomori, F. and T. Caponio. 2013. "Competing frames of immigrant integration in the EU: Geographies of social inclusion in Italian regions." *Policy Studies* 34(2): 162–179.
Carmel, E. 2011. "European Union migration governance: Utility, security and integration," in Carmel, A. Cerami and T. Papadopoulos (eds), *Migration and welfare in the new Europe: Social protection and the challenges of migration*. Bristol: Policy Press, 49–66.
——. 2014. "Governance analysis and reflections on risk." Presented at Law, Regulation and Governance (Workshop at the Law & Society Unit of the University of Bielefeld) 5–7 November.
Carmel, E., A. Cerami and T. Papadopoulos (eds.). 2011. *Migration and welfare in the new Europe: Social protection and the challenges of migration*. Bristol: Policy Press.
Carmel, E. and T. Papadopoulos. 2003. "The new governance of social security in Britain," in J. Millar (ed.), *Understanding social security: Issues for policy and practice*. Bristol: Policy Press, 31–52.
Carmel, E. and R. Paul. 2010. "The struggle for coherence in EU migration policy." *Italian Journal of Social Policy* 2010(1): 209–230 [in Italian].
——. 2013a. "Free movement in the European Union? An interdisciplinary policy appraisal." (editorial to special issue) *Policy Studies* 34(2): 113–121.
——. 2013b. "Complex stratification: Understanding the European Union governance of migrant rights." *Regions & Cohesion* 3(3): 56-85.
Carrera, S. et al. 2011. "Labour immigration policy in the EU: A renewed agenda for Europe 2020." *CEPS Policy Brief* No. 240.
Carrère, V. 2008. "Une armée de travailleurs de réserve." *Plein Droit* 76(March): 16–19.
Carrère, V. and M. Duval. 2009. "Des accords léonins." *Plein Droit* 83(December): 5 pp.
Castles, F. G. and D. Mitchell. 1993. "Worlds of welfare and families of nations," in Castles (ed.), *Families of nations: Patterns of public policy in western democracies*. Dartmouth: Aldershot, 93–128.
Castles, S. 1985. "The guests who stayed—The debate on 'foreigners policy' in the German Federal Republic." *International Migration Review* 19(3): 517–534.
——. 1986. "The guest-worker in Western-Europe—An obituary." *International Migration Review* 20(4): 761–778.
——. 1995. "How nation-states respond to immigration and ethnic diversity." *New Community* 21: 293–293.
——. 2006. "Guestworkers in Europe: A resurrection?" *International Migration Review* 40(4): 741–766.

———. 2011. "Migration, crisis, and the global labour market." *Globalizations* 8(3): 311–324.
Castles, S. and M. J. Miller. 2009. *The age of migration*, 4th ed. Basingstoke: Palgrave Macmillan.
Caviedes, A. 2010. "The sectoral turn in labour migration policy," in G. Menz and Caviedes (eds), *Labour migration in Europe*. Basingstoke: Palgrave Macmillan, 54–75.
Cento Bull, A. 2009. "Lega Nord: A case of simulative politics?" *South European Society and Politics* 14(2): 129–146.
Cerna, L. 2009. "The varieties of high-skilled immigration policies: Coalitions and policy outputs in advanced industrial countries." *Journal of European Public Policy* 16(1): 144–161.
———. 2013. "Understanding the diversity of EU migration policy in practice: The implementation of the Blue Card initiative." *Policy Studies* 34(2): 180–200.
Cerny, P. G. 1997. "Paradoxes of the competition state: The dynamics of political globalization." *Government and Opposition* 32(2): 251–274.
———. 2010. "The competition state today: From 'raison d'État' to 'raison du Monde.'" *Policy Studies* 31(1): 5–21.
Chauvin, S. and B. Garcés-Mascareñas. 2012. "Beyond informal citizenship: Exploring the new moral economy of migrant illegality." *International Political Sociology* 6(3): 241–259.
Chavez, L. R. 2007. "The condition of illegality." *International Migration* 45(3): 192–196.
Clarke, J. and J. Salt. 2003. "Work permits and foreign labour in the U.K.: A statistical review," in Office for National Statistics (ed.), *Labour Market Trends*. London.
Clasen, J. 2005. *Reforming European welfare states: Germany and the United Kingdom compared*. Oxford: Oxford University Press.
Coates, D. 2000. *Models of capitalism growth and stagnation in the modern era*. Cambridge: Polity Press.
Cohen, R. 1987. *The nw helots: Migrants in the international division of labour*. Gower: Avebury.
———. 2006. *Migration and its enemies: Global capital, migrant labour and the nation-state*. Aldershot: Ashgate.
Commission of the European Communities (CEC). 2000. *On a Community immigration policy*. Brussels.
———. 2004. *Green paper on an EU approach to managing economic migration*. COM(2004) 811 final. Brussels.
———. 2005. *Policy plan on legal migration*. Brussels.
———. 2008. *A common immigration policy for Europe: Principles, actions and tools*. Brussels.
Cornelius, W. A., P. L. Martin and J. F. Hollifield (eds.). 2004. *Controlling immigration: A global perspective*. Stanford, CA: Stanford University Press.
Cornelius, W. A. and T. Tsuda. 2004. "Controlling immigration: The limits of government intervention," in Cornelius, L. Martin, and J. F. Hollifield (eds), *Controlling immigration: A global perspective*. Stanford, CA: Stanford University Press, 2–48.
Council of the European Union (CEU). 2003a. *Directive concerning the status of third-country nationals who are long-term residents*. Brussels.
———. 2003b. *Directive on the right to family reunification*. Brussels.
———. 2009. *Directive on the conditions of entry and residence of third-country nationals for the purposes of highly qualified employment*. Brussels.
Cremers, J. 2011. *In search of cheap labour in Europe: Working and living conditions of posted workers*. Brussels: CLR Studies.

———. 2013. "Free provision of services and cross-border labor recruitment." *Policy Studies* 34(2): 201–220.

Crouch, C. 2005. *Capitalist diversity and change: Recombinant governance and institutional entrepreneurs.* Oxford: Oxford University Press.

Crowley, J. 2001. "Differential free movement and the sociology of the 'internal border,'" in E. Guild and C. Harlow (eds), *Implementing Amsterdam: Immigration and asylum rights in EC law.* Oxford and Portland, OR: Hart Publishing, 13–34.

Culpepper, P. D. 2006. "Capitalism, coordination, and economic change: The French political economy since 1985," in Culpepper, P. Hall and B. Palier (eds), *Changing France: The politics that markets make.* Basingstoke: Palgrave MacMillan, 29–49.

Cyrus, N. and D. Vogel. 2007. "Germany," in A. Triandafyllidou and R. Gropas (eds), *European immigration: A sourcebook.* Aldershot: Ashgate, 127–140.

DAAD (German Academic Exchange Service). 2012. "Foreign students studying at German universities number over quarter of a million for first time," Press release, 26 July. Available: www.daad.de.

Daily Mail. 2012. "Bus firm flew bosses to Poland to hire 50 foreign drivers after claiming they could not find Brits to fill the jobs," 25 April.

Dean, H. 2007. "The ethics of welfare-to-work." *Policy & Politics* 35(4): 573–589.

Della Porta, D. 2008. "Comparative analysis: Case-oriented versus variable-oriented research," in Della Porta and M. Keating (eds), *Approaches and methodologies in the social sciences.* Cambridge: Cambridge University Press, 198–222.

Dench, S. et al. 2006. *Employers' use of migrant labour* (Home Office report from the Institute of Employment Studies). London: Home Office.

Der Spiegel. 2012. "Mehr Asylbewerber kommen nach Deutschland," 12 October.

———. 2013. "EU-Parlamentspräsident Schulz: 'Europa ist ein Einwanderungskontinent,'" 14 October.

Devitt, C. 2011. "Varieties of capitalism, variation in labour immigration." *Journal of Ethnic and Migration Studies* 37(4): 579–596.

———. 2012. "Labour migration governance in contemporary Europe: The U.K. case." *FIERI Working Papers,* April 2012.

Dine, P. 2008. "Decolonizing the Republic." *Contemporary French and Francophone Studies* 12(2): 173–181.

Dølvik, J. E. and J. Visser. 2009. "Free movement, equal treatment and workers' rights: Can the European Union solve its trilemma of fundamental principles?" *Industrial Relations Journal* 40(6): 491–509.

Düvell, F. 2007. "United Kingdom," in A. Triandafyllidou and R. Gropas (eds), *European immigration: A sourcebook.* Aldershot: Ashgate, 347–359.

Dumont, J.-C. and M. Doudeijns. 2003. *Immigration and labour shortages: Evaluation of needs and limits to selection policies in the recruitment of foreign labour.* Paris: OECD.

Durrant, H. forthcoming. "Governing good, bad and ugly workplaces. Explaining the paradox of state-steered voluntarism in New Labour's Skills Strategy for England." *Journal of Education and Work.*

Dustmann, C., T. Frattini and C. Halls. 2010. "Assessing the fiscal costs and benefits of A8 migration to the U.K." *Fiscal Studies* 31(1): 1–41.

Ellermann, A. 2009. *States against migrants: Deportation in Germany and the United States.* Cambridge: Cambridge University Press.

Esping-Andersen, G. 1990. *The three worlds of welfare capitalism.* Cambridge: Polity Press.

Estevez, M., T. Iversen and D. Soskice. 2001. "Social protection and the formation of skills: A reinterpretation of the welfare state," in P. Hall and Soskice (eds), *Varieties of capital-

ism: The institutional foundations of comparative advantage. Oxford: Oxford University Press, 145–183.
Eurobarometer. 2011. *Eurobarometer 75: Public opinion in the European Union*. Brussels: CEC.
Eurostat. 2008. *In the spotlight: Demographic change: challenge or opportunity?* Brussels.
———. 2011. *European Labour Force Survey (1983–2011)*. Brussels.
Evans, G. 2006. "Is multiculturalism eroding support for welfare provision? The British case," in K. Banting and W. Kymlicka (eds), *Multiculturalism and the welfare state: Recognition and redistribution in contemporary democracies*. Oxford: Oxford University Press, 152–176.
Faist, T. and A. Ette. 2007. *The Europeanisation of national policies and politics of immigration: Between autonomy and the European Union*. Basingstoke: Palgrave Macmillan.
Favell, A. 2001. *Philosophies of integration: Immigration and the idea of citizenship in France and Britain*. Basingstoke: Palgrave Macmillan.
———. 2008a. *Eurostars and Eurocities: Free movement and mobility in an integrating Europe*. Oxford: Blackwell.
———. 2008b. "The new face of East-West migration in Europe." *Journal of Ethnic and Migration Studies* 34(5): 701–716.
Favell, A. and R. Hansen. 2002. "Markets against politics: Migration, EU enlargement and the idea of Europe." *Journal of Ethnic and Migration Studies* 28(4): 581–601.
Ferré, N. 2007. "Recherche 'compétences et talents.'" *Plein Droit* 73(July): 16–18.
Ferrera, M. 1996. "The 'southern model' of welfare in social Europe." *Journal of European Social Policy* 6(1): 17–37.
———. 2013. "Welfare-state transformations: From neo-liberalism to liberal neo-welfarism?" in V. A. Schmidt and M. Thatcher, (eds), *Resilient liberalism in Europe's political economy*. Cambridge: Cambridge University Press: 77-111.
Fischer, F. 2003. "Beyond empiricism: Policy analysis as deliberative practice." in M.A. Hajer and H. Wagenaar (eds), *Deliberative policy analysis: Understanding governance in the network society*. Cambridge: Cambridge University Press, 209–227.
———. 2007. "Policy analysis in critical perspective: The epistemics of discursive practices." *Critical Policy Studies* 1(1): 97–109.
Frankfurter Allgemeine Zeitung. 2002. "Union widerspricht Wirtschaft im Einwanderungsstreit," 1 January.
———. 2013. "Einwanderung in Deutschland 2012 auf Rekordniveau," 7 May.
Freedman, J. 2004. *Immigration and insecurity in France*. Aldershot: Ashgate.
Freeman, G. 1998. "The decline of sovereignty? Politics and immigration restriction in liberal states," in C. Joppke (ed.), *Challenge to the nation-state: Immigration in Western Europe and the United States*. Oxford: Oxford University Press, 86–108.
———. 1995. "Modes of immigration politics in liberal-democratic states." *International Migration Review* 29(4): 881–902.
Freeman, G. and A. E. Kessler. 2008. "Political economy and migration policy." *Journal of Ethnic and Migration Studies* 34(4): 655–678.
Geddes, A. 2000. *Immigration and European integration: Towards fortress Europe?* Manchester: Manchester University Press.
———. 2003a. "Migration and the welfare state in Europe," in S. Spencer (ed.), *The politics of migration: Managing opportunities, conflict and change*. Oxford: Blackwell, 150–162.
———. 2003b. *The Politics of Migration and Immigration in Europe*. London: Sage.
Geddes, A. and S. Scott. 2010. "U.K. food businesses' reliance on low-wage migrant labour: A case of choice or constraint?" in M. Ruhs and B. Anderson (eds), *Who needs migrant*

workers? Labour shortages, immigration, and public policy. Oxford: Oxford University Press, 193–218.

Gosh, B. 2000. "Towards a new international regime for orderly movements of people," in B. Ghosh (ed.), *Managing migration: Time for a new international regime?* Oxford: Oxford University Press, 6–26.

Glynos, J. and D. Howarth. 2007. *Logics of critical explanation in social and political theory.* London and New York: Routledge.

Gottweis, H. 2003. "Theoretical strategies of poststructuralist analysis: Towards an analytics of government," in M. A. Hajer and H. Wagenaar (eds), *Deliberative policy analysis: Understanding governance in the network society.* Cambridge: Cambridge University Press, 247–264.

Green, S. 2001. "Immigration, asylum and citizenship in Germany: The impact of unification and the Berlin Republic." *West European Politics* 24(4): 82–104.

Green, S. 2004. *The politics of exclusion: Institutions and immigration policy in contemporary Germany.* Manchester: Manchester University Press.

Green, S. 2007. "Zwischen Kontinuität und Wandel: Migrations- und Staatsangehörigkeitspolitik," in M. G. Schmidt and R. Zohlnhöfer (eds), *Regieren in der Bundesrepublik Deutschland. Innen- und Aussenpolitik seit 1949.* Wiesbaden: VS Verlag für Sozialwissenschaften, 113–134.

Gualmini, E. and V. A. Schmidt. 2013. "State transformation in Italy and France: Technocratic versus political leadership on the road from neo-liberalism to neo-liberalism". in Schmidt and M. Thatcher, (eds), *Resilient liberalism in Europe's political economy.* Cambridge: Cambridge University Press, 346–373.

Guild, E. 2005a. "The legal framework: Who is entitled to move?" in D. Bigo and Guild (eds), *Controlling frontiers: Free movement into and within Europe.* Aldershot: Ashgate, 14–48.

———. 2005b. "Who is entitled to work and who is in charge? Understanding the legal framework of European labour migration," in D. Bigo and Guild (eds), *Controlling frontiers: Free movement into and within Europe.* Aldershot: Ashgate, 100–139.

———. 2007. "Citizens without a constitution, borders without a state: EU free movement of persons," in A. Baldaccini, Guild, and H. Toner (eds), *Whose freedom, security and justice? EU immigration and asylum law and policy.* Oxford and Portland, OR: Hart Publishing, 25–55.

Guild, E. and S. Mantu. 2011. *Constructing and imagining labour migration: Perspectives of control from five continents.* Farnham and Burlington, VT: Ashgate.

Guiraudon, V. 2000. "European integration and migration policy: Vertical policy-making as venue shopping." *Journal of Common Market Studies* 38(2): 251–271.

Hajer, M. A. and H. Wagenaar (eds.). 2003a. *Deliberative policy analysis: Understanding governance in the network society.* Cambridge: Cambridge University Press.

———. 2003b. "Introduction," in Hajer and Wagenaar (eds), *Deliberative policy analysis: Understanding governance in the network society.* Cambridge: Cambridge University Press, 1–30.

Hall, P. A. and D. Soskice. 2001a. "An introduction to varieties of capitalism," in Hall and Soskice (eds), *Varieties of capitalism: The institutional foundations of comparative advantage.* Oxford: Oxford University Press, 1–68.

——— (eds.). 2001b. *Varieties of capitalism: The institutional foundations of comparative advantage.* Oxford: Oxford University Press.

Hammar, T. 1990. *Democracy and the nation-state: Aliens, denizens and citizens in a world of international migration.* Avebury: Aldershot.

Hancké, B. 2001. "Revisiting the French model: Coordination and restructuring in French industry," in P. Hall and D. Soskice (eds), *Varieties of capitalism: The institutional foundations of comparative advantage*. Oxford: Oxford University Press, 307–334.

Hancké, B., M. Rhodes and M. Thatcher. 2007. "Introduction: Beyond varieties of capitalism," in Hancké, Rhodes, and Thatcher (eds), *Beyond varieties of capitalism: Conflict, contradiction, and complementarities in the European economy*. Oxford: Oxford University Press, 3–38.

Hansen, P. 2000. "'European Citizenship', or where Neo-liberalism meets Ethno-culturalism." *European Societies* 2(2): 139–165.

———. 2010. "More Barbwire or more Immigration, or both? EU Migration Policy in the Nexus of Border Security Management and Neoliberal Economic Growth." *The Whitehead Journal of Diplomacy and International Relations* 11(1): 89–102.

———. 2014. "Immigration without incorporation: EU migration policy in a Post-citizenship Europe?" in E. Guild (ed.), *The reconceptualization of European Union citizenship*. Leiden and New York: Martinus Nijhoff, 361–380.

Hansen, P. and S. B. Hager. 2010. *The politics of European citizenship: Deepening contradictions in social rights and migration policy*. Oxford and New York: Berghahn.

Hansen, P. and S. Jonsson. 2011. "Demographic colonialism: EU–African migration management and the legacy of Eurafrica." *Globalizations* 8(3): 261–276.

———. 2012. "Imperial origins of European integration and the case of Eurafrica: A reply to Gary Marks' 'Europe and its empires.'" *Journal of Common Market Studies* 50(6): 1028–1041.

Hansen, R. 2000. *Citizenship and immigration in post-war Britain the institutional origins of a multicultural nation*. Oxford: Oxford University Press.

Hantrais, L. 1999. "Contextualization in cross-national comparative research." *International Journal of Social Research Methodology* 2(2): 93–108.

———. 2009. *International comparative research: Theory, methods and practice*. Basingstoke: Palgrave Macmillan.

Hargreaves, A. G. 2007. *Multi-ethnic France: immigration, politics, culture and society*. 2nd ed. Abingdon: Routlegde.

Hay, C. and D. Wincott. 2012. *The Political Economy of European Welfare Capitalism*. Basingstoke: Palgrave Macmillan.

Hay, C. and N. J. Smith. 2013. 'The resilience of Anglo-liberalism in the absence of growth: The UK and Irish cases'. in V. A. Schmidt and M. Thatcher, (eds), *Resilient liberalism in Europe's political economy*, Cambridge: Cambridge University Press, 289–312.

Hekman, S. 1983. "Weber's ideal type: A contemporary reassessment." *Polity* 16(1): 119–137.

Hensen, J. 2009. "Zur Geschichte der Aussiedler- und Spätaussiedleraufnahme," in C. Bergner and M. Weber (eds), *Aussiedler- und Minderheitenpolitik in Deutschland: Bilanz und Perspektiven*. Munich: Oldenbourg, 47–62.

Héritier, A. 2008. "Causal explanation," in D. Della Porta and M. Keating (eds), *Approaches and methodologies in the Social Sciences: A pluralist perspective*. Cambridge: Cambridge University Press, 61–79.

Hinrichs, K. 2010. "A social insurance state withers away: Welfare state reforms in Germany—Or: attempts to turn around in a cul-de-sac," in B. Palier (ed.), *A long Goodbye to Bismarck? The politics of welfare reform in continental Europe*. Amsterdam: Amsterdam University Press, 45–72.

Hollifield, J. F. 1992. *Immigrants, markets, and states: The political economy of postwar Europe*. Cambridge, MA: Harvard University Press.

———. 2004a. "The emerging migration state." *International Migration Review* 38(3): 885–912.

———. 2004b. "France: Republicanism and the limits of immigration control," in W. A. Cornelius, P. L. Martin and J. F. Hollifield (eds), *Controlling immigration: A global perspective*. Stanford, CA: Stanford University Press, 183–214.

Hollingsworth, J. R. 1997. "Continuities and changes in social systems of production: The cases of Japan, Germany, and the United States," in Hollingsworth and R. Boyer (eds), *Contemporary capitalism: The embeddedness of institutions*. Cambridge: Cambridge University Press, 265–310.

Hollingsworth, J. R. and R. Boyer. 1997. "Coordination of economic actors and social systems of production," in Hollingsworth and Boyer (eds), *Contemporary capitalism: The embeddedness of institutions*. Cambridge: Cambridge University Press, 1–47.

Home Office. 2011. "Control of immigration: Quarterly statistical summary United Kingdom quarter 4/2010, October–December." London.

———. 2012. *Admissions data tables Immigration Statistics (April–June 2012)*. London. http://www.homeoffice.gov.uk/publications/science-research-statistics/research-statistics/immigration-asylum-research/immigration-tabs-q2-2012/admissions-q2-2012-tabs (accessed 25 October 2012).

House of Commons. 2011. *Immigration: The points-based system, work routes*. HC 913. (published on 17 May 2011). London: Select Committee of Public Accounts.

Howard, M. M. 2009. *The politics of citizenship in Europe*. Cambridge: Cambridge University Press.

Howarth, D. and Y. Stavrakakis. 2000. "Introducing discourse theory and political analysis: identities, hegemonies and social change," in Howarth, A. Norval and Stavrakakis (eds), *Discourse theory and political analysis*. Manchester: Manchester University Press, 1–23.

Huddleston, T. and J. Niessen. 2011. *Migrant Integration Policy Index III*. Brussels.

Hüfner, F. and C. Klein. 2012. "The German labor market: Preparing for the future." *OECD Economics department Working Paper* No. 983. Paris.

Institut National de la Statistique et des Etudes Economiques (INSEE). 2005. *Les immigrés en France—Edition 2005*. Paris.

———. 2012. *Immigrés et descendants d'immigrés en France—Edition 2012*. Paris.

International Organization for Migration (IOM). 2008. "World migration 2008: Managing labour mobility in the evolving global economy." *IOM World Migration Report Series*. Geneva.

———. 2009. "Regional and country figures, regional trends and dynamics" [Statistics online]. Available: http://www.iom.int/jahia/Jahia/about-migration/facts-and-figures/regional-and-country-figures [accessed 1 June 2009].

Iversen, T. and J. D. Stephens. 2008. "Partisan politics, the welfare state, and three worlds of human capital formation." *Comparative Political Studies* 41(4–5): 600–637.

Jessop, B. 1997. "Capitalism and its future: Remarks on regulation, government and governance." *Review of International Political Economy* 4(3): 561–581.

———. 1999. "The changing governance of welfare: Recent trends in its primary functions, scale, and modes of coordination." *Social Policy and Administration* 33(4): 348–359.

———. 2002. *The future of the capitalist state*. Cambridge: Polity.

———. 2008. *State power: A strategic-relational approach*. Cambridge: Polity.

———. 2009. "Cultural political economy and critical policy studies." *Critical Policy Studies* 3(3–4): 336–356.

Jessop, B. and N.-L. Sum. 2006. "Towards a cultural international political economy: poststructuralism and the Italian school," in M. De Goede (ed.), *International Political Economy and Poststructural Politics*. New York: Palgrave Macmillan, 157–175.

———. 2010. "Cultural political economy: Logics of discovery, epistemic fallacies, the complexity of emergence, and the potential of the cultural turn." *New Political Economy* 15(3): 445–451.
Joppke, C. (ed.). 1998a. *Challenge to the nation-state: Immigration in Western Europe and the United States.* Oxford: Oxford University Press.
———. 1998b. "Immigration challenges the nation-state," in Joppke (ed.), *Challenge to the nation-state: Immigration in Western Europe and the United States.* Oxford: Oxford University Press, 5–46.
———. 1998c. "Why liberal states accept unwanted immigration." *World Politics* 50(2): 266–293.
———. 2005a. "Exclusion in the liberal state: The case of immigration and citizenship policy." *European Journal of Social Theory* 8(1): 43–61.
———. 2005b. *Selecting by origin: Ethnic migration in the liberal state.* Cambridge, MA: Harvard University Press.
———. 2010. *Citizenship and immigration.* Cambridge: Polity.
Joppke, C. and E. T. Morawska. 2003. *Toward assimilation and citizenship: Immigrants in liberal nation-states.* Basingstoke: Palgrave Macmillan.
Jordan, B. and F. Düvell. 2003. *Migration the boundaries of equality and justice.* Cambridge: Polity Press.
Kaiser, L. and R. Paul. 2011. "Differential inclusion in Germany's conservative welfare state: Policy legacies and structural constraints," in E. Carmel, A. Cerami and T. Papadopoulos (eds), *Migration and welfare in the new Europe: Social protection and the challenges of migration.* Bristol: Policy Press, 121–142.
Kim, A. 2010: "Foreign labour migration and the economic crisis in the EU: Ongoing and remaining issues of the migrant workforce in Germany." *IZA Discussion Papers* No. 5134, August.
King, R., G. Lazaridis and C. G. Tsardanides. 2000. *Eldorado or fortress? Migration in Southern Europe.* Basingstoke: Macmillan.
Kitschelt. H. et al. (eds.) 1999a. *Continuity and change in contemporary capitalism.* Cambridge: Cambridge University Press.
———. 1999b. "Convergence and divergence in advanced capitalist democracies," in Kitschelt et al. (eds), *Continuity and change in contemporary capitalism.* Cambridge: Cambridge University Press, 427–460.
Kiwan, D. 2010. "Highly-skilled 'guest-workers' in the U.K.: Implications for 'citizenship' in naturalisation policy and integration policy." *Policy and Society* 29(4): 333–343.
Kofman, E. 2002. "Contemporary European migrations, civic stratification and citizenship." *Political Geography* 21(8): 1035–1054.
Kohler-Koch, B. 2003. "Interdependent European governance," in B. Kohler-Koch (ed.), *Linking EU and national governance.* Oxford: Oxford University Press, 10–23.
Kolb, H. 2010. "Emigration, immigration, and the quality of membership: On the political economy of highly skilled immigration politics," in G. Menz and A. Caviedes (eds), *Labour migration in Europe.* Basingstoke: Palgrave Macmillan, 76–100.
Koopmans, R. 2010. "Trade-offs between equality and difference: Immigrant integration, multiculturalism and the welfare state in cross-national perspective." *Journal of Ethnic and Migration Studies* 36(1): 1–26.
Koopmans, R., et al. 2005. *Contested citizenship: Immigration and cultural diversity in Europe.* Minneapolis: University of Minnesota Press.
Koser, K. 2010. "The impact of the global financial crisis on international migration." *The Whitehead Journal of Diplomacy and International Relations* 11(1): 13–20.

Kunz, R. 2013. "Governing international migration through partnership." *Third World Quarterly* 34(7): 1227–1246.
Kuptsch, S. 2012: "The economic crisis and labour migration policy in European countries." *Comparative Population Studies* 37(1–2): 15–32.
Kymlicka, W., and K. G. Banting. 2006. *Multiculturalism and the welfare state: Recognition and redistribution in contemporary democracies.* Oxford: Oxford University Press.
Laubenthal, B. 2012. "Labour migration governance in contemporary Europe: The case of Germany." *FIERI working papers,* April.
Laurens, S. 2009. *Une politisation feutrée: Les haut fonctionnaires et l'immigration en France.* Paris: Belin.
Lavenex, S. 2005. "The politics of exclusion and inclusion in 'Wider Europe,'" in J. Debardeleben (ed.), *Soft or Hard Borders?* Aldershot: Ashgate, 124–143.
Lavenex, S. and E. M. Uçarer (eds.). 2002. *Migration and the externalities of European integration.* Lanham: Lexington Books.
Layton-Henry, Z. 2004. "Britain: From immigration control to migration management," in W. A. Cornelius, P. L. Martin, and J. F. Hollifield (eds), *Controlling immigration: A global perspective.* Stanford, CA: Stanford University Press, 297–333.
Le Monde. 2006. "Pour Nicolas Sarkozy, 'l'immigration choisie est un rempart contre le racisme.'" 28 April.
Leibfried, S. 1993. "Towards a European welfare state? On integrating poverty regimes into the European Community," in C. Jones (ed.), *New perspectives on the welfare state in Europe.* London: Routledge, 120–143.
Loriaux, M. 2003. "France: A new 'capitalism of voice'?" in L. Weiss (ed.), *State in the global economy: Bringing domestic institutions back in.* Cambridge: Cambridge University Press, 101–120.
Loughlin, M. 2003. *The idea of public law.* Oxford: Oxford University Press.
Lutz, H. and E. Palenga-Möllenbeck. 2010. "Care Work Migration in Germany: Semi-Compliance and Complicity." *Social Policy and Society* 9(3): 419–430.
Maas, W. 2010. "Unauthorized migration and the politics of regularization, legalization, and amnesty," in G. Menz and A. Caviedes (eds), *Labour migration in Europe.* Basingstoke: Palgrave Macmillan, 232–250.
MacCormick, N. 2007. *Institutions of law: An essay in legal theory.* Oxford: Oxford University Press.
Maroukis, T. 2013. "Economic crisis and migrants' employment: A view from Greece in comparative perspective." *Policy Studies* 34(2): 221–237.
Marthaler, S. 2008. "Nicolas Sarkozy and the politics of French immigration policy." *Journal of European Public Policy* 15(3): 382–397.
Mau, S. et al. 2012. *Liberal States and the Freedom of Movement: Selective Borders, Unequal Mobility.* Basingstoke: Palgrave Macmillan.
McDowell, L. 2003. "Workers, migrants, aliens or citizens? State constructions and discourses of identity among post-war European labour migrants in Britain." *Political Geography* 22(8): 863–886.
———. 2009. "Old and new European economic migrants: Whiteness and managed migration policies." *Journal of Ethnic and Migration Studies* 35(1): 19–36.
McDowell, L., A. Batnitzky and S. Dyer. 2009. "Precarious work and economic migration: Emerging immigrant divisions of labour in Greater London's service sector." *International Journal of Urban and Regional Research* 33(1): 3–25.
Menz, G. 2001. "Beyond the Anwerbestopp? The German-Polish bilateral labour treaty." *Journal of European Social Policy* 11(3): 253–269.

———. 2005. *Varieties of capitalism and Europeanization: National response strategies to the single European market.* Oxford: Oxford University Press.

———. 2009. *The political economy of managed migration: Nonstate actors, Europeanization, and the politics of designing migration policies.* Oxford: Oxford University Press.

———. 2010a. "Employers, trade unions, varieties of capitalism, and labour migration policies," in Menz and A. Caviedes (eds), *Labour migration in Europe.* Basingstoke: Palgrave Macmillan, 25–53.

———. 2010b. "The privatisation and outsourcing of migration management," in Menz and A. Caviedes (eds), *Labour migration in Europe.* Basingstoke: Palgrave Macmillan, 183–205.

Menz, G. and A. Caviedes. 2010a. "Introduction: Patterns, trends, and (ir-)regularities in the politics and economics of labour migration in Europe," in Menz and Caviedes (eds), *Labour migration in Europe.* Basingstoke: Palgrave Macmillan, 1–22.

——— (eds.). 2010b. *Labour migration in Europe.* Basingstoke: Palgrave Macmillan

Migration Observatory. 2011. "Thinking behind the numbers: Understanding public opinion on immigration in Britain." Report published 16 October, Oxford.

Miller, D. 2006. "Multiculturalism and the welfare state: Theoretical reflections," in W. Kymlicka and K. Banting (eds), *Multiculturalism and the welfare state.* Oxford: Oxford University Press, 323–338.

Ministère de l'Intérieur. 2013. "L'immigration professionelle." www.immigration.interieur.fr, (accessed 10 November 2013).

Morgan, G. and S. Quack. 2010. "Law as a governing institution," in Morgan et al. (eds), *The Oxford handbook of comparative institutional analysis.* Oxford: Oxford University Press, 275–308.

Morice, A. 1996. "Précarisation de l'économie et clandestinité: une politique délibérée." *Plein Droit* 31(April): 10pp.

Morice, A. and S. Potot. 2010. "Travailleurs étrangers entre émancipation et servitude." in Morice and Potot (eds), *De l'ouvrier immigré au travailleur sans papiers: Les étrangers dans la modernisation du salariat.* Paris: Édition Karthala, 5–21.

Morrisens, A. and D. Sainsbury. 2005. "Migrants' social rights, ethnicity and welfare regimes." *Journal of Social Policy* 34(4): 637–660.

Morris, L. 2002. *Managing migration: Civic stratification and migrants' rights.* London: Routledge.

Nannestad, P. 2007. "Immigration and welfare states: A survey of 15 years of research." *European Journal of Political Economy* 23(2): 512–532.

Neal, A. W. 2009. "Securitization and risk at the EU border: The origins of FRONTEX." *Journal of Common Market Studies* 47(1): 333–356.

Newman, J. (ed.). 2005. *Remaking governance: Peoples, politics and the public sphere.* Bristol: Policy.

O'Connor, J. S. 2005. "Policy coordination, social indicators and the social-policy agenda in the European Union." *Journal of European Social Policy* 15(4): 345–361.

OECD. 2008a. *International Migration Outlook 2008.* Paris.

———. 2008b. *OECD Factbook 2008: Economic, Environmental and Social Statistics.* Paris.

———. 2009. *Workers crossing borders: A road-map for managing labour migration* (part II of the International Migration Outlook 2009). Paris.

———. 2011. *International Migration Outlook 2011.* Paris.

———. 2012. *International MIgration Outlook 2012.* Paris.

———. 2013. *International Migration Outlook 2013.* Paris.

Office de l'immigration et de l'intégration (OFII). 2012a. *Métiers en tension* (shortage occupations). http://www.immigration-professionnelle.gouv.fr/en/procedures/shortage-occupations (accessed 23 October 2012).

———. 2012b. *Pour la promotion de l'immigration professionnelle* (web portal on labor migration to France). http://www.immigration-professionnelle.gouv.fr (accessed 23 October 2012).

———. 2013. *Accords bilatéraux sur les migrations professionnelles et échanges de jeunes professionnels* (web portal on labor migration to France). http:\\immigration-professionnelle.gouv.fr (accessed 10 November 2013).

Office for National Statistics. 2008. *Long-term international migration* (long-term international migration estimates from the International Passenger Survey [IPS]: 1975–1990). London.

———. 2009. *Migration Statistics 2008*. Annual Report. London.

———. 2011. *Long-term international migration* (long-term international migration estimates from the International Passenger Survey [IPS]: 1991–2010). London.

Pai, H.-H. 2008. *Chinese whispers: The true story behind Britain's hidden army of labour.* London: Penguin Non-fiction.

Palier, B. 2006. "The long good-bye to Bismarck? Changes in the French welfare state," in P. D. Culpepper, P. Hall and Palier (eds), *Changing France: The politics that markets make.* Basingstoke: Palgrave MacMillan, 107–128.

———. 2010a. "The dualization of the French welfare system," in Palier (ed.), *A long Goodbye to Bismarck? The politics of welfare reform in continental Europe.* Amsterdam: Amsterdam University Press, 73–100.

———. 2010b. "Ordering change: understanding the 'Bismarckian' welfare reform trajectory," in Palier (ed.), *A long Goodbye to Bismarck? The politics of welfare reform in continental Europe.* Amsterdam: Amsterdam University Press, 19–44.

Palmowski, J. 2008. "In search of the German nation: Citizenship and the challenge of integration." *Citizenship Studies* 12(6): 547–563.

Papadopoulos, T. 2011. "Immigration and the variety of migrant integration regimes in the European Union," in E. Carmel, A. Cerami and Papadopoulos (eds), *Migration and welfare in the new Europe: Social protection and the challenges of migration.* Bristol: Policy Press, 23–47.

Pascouau, Y. 2013. "Intra-EU mobility: The second 'building block' of EU labor migration policy." Issue Paper 74 of the *European Policy Centre,* May.

Parusel, B. and J. Schneider. 2010. *Deckung des Arbeitskräftebedarfs durch Zuwanderung.* Nürnberg: BAMF.

Paul, R. 2011. "European labor geography in crisis: The variable governance of foreign workers in Germany, France and Britain." *Perspectives on Europe* 41(2): 47–53.

———. 2012a."Limits of the competition state: The cultural political economy of European labour migration policies." *Critical Policy Studies* 6(4): 379–401.

———. 2012b. "Managing diverse policy contexts: The welfare state as repertoire of policy logics in German and French labour migration governance." in Vad Jønsson et al. (eds), *Migrations and welfare states: Policies, discourses and institutions.* Helsinki and Jyväskylä: Bookwell, 139–174.

———. 2013. "Strategic contextualization: EU free movement, labour migration policies and the governance of foreign workers in Europe." *Policy Studies* 34(2): 122–141.

———. 2014. "Beyond varieties of capitalism? Crisis and policy change in contemporary British and German labour migration governance." paper presented at final conference of the Collaborative Research Centre 597 *Transformation of the State,* Bremen, 3-5 April 2014, submitted as part of a special issue to the *Journal of Ethnic and Migration Studies.*

Peck, J. 2001. *Workfare states.* New York: Guilford Press.

Peers, S. 2001. "Aliens, workers, citizens or humans? Models for Community immigration law," in E. Guild and C. Harlow (eds), *Implementing Amsterdam: Immigration and asylum rights in EC law*. Oxford and Portland, OR: Hart Publishing, 291–308.

Peixoto, J. 2002. "Strong market, weak state: The case of recent foreign immigration in Portugal." *Journal of Ethnic and Migration Studies* 28(3): 483–497.

Pierre, J. and B. G. Peters. 2000. *Governance, politics and the state*. Basingstoke: Palgrave Macmillan.

Pierson, P. 1998. "Irresistible forces, immovable objects: Post-industrial welfare states confront permanent austerity." *Journal of European Public Policy* 5(4): 539–560.

———. 2001. *The new politics of the welfare state*. Oxford: Oxford University Press.

Polanyi, K. 2001 [1944]. *The great transformation: The political and economic origins of our time*. Boston: Beacon Press.

Quassoli, F. 1999. "Migrants in the Italian underground economy." *International Journal of Urban and Regional Research* 23(2), 212–231.

Reyneri, E. 1998. "The mass legalization of migrants in Italy: Permanent or temporary emergence from the underground economy?" *South European Society and Politics* 3(3): 83–104.

———. 2004. "Immigrants in a segmented and often undeclared labour market." *Journal of Modern Italian Studies* 9(1): 71–93.

Rhodes, M. 2000. "Restructuring the British welfare state: Between domestic constraints and global imperatives," in F. W. Scharpf and V. A. Schmidt (eds), *Welfare and work in the open economy*. Vol. II: *Diverse responses to common challenges*. Oxford: Oxford University Press, 19–69.

Rhodes, R. 1996. "The New Governance: Governing without Government." *Political Studies* 44(4): 652–667.

Rogers, R. 1985. *Guests come to stay: The effects of European labour migration on sending and receiving countries*. Boulder and London: Westview.

Roos, C. 2013. *The EU and immigration policies. Cracks in the walls of fortress Europe?* Basingstoke: Palgrave MacMillan.

Ruhs, M. 2013. *The price of rights: Regulating international labor migration*. Princeton: Princeton University Press.

Ruhs, M. and B. Anderson. 2010a. "Semi-compliance and illegality in migrant labour markets: an analysis of migrants, employers and the state in the U.K." *Population, Space and Place* 16(3): 195–211.

———. 2010b. *Who needs migrant workers? Labour shortages, immigration, and public policy*. Oxford: Oxford University Press.

Ryan, B. 2007. "The European Union and labour migration: Regulating admission or treatment?" in A. Baldaccini, E. Guild and H. Toner (eds), *Whose freedom, security and justice? EU immigration and asylum law and policy*. Oxford and Portland, OR: Hart Publishing, 489–515.

Ryner, M. 2000. "European welfare state transformation and migration," in M. Bommes and A. Geddes (eds), *Immigration and welfare: Challenging the borders of the welfare state*. London: Routledge, 51–71.

Sainsbury, D. 2006. "Immigrants' social rights in comparative perspective: Welfare regimes, forms in immigration and immigration policy regimes." *Journal of European Social Policy* 16(3): 229–244.

Saint-Paul, G. 2009. *Immigration, qualifications et marché du travail*. Paris: Conseil d'Analyse Economique.

Sales, R. 2002. "The deserving and the undeserving? Refugees, asylum seekers and welfare in Britain." *Critical Social Policy* 22(3): 456–478.

Salt, J. 2009. *International migration and the United Kingdom* (country report to the OECD). London.
———. 2010. *International migration and the United Kingdom* (country report to the OECD). London.
Samers, M. 2003. "Invisible capitalism: Political economy and the regulation of undocumented immigration in France." *Economy and Society* 32(4): 555–583.
———. 2010. "Strange castle walls and courtyards: Explaining the political economy of undocumented immigration and undeclared employment." in G. Menz and A. Caviedes (eds), *Labour migration in Europe*. Basingstoke: Palgrave Macmillan, 209–231.
Sassen, S. 1996. *Losing control? Sovereignty in an age of globalization*. New York and Chichester: Columbia University Press.
Schain, M. 2008. *The politics of immigration in France, Britain, and the United States: A comparative study*. Basingstoke: Palgrave Macmillan.
Schierup, C.-U. and A. Ålund. 2011. "The end of Swedish exceptionalism? Citizenship, neoliberalism and the politics of exclusion." *Race & Class* 53(1): 45–64.
Schierup, C.-U., P. Hansen and S. Castles. 2006. *Migration, citizenship, and the European welfare state: A European dilemma*. Oxford: Oxford University Press.
Schmidt, V. A. 2002a. "Does discourse matter in the politics of welfare state adjustment?" *Comparative Political Studies* 35(2): 168–193.
———. 2002b. *The futures of European capitalism*. Oxford: Oxford University Press.
———. 2008. "Discursive institutionalism: The explanatory power of ideas and discourse." *Annual Review of Political Science* 11(1): 303–327.
Schmidt, V.A. and M. Thatcher. (eds.) 2013. *Resilient liberalism in Europe's political economy*. Cambridge: Cambridge University Press.
Schmidt, V. A. and C. Woll. 2013. "The state: The bête noire of neo-liberalism or its greatest conquest?" in Schmidt and M. Thatcher, (eds), *Resilient liberalism in Europe's political economy*. Cambridge: Cambridge University Press, 112–141.
Schnyder, G. and G. Jackson. 2013. "Germany and Sweden in the crisis: Re-coordination or resilient liberalism?" in V. A. Schmidt and M. Thatcher, (eds), *Resilient liberalism in Europe's political economy*. Cambridge: Cambridge University Press, 313–345.
Schönwälder, K. 2004. "Why Germany's guestworkers were largely Europeans: The selective principles of post-war labour recruitment policy." *Ethnic and Racial Studies* 27(2): 248–265.
Schwenken, H. 2006. *Rechtlos, aber nicht ohne Stimme: Politische Mobilisierungen um irreguläre Migration in die Europäische Union*. Bielefeld: transcript.
———. Forthcoming. "Multiple paths and dead ends towards extended rights for undocumented migrant women workers in the European Union," in U. Ruppert, A. Jung and B. Schwarzer. *Beyond the merely possible: Transnational women's movements today*. Baden-Baden: Nomos
Scruggs, L. and J. P. Allan. 2006. "The material consequences of welfare states benefit generosity and absolute poverty in 16 OECD countries." *Comparative Political Studies* 39(7): 880–904.
Shen, W. 2005. "A study on Chinese student migration in the United Kingdom." *Asia Europe Journal* 3(3): 429–436.
Solano, D. and A. M. Rafferty. 2007. "Can lessons be learned from history? The origins of the British imperial nurse labour market: A discussion paper." *International Journal of Nursing Studies* 44(6): 1055–1063.
Somerville, W. 2007. *Immigration under New Labour*. Bristol: Policy Press.
Spire, A. 2005. *Étrangers à la carte*. Paris: Édition Grasset & Fasquelle.

———. 2007. "Le grand bond en arrière." *Plein Droit* 73(July): 3–6.
Starke, P., H. Obinger and F. G. Castles. 2008. "Convergence towards where: in what ways, if any, are welfare states becoming more similar?" *Journal of European Public Policy* 15(7): 975–1000.
Statistisches Bundesamt. 2011. *Statistics on foreign population and migration online.* www.destatis.de (accessed 22 April 2011).
———. 2013. *Statistics on foreign population and migration online.* www.destatis.de (accessed 26 October 2013).
Stone, D. 1988. *Policy paradox and political reason.* Glenview: Scott, Foresman and Company.
———. 2012. *Policy paradox. The art of political decision-making.* 3rd ed. New York and London: Norton.
Süddeutsche Zeitung. 2011. "Zuwanderung aus Spanien und Griechenland: Die Krise treibt sie nach Deutschland," 22 December.
Sum, N.-L. 2009. "The production of hegemonic policy discourses: 'Competitiveness' as a knowledge brand and its (re-)contextualizations." *Critical Policy Studies* 3(2): 184—203.
Sum, N.-L. and B. Jessop. 2013. *Towards a cultural political economy. Putting culture in its place in political economy.* Cheltenham: Edward Elgar Publishing.
Sunderhaus, S. 2007. "Regularization programs for undocumented migrants." *Migration Letters* 4(1): 65–76.
Taylor-Gooby, P., T. Larsen and J. Kananen. 2004. "Market means and welfare ends: The U.K. welfare state experiment." *Journal of Social Policy* 33(4): 573–592.
Terray, E. 1999. "Le travail des étrangers en situation irrégulière ou la délocalisation sur place," in E. Balibar et al. (eds), *Sans-papiers: L'archaïsme fatal.* Paris: Éditions La Découverte, 9–34.
Thatcher, M. (2013) "Supranational neo-Liberalization: The EU's regulatory model of economic markets". in V. A. Schmidt and M. Thatcher, (eds), *Resilient liberalism in Europe's political economy.* Cambridge: Cambridge University Press, 171–200.
The Guardian. 2012. "London Metropolitan University challenges loss of sponsorship licence," 3 September.
———. 2013. "David Cameron: blame education not migration for factories' foreign labour," 28 October.
Thränhardt, D. 2004. "Immigrant cultures, state policies and social capital formation in Germany." *Journal of Comparative Policy Analysis: Research and Practice* 6(2): 159–183.
Thrift, N. 2010. "A perfect innovation engine: The rise of the talent world," in J. Best and M. Paterson. (eds), *Cultural Political Economy.* Oxford: Routledge, 197–221.
Torpey, J. 2000. *The invention of the passport: Surveillance, Citizenship and the State.* Cambridge: Cambridge University Press.
Triadafilopoulos, T. and K. Schönwälder. 2006. "How the Federal Republic became an immigration country: Norms, politics and the failure of West Germany's guest-worker system." *German Politics and Society* 24(3): 1–19.
Tribalat, M. 2010. *Les yeux grands fermés. L'immigration en France.* Paris: Éditions Denoël.
UK Border Agency (UKBA). 2012. *Annual tier 2 limit announcement.* London. http://www.ukba.homeoffice.gov.uk/sitecontent/newsarticles/2012/april/18-Tier2-limit (accessed 25 October 2012).
Van Dijk, T. A. 1997. "Discourse as interaction in society," in Van Dijk (ed.), *Discourse as social interaction.* London: Sage, 1–37.
Van Houtum, H. and R. Pijpers. 2007. "The European Union as a gated community: The two-faced border and immigration regime of the EU." *Antipode* 39(2): 291–309.

Van Oorschot, W., M. Opielka and B. Pfau-Effinger. 2008. *Culture and welfare state: Values and social policy in comparative perspective.* Cheltenham: Edward Elgar.
Verwiebe, R. 2004. *Transnationale Mobilität innerhalb Europas.* Berlin: edition sigma.
Von Below, S. 2007. "What are the chances of young Turks and Italians for equal education and employment in Germany? The role of objective and subjective indicators." *Social Indicators Research* 82(2): 209-231.
Wagenaar, H. 2011. *Meaning in action: Interpretation and dialogue in policy analysis.* New York: M.E. Sharpe.
Weber, M. 1994 [1919]. *Politik als Beruf.* Tübingen: Mohr Siebeck.
Weil, P. 2005. *La France et ses étrangers: L'aventure d'une politique de l'immigration de 1938 à nos jours.* Paris: Gallimard.
Weiner, M. 1995. *The global migration crisis: Challenge to states and to human rights.* New York: HarperCollinsCollege.
Weishaupt, J. T. 2010. "Germany after a decade of Social Democrats in government: The end of the Continental model?" *German Politics* 19(2): 105-122.
Wendt, A. 1998. "On constitution and causation in international relations." *Review of International Studies* 24(5): 101-118.
Werner, H. 2001. "From temporary guests to permanent settlers? From the German 'guestworker' programmes of the Sixties to thec 'Green Card' initiative for IT specialists." *ILO International Migration Papers* 42: 1-25.
Wilkinson, M. and G. Graig. 2011. "Willful negligence: Migration policy, migrants' work and the absence of social protection in the U.K.," in E. Carmel, A. Cerami and T. Papadopoulos (eds), *Migration and welfare in the new Europe: Social protection and the challenges of migration.* Bristol: Policy Press, 177-190.
Wimmer, A. 2008. "The making and unmaking of ethnic boundaries: A multilevel process theory." *American Journal of Sociology* 113(4): 970-1022.
Woolfson, C. and J. Sommers. 2006. "Labour mobility in construction: European implications of the Laval un Partneri dispute with Swedish labour." *European Journal of Industrial Relations* 12(1): 49-68.
Yanow, D. 2000. *Conducting interpretive policy analysis.* Thousand Oaks: Sage.
———. 2006. "Thinking interpretively: Philosophical presuppositions and the human sciences," in Yanow and P. Schwartz-Shea (eds), *Interpretation and method: Empirical research methods and the interpretive turn.* New York: M.E. Sharpe, 5-26.
———. 2007. "Interpretation in policy analysis: On methods and practice." *Critical Policy Analysis* 1(1): 110-122.
Zaletel, P. 2006. "Competing for the highly skilled migrants: Implications for the EU common approach on temporary economic migration." *European Law Journal* 12(5): 613-613.
Zimmermann, K. F. 2005. "European labour mobility: Challenges and potentials." *Economist-Netherlands* 153(4): 425-450.
Zincone, G. and T. Caponio. 2006. "The multilevel governance of migration," in R. Penninx, M. Berger and K. Kraal (eds), *The dynamics of international migration and settlement in Europe: A state of the art.* Amsterdam: Amsterdam University Press, 269-304.

Index

Algerian exceptionalism, 85, 117, 120, 132, 173. *See also* legislation: France; migration policy legacies: France
Amsterdam Treaty, 24
Anderson, Bridget, 7, 8, 28, 39, 52, 56
annual caps on entries. *See* selection with annual caps
assimilationist integration, 64–69, 82–83, 86–88, 176, 187. *See also* integration theories
asylum migration, 4, 12, 24–25, 33, 56, 74, 76, 78–79, 95, 109, 113, 198

bilateral migration agreements
    Britain, 180
    France, 44, 85, 119–121, 174–176
    Germany, 74, 76, 107, 112–113, 131, 133, 158–159
Bismarckian welfare provision, 58–61, 78, 81, 83, 109, 133–136, 165–169, 179, 188. *See also* welfare state regimes
Blair, Tony, 97, 105, 121, 143
border concepts
    in economics, 13, 23
    in legal studies, 7, 9, 40
    in political economy, 8, 9, 23–24, 40
    in political sciences, 8, 23–25
    in political sociology, 8, 9, 40
border drawing
    allocation effects of (*see* distribution of mobility rights)
    concept of, 27–39, 192–196
    ontology of, 33–40, 193–195
    principles of, 30–33, 43, 52–54, 59–62, 66–68, 70
    through public law, 30–33

border-drawing dimensions
    civic, 45, 55, 62–69, 133, 164–191
    economic, 45, 46–54, 139–163, 164–165, 169, 181, 187–189, 203
    social, 45, 54–62, 68, 164–191
borders
    internal/multidimensional, 26–27, 55, 68–70, 193–195
    physical/dichotomous, 22–25
Bosbach, Wolfgang, 1
Boswell, Christina, 23, 65, 66, 161
Bourdieu, Pierre, 20, 27–31, 37, 38, 40, 44, 193, 195
brain drain. *See* development aid

Cameron, David, 2, 99, 124, 128, 153
Carmel, Emma, 6, 27, 35, 45, 48, 49, 66, 159, 197
Castles, Stephen, 1, 4, 22
Caviedes, Alexander, 46, 49
Cerny, Phil, 47–48
Chauvin, Sébastien, 24, 29–30
circular migration, 67, 110, 112, 116–117, 119, 130, 144, 155
citizenship regimes, 62–69, 74–75, 82–83, 90–91, 93, 110, 159–160, 170, 189
civic citizenship, 63–66, 82–83, 90–91, 176, 188
classification
    concept of, 27–33, 193–195 (*see* Bourdieu, Pierre)
    criteria, 31–32, 106–113; Germany, 114–121; France, 121–129; Britain, 129–137
    in public law, 31–32
    See also selection

coalition government, 90, 97–98, 122, 164, 184–187, 202. *See also* policy reforms: Britain
comparative methodology, 10–11, 45–46, 69–70, 73–74, 187
competition state theory, 46–49, 140–146, 160–161, 197–198, 203–204
composition of foreign workforce
 Britain, 91–98
 France, 83–89
 Germany, 75–81
Conservative Party
 Britain (*see* coalition government)
 Germany, 1, 80
cultural political economy, 35–40, 56, 69, 126, 139–163, 164, 193–195. *See also* Jessop, Bob; Sum, Ngai-Ling

Della Porta, Donatella, 10–11, 73
demographic change, 4, 11, 46, 59, 65, 75–80–81, 84, 88, 92, 96, 152, 154, 159, 165–168, 180, 196, 203–205
development aid, 3, 119–120, 175, 198–199, 205
distribution of mobility rights, 9, 15, 113, 129–136, 192, 196–201

earned citizenship, 60–61, 79, 109, 133–136, 166–169, 178, 188
earning requirements, 5, 33, 98, 116, 117, 125, 127, 131, 202
Eastern European migration. *See* EU enlargement; EU mobility
economic crisis, 47, 55, 66, 82, 97, 150, 183, 192, 201–206
economic imaginaries, 37, 139–141, 194. *See also* cultural political economy
economic utilitarianism, 15, 44, 46–49, 53, 80, 84–89, 91, 93, 95–97, 99, 126, 136–137, 141–154, 165–169, 176, 183, 186, 188, 193–194, 196, 197–199, 205–206
electoral politics. *See* public opinion
entry quota, on migration. *See* selection with annual caps
Esping-Andersen, Gøsta, 57–59
ethnic citizenship, 11, 46, 63–68, 77–78, 169, 170
ethno-culturalism, 44, 62–63, 65–67, 88, 171, 176, 181–183, 187–190, 194, 199, 205

EU citizenship, 8, 29, 49, 66, 68, 157, 169, 184–185, 198–201
EU Commission, 4, 6, 24, 48–49
EU Council, 24–25
EU enlargement, 79, 89, 97, 99, 113, 120–121, 128, 132, 157–160, 177, 183–184, 186, 188, 195, 199, 205
EU migration policies
 Blue Card for high-skilled workers, 111, 116, 141, 203
 on family members, 25
 on long-term residents, 25, 55, 124
EU mobility, 6, 12, 15, 55, 63, 66–68, 89, 97, 120–121, 127–128, 131–132, 157–160, 169–171, 177, 180–184, 187–188, 195–196, 196–202
EU Parliament, 2, 6, 25
European common market, 4, 6–7, 66, 195, 198–201, 205
Europeanization of migration policies, 4–6, 8, 25, 205–206

family reunion migration, 2–4, 12, 24–25, 54, 56, 66–67, 77, 86, 88–89, 93–94, 97, 124, 129, 166, 175–176, 184–185. *See also* EU migration policies
Favell, Adrian, 6, 63, 65, 80, 91, 94, 182, 187, 199
Fischer, Frank, 9, 34–35, 39
Freeman, Gary, 23–24
Front National, 86, 180, 205. *See also* migration policy legacies: France; public opinion
free movement. *See* EU mobility

Garcés-Mascareñas, Blanca, 24, 29–30
"gap hypothesis" in migration policy studies, 22–25
Geddes, Andrew, 6, 12, 23, 44, 55–56, 66, 93–95, 161
geopolitics, of labor migration policies, 75–79, 99, 169–171, 188
governance studies, 34–35
Green Card, 4–5, 112. *See also* shortage lists: Germany
Green Party, Germany, 1, 64, 80
guest workers, 4–5, 22, 32, 54, 63, 65, 67, 75–78, 82–86, 99, 110, 120, 133, 168–169, 172, 176. *See also* migration policy legacies

Guild, Elisabeth, 7, 66

Hager, Sandy B., 8, 20, 29, 99, 199
Hall, Peter, 50–51, 74–75, 90
Hammar, Thomas, 55, 62
Hansen, Peo, 8, 20, 29, 54–55, 99, 170, 186, 199
Hay, Colin, 49, 55, 59, 61, 91, 161
high-skilled migration
    Britain, 122–124, 141–148, 182–183, 186
    France, 114–117, 141–148, 176
    Germany, 109–111, 141–148, 166–167
Hollande, François, 205
Hollifield, James F., 24
Hortefeux Laws, 88–89, 118
Howard, Marc, 64

"immigration choisie," 2, 88–89, 99, 112, 114–121, 173–180, 188, 198. *See also* legislation: France
inequalities. *See* distribution of mobility rights
informal migrant workers, 5, 12, 15, 29, 33, 51–52, 79, 82, 87, 95, 98, 99, 118, 120, 159–161, 166–168, 175–180, 186, 188, 195, 197. *See also* regularizations
integration theories, 62–69, 74–75, 82–83, 86–88, 90–92, 94, 182, 187. *See also* assimilationist integration; multiculturalist integration
interdisciplinary approach, 7–9, 40
interpretive policy analysis, 9–10, 34–35, 182, 192–193
intra-corporate transfers, 111–112, 116, 124–128, 130, 144–146, 148, 184, 202

Jessop, Bob, 35, 36–40, 47–49, 140, 193–195
Jonsson, Stefan, 170
Joppke, Christian, 24, 62, 64–66, 75

Koopmans, Ruud, 60

labor migration management, concept of, 3–7
legislation
    Britain, 121–129
    France, 114–121
    Germany, 106–113

Lisbon Agenda, 48
Lisbon Treaty, 6, 25
low-skilled migration, 4, 48
    Britain, 124, 127–129, 154–160, 183–184
    France, 117–121, 154–160, 177–180
    Germany, 111–113, 154–160

Maastricht Treaty, 66
Maghreb, migration from the. *See* Algerian exceptionalism; migration policy legacies: France; North-African migration
Mau, Steffen, 3, 21
May, Theresa, 98, 202
McDowell, Linda, 181–182
meaning making/semiosis, 33–40
media stories on migration, 1–3
Menz, Georg, 5, 8, 46–48, 53, 163
Merkel, Angela, 110
migration, definition, 11–12
migration partnerships, 175, 179
migration policy legacies
    Britain, 89–98
    France, 81–89
    Germany, 74–81
migration policy theories
    globalization-related, 23
    multi-level governance, 24–25
    neo-classic political economy, 23
    neo-institutionalist, 24
    post-Marxist, 23
    rational choice, 23
multiculturalist integration, 65–69, 91–92, 94, 98. *See also* integration theories

national unemployment. *See* selection: by social concerns
nation-state, concept of the, 19–22
New Commonwealth migration, 91–94, 181–183. *See also* migration policy legacies: Britain
New Labour, 90, 95–97, 121, 180, 184, 186
North-African migration, 82, 83–87, 176. *See also* Algerian exceptionalism; migration policy legacies: France

OECD, 3–5, 10, 36, 47, 67, 145, 172, 200, 203, 204

Old Commonwealth migration, 91–93, 181. *See also* migration policy legacies: Britain

Palier, Bruno, 59, 83
Papadopoulos, Theo, 35, 38, 79, 87
points-based system, 33, 94, 96–97, 121–128, 176, 184–185, 202. *See also* legislation: Britain
Polanyi, Karl, 54
policy meanings. *See* interpretive policy analysis
policy reforms
    Britain, 95–98, 202–203
    France, 88–89, 205
    Germany, 80–81, 203–205
post-colonialism, 43, 62–69, 82–83, 85–86, 91–95, 99, 119–121, 127–128, 132–133, 159–160, 173–180, 180–183, 188, 196, 198–201. *See also* migration policy legacies
Post-Fordism, 5–6, 8, 39, 46–49, 54, 81
public opinion, 23, 82, 86–87, 128, 178–180, 180–181, 184–187, 188, 200–201, 204–205

"recruitment stop," 4, 54, 77, 86, 87, 114. *See also* "zero" immigration policies
regularization/legalization, 5, 22, 24, 87, 89, 95, 99, 117–120, 136, 167, 173, 176–180, 186, 187, 195, 198. *See also* informal migrant workers
repatriation policies, 65, 67–68, 74–78, 169, 171. *See also* ethnic citizenship; migration policy legacies: Germany
resident labor market test
    Britain, 125–127
    France, 114–119
    Germany, 107–112, 203
Roos, Christof, 25
Ruhs, Martin, 7, 55, 197

Sainsbury, Diane, 59–60, 166, 168
"sans-papiers." *See* informal migrant workers
Sarkozy Laws, 88–89. *See* "immigration choisie"
Sarkozy, Nicolas, 2, 82, 88–89, 147
Sassen, Saskia, 23
Schierup, Ulrik, 49, 56, 61, 69

Schmidt, Vivien, 47, 49, 51, 74, 82, 90, 146–148, 161–163
Schröder, Gerhardt, 80
Schulz, Martin, 2
Schumpeterian economic coordination, 47–48, 141, 161. *See also* Jessop, Bob
Schwenken, Helen, 168
selection
    by origin, 44, 65–66, 84–89, 91, 93, 99, 112–113, 119–121, 127–128, 132–133, 134–135, 169–173, 174–180, 180–183, 198–201
    by origin of skills, 107–109, 122, 133–136, 167, 203–204
    by scarcity of skills, 80–81, 88–89, 107, 111–112, 117–119, 125–127, 130–132, 134–135, 139–163, 188, 201–205
    by skill level, 107–111, 114–117, 122–124, 129–132, 134–135, 139–163, 179, 182–183, 188, 194, 197–198, 202–205
    by social concerns, 54–57, 91, 97–98, 112, 126, 134–135, 150, 152–154, 154–160, 165–173, 176–180,183–187, 187–190, 201–206
    with annual caps, 78, 93, 96, 98, 119, 128–129, 134–135, 183, 184–187, 202–203
    See also legislation
shortage lists
    Britain, 126, 152–154, 202
    France, 89, 117–120, 157–158, 176–178, 195, 196, 199
    Germany, 111–112, 187
skilled migration
    Britain, 124–127, 148–154, 186, 202–203
    France, 117–121,148–154
    Germany, 111–113, 148–154, 203–205
skills policies, 126, 148, 152–154
Social Democrats, Germany, 1, 64, 80
Soskice, David, 50–51, 74–75, 90
sovereignty. *See* nation-state, concept of the
statehood. *See* nation-state, concept of the
Stone, Deborah, 3, 34
structured complexity, 193–195. *See also* cultural political economy; Jessop, Bob; Sum, Ngai-Ling

student migration, 12, 94, 97–98, 111, 121, 129, 173, 184–185, 198, 201, 203–204
Sub-Saharan migration, 82, 83–87, 176. *See also* migration policy legacies: France
Sum, Ngai-Ling, 36–40, 48, 49, 140, 193–195
Süßmuth-Commission, 81
symbolic capital, 30
symbolic power, 28–30, 37

third country nationals, definition, 12. *See also* migration, definition
Thrift, Nigel, 48, 143
Turkish migration, 74, 75–79, 113, 133, 171–173, 205. *See also* migration policy legacies: Germany

undocumented migrant workers. *See* informal migrant workers

varieties of capitalism, 49–54, 74–75, 82–83, 90–91, 131, 140, 146–148, 151–152, 161–163, 188, 189
von der Leyen, Ursula, 1

Wagenaar, Henk, 10, 20, 34, 38, 73, 196
Weber, Max, 13, 21, 45, 62
welfare state regimes, 57–62, 74–75, 82–83, 90–91, 189
Wimmer, Andreas, 28, 32, 44
Wincott, Daniel, 49, 55, 59, 61, 91, 161
Woll, Cornelia, 47

Yanow, Dvora, 34–35

"zero" immigration policies, 87, 94, 97–98, 173, 179–180. *See also* "recruitment stop"
"Zuwanderungsgesetz," 81, 106–111. *See also* legislation: Germany